Harrington on Hold 'em

Expert Strategy for No-Limit Tournaments; Volume III: The Workbook

By

DAN HARRINGTON
1995 World Champion

BILL ROBERTIE

A product of Two Plus Two Publishing LLC

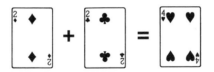

FIRST EDITION

FIRST PRINTING
JUNE 2006

Printing and Binding
Creel Printing, Inc.
Las Vegas, Nevada

Printed in the United States of America

D0171809

Harrington on Hold 'em:
Expert Strategy for
No-Limit Tournaments;
Volume III: The Workbook
COPYRIGHT © 2006
Two Plus Two Publishing LLC

For information contact: **Two Plus Two Publishing LLC**
32 Commerce Center Drive
Suite H-89
Henderson, NV 89014

ISBN: 1-880685-36-1

Slade: How the hell did you know I didn't have
the king or the ace?
The Man: I recollect a young man
putting the same question to Eddie the Dude.
"Son," Eddie told him,
"all you paid was the looking price.
Lessons are extra."

From *The Cincinnati Kid* (1965)

Table of Contents

iv Table of Contents

About Dan Harrington

Dan Harrington began playing poker professionally in 1982. On the circuit he is known as "Action Dan," an ironic reference to his solid but effective style. He has won several major no-limit hold 'em tournaments, including the European Poker Championships (1995), the $2,500 No-Limit Hold 'em event at the 1995 World Series of Poker, and the Four Queens No-Limit Hold 'em Championship (1996).

Dan began his serious games-playing with chess, where he quickly became a master and one of the strongest players in the New England area. In 1972 he won the Massachusetts Chess Championship, ahead of most of the top players in the area. In 1976 he started playing backgammon, a game which he also quickly mastered. He was soon one of the top money players in the Boston area, and in 1981 he won the World Cup of Backgammon in Washington D.C., ahead of a field that included most of the world's top players.

He first played in the $10,000 No-Limit Hold 'em Championship Event of the World Series of Poker in 1987. He has played in the championship a total of 14 times and has reached the final table in four of those tournaments, an amazing record. Besides winning the World Championship in 1995, he finished sixth in 1987, third in 2003, and fourth in 2004. He is widely recognized as one of the greatest and most respected no-limit hold 'em players, as well as a feared opponent in limit hold 'em side games. He lives in Santa Monica, Ca. where he is a partner in Anchor Loans, a real estate business.

About Bill Robertie

Bill Robertie has spent his life playing and writing about chess, backgammon, and now poker. He began playing chess as a boy, inspired by Bobby Fischer's feats on the international chess scene. While attending Harvard as an undergraduate, he became a chess master and helped the Harvard Chess Team win several intercollegiate titles. After graduation he won a number of chess tournaments, including the United States Championship at Speed Chess in 1970. He also established a reputation at blindfold chess, giving exhibitions on as many as eight boards simultaneously.

In 1976 he switched from chess to backgammon, becoming one of the top players in the world. His major titles include the World Championship in Monte Carlo in 1983 and 1987, the Black & White Championship in Boston in 1979, the Las Vegas Tournaments in 1980 and 2001, the Bahamas Pro-Am in 1993, and the Istanbul World Open in 1994.

He has written several well-regarded backgammon books, the most noted of which are *Advanced Backgammon* (1991), a two-volume collection of 400 problems, and *Modern Backgammon* (2002), a new look at the underlying theory of the game. He has also written a set of three books for the beginning player: *Backgammon for Winners* (1994), *Backgammon for Serious Players* (1995), and *501 Essential Backgammon Problems* (1997).

From 1991 to 1998 he edited the magazine *Inside Backgammon* with Kent Goulding. He owns a publishing company, the Gammon Press (www.thegammonpress.com), and lives in Arlington, Massachusetts, with his wife Patrice.

Introduction

In *Volumes I* and *II* of *Harrington on Hold 'em,* we gave a pretty complete overview of how no-limit hold 'em tournaments should be played. *Harrington on Hold 'em: Volume I* covered general advice about selecting starting hands, playing before and after the flop, reading the table, and using pot odds as a guide to making calls and folds. *Harrington on Hold 'em: Volume II* covered the unique problems that occur toward the end of tournaments, when stacks get small relative to the blinds and play becomes much more aggressive.

This book is a companion volume to the first two. It consists of fifty problems from no-limit hold 'em tournaments, both live and online. Some of the problems are fairly simple, illustrating and reinforcing points covered in the first two volumes. Other problems extend the discussion from the original books, introducing some new ideas while elaborating on others. We've also included some problems from televised tournaments, which provide a chance to comment on the styles and strategies of some of today's best-known players.

The book is laid out as a big quiz. In each problem, you the reader are presented with the decisions faced by one of the participants in the hand. As with the problems in *Volumes I* and *II,* you'll see the chip stacks and actions of the other players, as well as some information on their styles and habits. In the case of hands involving famous players, you may know something about their styles from television. Your job is to pick the play you would make in the given situation. In most cases the hand continues through many decision points. As we move from decision to decision, we'll tell you the plays that were actually made in the hand, which may be different from the plays you wanted to make. Don't be discouraged if your play differs from the play actually made. The problems contain many examples of incorrect (in our view) plays, and your decisions may well be better. Just follow along with the problem, answering the questions as they occur.

When the hand ends, we'll discuss the decisions that were made and award points for the different choices. In some cases, we'll also critique the play of the other players. After each hand, total up the points you earned. There's a scoresheet at the end where you can record your results and get an evaluation of your play. There's also a section on categorizing your errors, where you can see if your mistakes fall into particular patterns.

If quizzes aren't your thing, don't worry. You can go through the book as a straight problem collection, ignoring the quiz parts, and just enjoying the discussion.

Fear of Flopping

In putting this workbook together, we've tried to include a representative sampling of problems covering issues from different parts of the game. However, we did choose to focus on one part of the game in particular: playing after the flop.

Post-flop play in no-limit hold 'em is probably the biggest single weakness of beginners and intermediates. To the uninitiated, it seems complicated and threatening. When do you bet? When do you check? What can you deduce from your opponent's actions? It's a big, complex, and important topic, and most players taking their first steps in no-limit play feel lost in this area. But fear of playing after the flop leads to a dangerous remedy — what we call "fear of flopping," or an unreasonable desire *to end all decision-making before the flop arrives.*

Unfortunately, a number of recent books and articles on no-limit play treat the symptom rather than the problem, by offering mechanical strategies for moving all-in at different stages of the tournament. As a quick fix, these strategies have something to recommend them; if you're a weak player, you'll become less weak and make fewer mistakes by relying on a well-crafted mechanical strategy.

However, becoming less weak is a lot different from becoming strong. To become a really good player, you have to learn to play after the flop. Along with correctly choosing your starting hands and adjusting your play to decreasing Ms, it's one of the three key skills of no-limit play. That's what we're going to try to teach you here in *Harrington on Hold 'em: Expert Strategy for No-Limit Tournaments; Volume III: The Workbook*. We've selected an assortment of hands from both big live tournaments with all-star players, and online tournaments with large but weaker fields, chosen to illustrate the decision-making process in post-flop play. Work carefully through the problems in this book, and your post-flop play should improve dramatically.

Thanks to the Forums and Others

The Two Plus Two Online Forums (www.twoplustwo.com) are an excellent source of poker advice and commentary. We'd like to thank all the contributors who submitted comments and suggestions following the release of *Harrington on Hold 'em: Volumes I* and *II,* as well as those who submitted interesting problems and commentary. Bill and I read these forums regularly, and some of the problems in this book were inspired by discussions that occurred there.

We'd also like to thank the developers of a couple of excellent software tools for analyzing hand strength and all-in play at the end of tournaments: *Pokerstove* and *Sit-and-Go Power Tools.* (www.pokerstove.com and www.sitngo-analyzer.com.) These are very useful programs which we used in performing calculations for some of the situations in this book. We recommend them highly to any serious students of the game.

Finally, I want to thank David Sklansky and Mason Malmuth for their comments throughout this manuscript, Ed Miller for his help in creating the index, Gary Alstatt of Creel Printing for his back cover design and art work throughout this book, and Christy Creel and Tom Lesher, also of Creel Printing, for their help in

4 Introduction

putting this project together. And a special thanks goes to Patrick Nguyen of the Two Plus Two Forums for his front cover design.

Dan Harrington
Bill Robertie

Problem 1
Loose or Tight Pre-Flop?

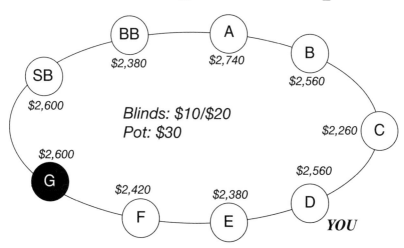

Situation: Large multi-table online tournament. A few hands have been played. So far you have observed that Players A and B seem loose, while Player G and the big blind appear tight.

Your hand: T♦8♣

Action to you: Players A, B, and C all fold.

Question 1: *Which of the following statements represents your point of view?*

A.   *I have a weak hand and there are still five players to act behind me. I fold.*

B.   *The active players have already folded, and the tight players are behind me. I raise to $60.*

C. *I agree with Choice B, but I really want my opponents to fold, so I raise to $120.*

D. *I call. It costs me less than 1 percent of my stack, and if I flop a big hand I could break someone. On TV the aggressive players call with hands like this and then outmaneuver their opponents after the flop. I can do that too.*

Action: You actually fold. Player F raises to $60 in the cutoff seat and wins the pot as the players behind him fold.

Solution to Problem 1

Give yourself 3 points for Choice A, folding a weak hand. If you've read the section on starting hands in *Harrington on Hold 'em: Volume I,* you know that in fourth position my hand requirements are pretty strict. To play I need a pair above sixes, ace-eight or better suited, ace-ten or better unsuited, and some of the high suited connectors or king-queen offsuit.

However, many players, especially online, do like to mix it up with these sorts of hands. Let's look at the other choices one by one and see what's wrong with the reasoning:

Choice B: Raise to $60 because the active players have already folded and the tight players are behind me.

If you picked this choice, remember that while it's good to observe the other players at the table, you're still very early in the tournament, just a few hands into the first round. Your judgments at this point need to have a wide margin of error. The player you're characterizing as "loose" may have just picked up an early rush of cards. The "tight" player behind you may just be prudently taking a little time to size up the table before making a move. Unless you know something about the other players from previous events, just play solid hand values while you observe tendencies and betting patterns.

Note that an aggressive player might elect to raise with this hand. Aggressive players like to be involved in pots early in the tournament, and they're not content to wait for premium hands. Instead, they're confident in their ability to smell danger after the flop and outmaneuver their opponents. Score 2 points for this play.

How much will aggressive players raise with a hand like ten-eight? Most don't like to make big raises with these hands. Their style is to raise just two and a half to three times the big blind. Gavin Smith, a member of the Full Tilt Team who's been quite successful recently, prefers these small raises as a way to put constant pressure on his opponents without committing a lot of chips. Chris Ferguson also likes this approach.

Choice C: Same reasoning as Choice B but raise to $120, since you don't want to be called.

If no one behind you has anything, your $60 raise should be enough to take down the pot. If someone behind you wakes up with a big hand and reraises, you've booted $120 instead of $60.

Choice D: Call, because it costs less than 1 percent of your stack to see a flop.

I don't mind seeing cheap flops with marginal hands, provided I have some assurance that the flop is, in fact, cheap. This is an argument for tossing in some money on the button or the small blind, when almost everyone has already acted. Here five players remain to act, so there's a reasonable chance that someone will raise and force you to throw your hand away.

The other problem with the "1 Percent" Theory is that these hands typically cost you much more than 1 percent of your stack to play. Here are a few illustrative scenarios:

8 Problem 1

- You call $20. Player E folds but Player F raises to $60. Player G calls, as do the small blind and the button. The pot now contains $260. It costs you $40 to call. You're being offered 6.5-to-1 pot odds. Do you fold? Probably not, but now you've invested almost 3 percent of your stack, and you're third to act among five players after the flop.

- You call $20 and so does the button. The small blind and big blind stay in as well. The pot now contains $80. The flop comes king-jack-eight. Are you happy? You've caught a piece of the flop, but will you call if the small blind checks and the big blind bets? I think not.

- As before, you call $20 and the button and the blinds stick around. The flop comes ace-ten-deuce. Are you happy? The blinds check, and you bet $60. The button raises you to $200. Do you call? Very difficult.

These scenarios illustrate a simple lesson. As soon as you enter a pot with a marginal hand, there are a lot of ways that things can go wrong, and a lot of ways that more money can flow from your stack into the pot. The real danger comes not when you miss your hand, but when you flop middle or bottom pair plus some nebulous runner-runner draws. You'll have great difficulty establishing where you stand and quantifying your downside. When your opponents bet at you, you'll constantly wonder how many chips you're willing to risk before pulling the plug. The game is called no-limit for a reason.

One other scenario deserves mentioning, because it's quite common yet goes unnoticed by most players. You start with $2,000 in chips. You fool around a bit at the beginning with loose calls, and your stack drops to $1,600. Now you catch a pair of kings and get all-in against the big stack at your table, who has queens. Your kings prevail, and you double up. Perfecto! What's the problem?

You now have $3,200. The problem? You would have $4,000 if you hadn't squandered those chips earlier. Your early loose play has, almost invisibly, cost you $800, or about a quarter of your current stack.

When learning your poker from television, keep one fact firmly in mind: you're only seeing a small percentage of the hands actually played. Stealing pots with nothing looks trivially easy on television. You raise with a marginal hand pre-flop and get called by someone with a better hand. You miss the flop, but bet and get a reluctant call. On the turn you continue to miss, but make a large bet anyway. Your opponent finally folds his medium pair in the face of your three bets. Easy, yes?

Not really. What you haven't seen is all the hard work and careful observation that led to this seemingly simple hand. The aggressive player who pulled off this elaborate coup may have spent hours cataloging the sort of hands his opponent liked to play in certain positions and how he responded to various flops. He may have concluded that a bluff in this position, with this flop, against this opponent, had an 80 percent chance of succeeding, and consequently raising with the

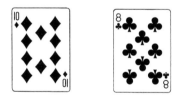

pre-flop was actually a positive-equity play *in this specific situation*. That's a far cry from randomly tossing in a few chips with a weak hand and expecting to bluff your opponent out.

Keep in mind as well that these sorts of moves are more effective in live play than online, because you have a chance to notice physical tells that can give you information above and beyond the betting patterns you've seen. Online, betting patterns are pretty much all the information you have. That's a strong argument for just playing straightforward poker, especially in the early stages of a tournament.

Problem 2
Fear of Flopping

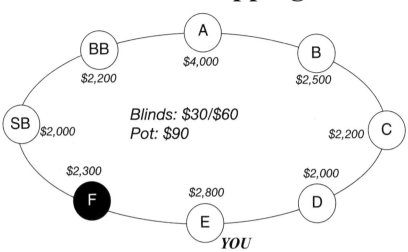

Situation: Single table online tournament with a modest entry fee. Table has been loose so far. The players don't seem very competent at this level.

Your Hand: A♣Q♣

Action to you: Players A and B limp. Players C and D fold.

Question 2: *What do you do?*

A. *Fold*
B. *Call $60*
C. *Raise to $240*
D. *Push all-in*

Action: You actually push all-in. Player F and the blinds fold. Player A calls. Player B folds. Player A turns over A♦A♥, and his hand holds up to knock you out.

Solution to Problem 2

Many beginners and intermediates go astray in positions of this sort. They like to move all-in, reasoning as follows:

● Players A and B only limped, so they can't have much of a hand.

● There's already $210 in the pot, so it's definitely worth winning.

● The players behind me aren't likely to have a hand that can call an all-in bet.

● Even if I get called, I have a huge hand, so

● I'm all-in!

Let's work through the logic point by point, and spotlight the flaws.

Players A and B can't have much of a hand. This might be true, but it's not guaranteed. Some players like to limp in early position with aces or kings, hoping that a couple of others will limp, then some greenhorn will raise big to steal the pot, after which they pounce. A variation on this play is to limp with ace-king, hoping for the same sequence, then raise, representing aces!

The assumption is most often true at a loose, weak table, where players routinely limp with any two suited cards or small pairs. But loose, weak tables have a different problem: you're likely to get called by someone with a small pair, who thinks he's calling for value!

There's already $210 in the pot. True, but there's also $2,800 in your stack, which you're putting at risk. You have to win immediately quite often to make up for those times you risk your stack as a big underdog. Those are tough odds to beat.

The players behind me aren't likely to have a hand. The hands you really fear are AA, KK, QQ, and AK. There's about a 2 percent chance that any particular player has one of these hands, so the total chance that one of the three players behind you has a monster is 6 percent. At a weak table, however, players might call with jacks, or tens, or even lower pairs, all of which are favorites against you.

I have a huge hand. Beginners think

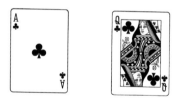

is a monster, but it's not. You're an underdog to any pair or ace-king, and even hands like nine-seven offsuit are about 34 percent to win against you. You need to dominate another hand before your winning chances rise above 70 percent.

The real reason players push all-in with this situation is what I like to call "fear of flopping." They're afraid if they make a normal-sized raise, someone will call them, and they won't know what to do after the flop. It's not an unreasonable fear, because playing after the flop is difficult and requires plenty of skill and practice. But the right approach is to work and improve your

skills, not to shove all your chips in the middle at the first opportunity.
So what should you do here? My top choice is B, calling $60.
You have a reasonable hand, and position over everyone who's in
the pot so far. Just call, and see what the flop brings. Score 4
points for that choice.

My second choice is C, raising to $240. Almost everyone
who would fold to an all-in bet would also fold to this bet. You
may steal the pot, but if you don't, you haven't invested your
whole stack in the hand. Score 3 points for this choice.

No credit for pushing all-in, for the reasons already discussed,
and no credit for folding a good hand.

Problem 3
Betting for Value

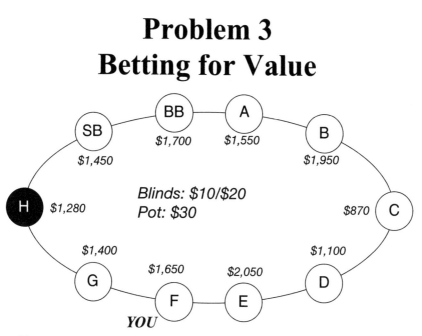

Situation: High-stakes single-table online tournament. A few hands have been played. The table is playing very tight, with a couple of hands folded around to the big blind.

Your hand: 9♠8♠

Action to you: Players A through E all fold.

Question 3A: *What do you do?*

A.   Fold
B.   Call $20
C.   Raise $60
D.   Raise $85

Action: You actually raise $85. Players G and H fold. The small blind calls. The big blind folds. The pot is now $190.

15

16 Problem 3

Flop: K♥5♦4♠

Action: The small blind checks.

Question 3B: *What do you do?*

A. *Check*
B. *Bet $100*
C. *Bet $180*

Action: You bet $100. The small blind calls. The pot is now $390.

Turn: 8♣

Action: The small blind checks.

Question 3C: *What do you do?*

A. *Check*
B. *Bet $200*
C. *Bet $400*

Action: You check. The pot remains $390.

River: 9♥

Action: The small blind bets $200. The pot is now $590.

Question 3D: *What do you do?*

A. *Fold*
B. *Call $200*
C. *Raise to $400*
D. *Raise to $700*
E. *Raise all-in*

Action: You actually call. Your opponent turns over a pair of fours and wins with a set of fours.

Solution to Problem 3

Question 3A: There is no really incorrect play here with the

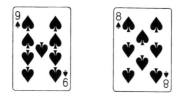

You can fold, because your hand is objectively weak. You can call and try to see a cheap flop; your hand will be disguised and position may favor you if no one behind you comes along. Or you can raise a bit and try to take the pot down right here given that five players have already folded.

In situations like this, I make my decisions based on my knowledge of the table. Here the table is tight, so I prefer raising or calling to folding. Since my preference is to win the pot right now, my top choice is the larger raise.

Score 3 points for Choice D, raising $85. Score 2 points for either Choice B, calling, or Choice C, raising $60. Score 1 point for folding.

You actually raise $85. Only the small blind calls, and the pot becomes $190.

The flop comes

18 Problem 3

The small blind checks.

Question 3B: The small blind called you, knowing he would be out of position. Although he got a small discount because he already had $10 in the pot, he still had to call $75.

Your first job is to start thinking about the hands he might have used to call. Top players try to be very specific at this stage. You don't want to fall into the habit of thinking "He called, so maybe he has something." Instead, you want to narrow his range down to some reasonable group of hands. Here, for example, he didn't reraise you, so he's probably not holding a big pair or ace-king. His most likely holdings are the following:

- Ace-x, where 'x' is a queen or lower, but probably higher than a four or five

- Medium pairs

- Low pairs

- Hands like KQ, KJ, QJ

If you knew a lot about your opponent, you could narrow this down a little further. Against a strong, tight-aggressive opponent, for instance, you could probably ignore low pairs as a possible hand. Good players don't like playing low pairs out of position against a raiser. But weak players do it all the time. Here we don't know anything, so we'll leave the low pairs on the table for awhile.

Notice that you're an underdog against every single hand on this list! Of course, that's one of the consequences of raising with 9♠8♠. But your opponent doesn't know that, so there's no reason to panic. As far as he knows, you could have any strong hand, and most of the hands he might hold were not helped by this flop.

As the pre-flop aggressor, you need to make a continuation bet here. If you bet about half the pot, you'll be getting a good price. (If he folds one time in three, you'll break even; more than that and your bet will show a profit.) Given his list of possible hands, a bet should work more than one time in three. Note, too, that this is a good flop for attacking: a king, two low cards, and three different suits mean you don't have to worry much about facing straight or flush draws.

Don't, however, make the mistake of betting the whole pot, or something close to it. The hands that will lay down to a full pot bet will mostly also lay down to a half-pot bet. The slight gain you get from the extra folds doesn't balance the loss of extra money invested in the calls.

Score 3 points for Choice B, betting $100. No credit for checking or betting too much.

You actually bet $100, and the small blind calls. The pot is now $390.

The turn comes an 8♣. The small blind checks.

Question 3C: The small blind called, which is bad. Then the turn hit your hand, which is good. Then the small blind checked, which is also good, unless he's trapping with a big hand, which is bad. Now what?

Our first job is to narrow his hand spectrum a little more since we have new information. (He called our bet on the flop but didn't raise.) Let's first see what pairs he could hold.

- AA, KK, QQ: Not likely because he only called pre-flop.

- JJ, TT: Possible. These pairs might just call pre-flop and would very likely call post-flop with just one overcard.

- 99, 88: Nines are less likely since you hold a nine, and eights are even less likely since two are accounted for.

- 77, 66: Could make both calls.

- 55, 44: Might have called pre-flop and is now trapping with a set.

- 33, 22: Unlikely pre-flop callers and impossible post-flop callers.

Of the likely pairs, you're beating the sevens and sixes, and losing to the jacks, tens, fives, and fours. You'd like to charge more money to the sevens and sixes, while a bet just might chase the tens away, although probably not the jacks.

You're now beating most of the ace-x type hands, and you certainly want to charge them, although a bet will chase most of those hands away.

If he originally called with KQ, KJ, or KT, you're losing, and he won't lay the hand down. But these hands would probably have bet on the flop and/or the turn, so they're getting less likely. Ace-king is possible, but even less likely since he didn't reraise pre-flop.

The odds still look good for another half-pot-sized bet. You need to charge the hands you're beating, and there are still a considerable number of those. You don't want to bet more than half the pot, since there are still some hands that beat you, and you want to get the best odds you can.

Score 3 points for Choice B, betting $200. 2 points for Choice A, checking. No credit for Choice C, making a big bet.

You actually check, and the pot remains at $390.

The river comes a 9♥, and the small blind bets $200. The pot is $590.

Question 3D: You make a second pair, and now the small blind bets at you! Fold, call, or raise?

Folding is out of the question with two pair. You're going to at least call, as you're getting 3-to-1 odds, and you can't be sure that you're not up against someone with a pair of kings who just decided to slow-play this hand. You could also be facing ace-nine, and your opponent just decided to bet on the end with second pair and top kicker.

Of course, your opponent's play is also consistent with having a pair of fives or fours in the hole, and he's now decided to bet on the end because it's his last chance to extract some value.

Calling versus raising is a question that hinges as much on stack size as the strength of the hand. Here you have $1,465 left, and with the blinds totaling $30, your M is just under 50. That's a deep stack, and rather than get too involved in what may be a toss-up situation, I would just call. If my M were 10 or lower, I would probably raise, even if that committed me to the pot. Here I favor calling.

Score 3 points for Choice B, calling $200, and 1 point for Choice C, raising to $400. No credit for other choices.

You actually call, and your opponent wins with a set of fours.

Problem 4
Negreanu Versus Farha —
Aggression Meets Aggression

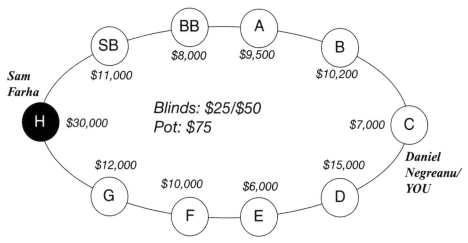

Situation: Early in the first round of the 2005 World Series of Poker. Your playing partner is "Kid Poker," Daniel Negreanu, considered one of the best no-limit tournament players in the world. Most of the players at the table are new, inexperienced faces, including many internet qualifiers. A notable exception is Sam Farha on the button, a very aggressive and dangerous opponent, who finished second to Chris Moneymaker in the 2003 World Series. Sam has knocked two players out already, and is one of the early chip leaders with $30,000.

Your hand: 9♥8♥

Action to you: Players A and B both fold.

24 Problem 4

Question 4A: *What do you do?*

A.   *Fold*
B.   *Call $50*
C.   *Raise to $150*

Action: You raise to $150. Players D and E fold. Player F raises to $400. Player G folds. Sam Farha on the button calls. The blinds fold. The pot is $1,025.

Question 4B: *What do you do?*

A.   *Fold*
B.   *Call $250*
C.   *Reraise to $1,200*

Action: You call. The pot is now $1,275.

Flop: 7♠6♠5♦

Question 4C: *What do you do?*

A.   *Check*
B.   *Bet $600*
C.   *Bet $1,000*
D.   *Push all-in*

Action: You check. Player F checks. Sam Farha bets $1,000.

Question 4D: *What do you do?*

A.   *Call*
B.   *Raise to $3,000*
C.   *Push all-in*

Action: You call. Player F calls behind you. The pot is now $4,275.

Turn: K♥

Question 4E: *What do you do?*

A. *Check*
B. *Bet $2,000*
C. *Push all-in*

Action: You bet $2,000. Player F folds. Sam Farha calls. The pot is now $8,275. You have $3,600 left in your stack.

River: 5♠

Question 4F: *What do you do?*

A. *Check*
B. *Bet $2,000*
C. *Push all-in*

Action: You check. Sam Farha puts you all-in. The pot is now $11,875.

Question 4G: *What do you do?*

A. *Call $3,600*
B. *Fold*

Action: You actually fold. Sam Farha held the 9♠2♠ for a flush.

Solution to Problem 4

We've already seen examples of Daniel Negreanu's play in *Harrington on Hold 'em: Volume II*. Sammy's a dangerous, trappy opponent who attacks often enough with weak hands that his really big hands have an excellent chance of being paid. (His style is similar to Phil Ivey's in that respect — he attacks with weak hands and strong hands alike.) He's especially effective with a big stack, and in the early stages of a tournament, he'll push some long-shot hands to see if he can break people when his hands connect.

In the 2005 World Series, Sammy actually doubled up on the very first hand of the event when he picked up ace-ten (nice way to start hand #1), ran into someone with a pair of tens, and flopped ace-ace-ten! A little later in the first round he busted another opponent, and by the time this hand was played (still in Round 1!), he was sitting with $30,000 in chips.

Question 4A: Aggressive players don't restrict themselves to narrow categories of hands for calling and raising. The guidelines I described in *Harrington on Hold 'em: Volume I* are too constricting for generating the number of hands that aggressive players like to play. In addition to the standard hands for raising in early middle position, the high pairs and the ace-king and ace-queen hands, aggressive players will make moves with high and middle suited and unsuited connectors, hands like jack-nine and ten-eight, and some of the medium and low pairs.

Aggressive players aren't playing these hands because they think it's "theoretically correct" to do so. Instead, they believe their skills in hand reading, analysis, and post-flop play will compensate for the inherent weakness of the hand.

Whether you should play these hands or not depends on the style you're trying to perfect and your skill level. Often with these hands you'll be sitting with middle or bottom pair after the flop, and facing some tough decisions when your opponents play at you. One approach is to try to mix these hands into your repertoire and see what happens. If your results deteriorate, go back to a more conservative style of play. If, on the other hand, your results improve, so much the better.

Score 3 points for Choice A, folding your

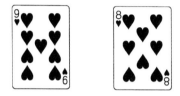

which is a perfectly "correct" play. Also score 3 points for Choice C, raising to $150, which is both a very aggressive play and a play that effectively masks your hand. Score 2 points for Choice B, calling, which may encourage someone behind you to raise. Then you'd have an unpleasant choice between folding and calling with a weak hand out of position. I wouldn't denote any play here a real mistake, but calling is my least favorite option.

You actually raise to $150. Players D and E fold. Player F raises to $400. Player G folds.

Sam Farha calls $400, with a hand of 9♠2♠. Needless to say, this is not a conventional play. He's seen a raise and a reraise in front of him, and he's electing to call with one of the poorest hands he could be holding. So what's going on?

Basically Sammy is playing with three big weapons: his position, his stack size, and his skill at post-flop play. Since he has far more chips than either of the other players in the hand, he'll represent whatever holding the flop allows and try to take the other players off the hand. With his position, he'll get to see what both players do before he has to react. Essentially, he's saying those three advantages alone are worth $400 to him.

Is he right? It's a judgment call. Very aggressive players like to finish the first couple of days' play with a big stack, which they can use to accumulate even more chips as the players race to the final table. They're not interested in grinding along with a small stack for most of the tournament; small stacks don't allow them to make use of most of their skills. But in order to accumulate those big stacks, they have to gamble along the way with sub-par (or in some cases, very sub-par) starting hands. That's how the aggression game is played.

The pot is now $1,025.

Question 4B: Daniel has to call another $250, so he's getting better than 4-to-1 odds from the pot. He seems to be against a couple of real hands, although he's played with Sammy enough to know that Sammy could be playing a lot of different cards in position. Still, his goal is the same as Sammy's — pile up a lot of chips by the end of the day. He's already off to a bad start, as he's lost 30 percent of his starting chips, and it's just the middle of the first round. So he elects to play, and calls.

Score 3 points for Choice A, folding. No one could fault you for giving up the hand, out of position against a raiser and a caller, with just a medium suited connector. Do you think you can play after the flop as well as Daniel? If so, score 3 points for Choice B, calling. No? Then score 1 point for calling. In any case, no credit for Choice C, reraising.

Negreanu calls $250. The pot now contains $1,275. The flop comes

Question 4C: Jackpot for Negreanu. He's hit the nut straight, and his hand is well-disguised by the pre-flop raise and subsequent call of the reraise. Now his job is to extract the maximum from the

hand to compensate for all the times when playing medium suited connectors leads to nothing.

Since the two players behind him showed strength before the flop, there's no reason to bet here. One of those two players will take the lead in the betting. This flop would miss most of the hands that Daniel could have played for value before the flop. A bet just announces that his hand is not what might be expected. Much better to check instead. Score 4 points for Choice A, checking, and no credit for any of the bets.

You just check. Player F also checks.

For Sammy Farha, this is all good news. He's picked up a flush draw and an inside straight draw, 12 outs in all. If his two opponents were playing high pairs or two high cards, this flop missed them. Both players checked, which decreases the chance that either has a high pair, and increases the chance that he's up against two high cards. Of course, Daniel is very tricky, so he could really have almost anything at this point. Still, the door is open, so Sammy charges on through and bets $1,000. The pot increases to $2,275.

Question 4D: Time for Negreanu to survey the table again. Player F checked, which was significant. Had he raised pre-flop with a high pair, he could be expected to bet with an overpair to the board. So for now we'll put him on a couple of high cards, maybe ace-king or ace-queen.

What about Sammy's bet? Sammy's style is similar to Phil Ivey's. He bets when he has nothing, and he guards those bets by also betting when he has something. If the pot is checked to him, you can be pretty sure Sammy's going to take a poke at it. So we can't deduce much of anything from his bet. He probably, however, doesn't have a high pair. With a high pair, he would have reraised pre-flop to chase one of his opponents away. Best guess at this point is that Sammy has a pair and a straight draw, or two high cards with a flush draw, or he's just flat-out bluffing.

You still have the nuts, and no reason yet to believe that there's a threatening hand out there. It would be premature to raise. Player F might be slow-playing a high pair, in which case he's about to raise! In the absence of Player F, you'd want to raise a little bit against Sammy. A small raise shouldn't chase him away from the pot, and by building the pot slowly, you'll facilitate Sammy's calling you on the end with good pot odds. Remember that you'd like to get all your chips in the center this hand (flopped straights don't come around every day), and the surest way to get your chips in the center is to move them in gradually.

Here, however, the possible involvement of Player F negates that plan. Let's just call, and see if Player F does our work for us. Score 3 points for Choice A, calling. No credit for any raise.

You call, and Player F calls as well. The pot becomes $4,275. The turn card is the K♥.

Question 4E: The king is a great card for you. If Sammy is on a draw, it didn't help any possible draw. If Player F or Sammy is playing ace-king, they just made a pair of kings. The king couldn't hurt you, and it may have given someone a hand that could call you.

Now it's time to start seriously building the pot. You still have $5,600 in your stack, and if you start the process now, you won't have to make a huge (and perhaps uncallable) bet on the river. Score 4 points for Choice B, betting $2,000. It's a nice, solid amount that gives both opponents 3-to-1 express pot odds. No credit for checking. You have the best hand, and your call last turn indicated you're sticking around. You can't assume that the other two players will continue to bet the hand for you. Also no credit for Choice C, pushing all-in. It's not an absurd play, since your stack is only 25 percent larger than the pot. But if you want all the money in the middle, a two-stage bet is more likely to succeed. Don't worry about pricing out a flush draw — your opponent may not have a flush draw. All the other possible hands are more likely.

You actually bet $2,000. Player F folds. (He held the A♣J♦.) Farha now looks at a pot of $6,275 and needs $2,000 to call. The pot's offering him 3.1-to-1 odds to call. He has nine outs to make a flush, and the three eights which are not spades to make a straight; 12 outs in all. They aren't, of course, guaranteed to be outs. But Negreanu's bets don't seem to put him on a drawing hand. It's more likely that he has a made hand now, in which case the flushes and straights should be good. (We know, of course, that Negreanu has a made hand, but it's not one of the hands Sammy is thinking about.) A total of 12 outs in 46 unseen cards makes Sammy a 2.8-to-1 underdog on the express odds, and the implied odds are much better because Negreanu has become pot-committed. So he calls. The pot is now $8,275.

The river is the 5♠.

Question 4F: The pot has $8,275, and you have about $3,600 left in your stack. But the river was a bad card. If Sammy was on a flush draw, it just hit. It's also possible he was playing something like seven-five suited or six-five suited, in which case his two pair just became a full house.

You still, however, have a straight, not a bad hand. So, should you bet? To answer, let's consider three key questions governing bets on the river.

1. **Are you sure you have the best hand?** Not any more.

2. **If you bet, can you get any stronger hands to fold?** No. The only stronger hands are flushes and full houses, and they're certainly calling.

3. **If you bet, can you get any weaker hands to call?** Theoretically, yes. If you thought your opponent had trips or two pair, there would certainly be some chance they would call. But when we look at the likely hands, it's almost impossible that Sammy has one of these holdings. For

example, what trips can he hold? He can't have trip kings or sevens or sixes, because all those hands just became full houses. So he can only have trip fives. But if he has trip fives, what's the other card in his hand? Would he have called pre-flop with ace-five or five-four? And if he has two pair, independent of the pair of fives on board, then he must have started with king-seven, king-six, or seven-six. Did he call a raise and a reraise pre-flop with one of those hands?

(In fact Sammy actually called pre-flop with 9♠2♠, a *worse* hand than anything we're considering. So of course he *could* have called with any of those hands. But neither Daniel nor anyone else is going to make that assumption with his tournament hanging in the balance. Instead, he'll make the completely reasonable, and almost always correct, assumption that Sammy can't have trips or two pair given how the hand was played.)

One weaker hand that fits all the action so far is ace-king, suited or unsuited. It matches the pre-flop call, the bet on the flop after two checks, and the call on the turn with top pair, top kicker. But would the hand call an all-in bet on the end? Perhaps. In general, Sammy likes to push the action, rather than respond to someone's else's bets. I would expect him to fold this hand to an all-in, but not always, and particularly not always to a tricky and aggressive player like Negreanu.

One last question needs to be answered before we decide what to do: *If you check, will your opponent bluff at the pot?* Given a player as aggressive as Sammy, and given how he plays with a big stack, the answer is "possibly." Sammy is certainly capable of cranking up the pressure and moving at the pot, so there is some chance that a check will induce a bluff.

The conclusion? The preponderance of the evidence lies on the side of checking. Score 4 points for Choice A, checking, and 2 points for Choice C, pushing all-in. No credit for the mini-bet of $2,000. If you play at all, you're pot-committed.

You actually check. Sam Farha, now with a made flush, puts you all-in. Sam had to bet $3,600 to put you in, so you're looking at a pot of $11,875.

Question 4G: So should you call or not? We know that Sam has made his improbable flush, but you don't know that fact when decision time comes, so let's look at the considerations that factor into your decision.

1. **Pot odds.** The pot is offering you odds of 3.3-to-1. Those are big odds. If you fold you'll have $3,600 in your stack, but if you call and win, you'll have $15,475. Another way of expressing those odds is to say that if you call and your straight is best 23 percent of the time, you'll do better by calling.

2. **Hand strength.** You have the best possible straight, which is, by itself, a very strong hand. However, as we just discussed, given the board and the betting, most of the hands you can beat — a weaker straight, or trips, or two pair — don't jibe with the actions you've seen. The hands that beat you, however, make complete sense.

3. **Your opponent.** Is your opponent capable of playing hands very creatively and/or bluffing on the river? Yes, Sammy is completely capable of that. (As a result, Sammy often gets paid off on his big hands.)

4. **Your position in the tournament.** You're still in the first round of the tournament, so the $3,600 stack you'll have if you fold is still large enough (M=48) to keep playing for awhile. Of course, a $15,000 stack is much, much better.

Daniel actually folded, deciding that his hand analysis (which as usual was extremely accurate) trumped all other considerations.

He simply didn't believe that Sammy was bluffing without a hand, and he was right. Score 5 points if you elected to fold.

Sammy was incredulous when Daniel revealed his hand. "You folded a straight? *You folded a straight?*" But his surprise reveals another important lesson. Against a very strong player who is skilled at reading hands and playing after the flop, you may not be able to play hands that rely on implied odds, because the implied odds may not be there. Against Daniel, they weren't.

Score 3 points if you made the human play and called. I would have called with a straight. The combination of the pot odds and Sammy's playing style would have sucked me in, and most other good players as well, I suspect. Daniel made an amazing fold; hats off to him.

Problem 5
Facing an Early Limper

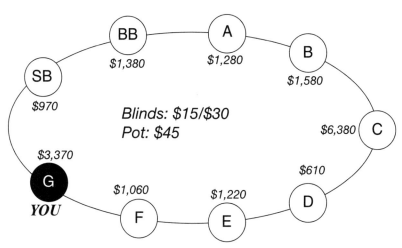

Situation: Large multi-table online tournament. You're in the second round. The big blind and Player C seem a little loose. You don't have any information yet on Player A. You flopped a straight in a multiway pot and doubled up early.

Your hand: 6♣6♥

Action to you: Player A limps for $30. Players B, C, D, E, and F all fold.

Question 5A: *What do you do?*

A. Fold
B. Call $30
C. Raise to $120
D. Raise to $200

36 Problem 5

Action: You actually call $30. The small blind folds and the big blind checks. The pot is now $105.

Flop: K♥7♦3♣

Action: The big blind checks and Player A checks.

Question 5B: *What do you do?*

A. *Check*
B. *Bet $55*
C. *Bet $80*
D. *Bet $100*

Action: You actually bet $80. The big blind folds, but Player A calls.

Turn: 3♠

Action: Player A checks. The pot is $265.

Question 5C: *What do you do?*

A. *Check*
B. *Bet $100*
C. *Bet $200*

Action: You actually check. The pot remains $265.

River: T♥

Action: Player A checks.

Question 5D: *What do you do?*

A. *Check*
B. *Bet $100*
C. *Bet $200*

Action: You actually check. Player A turns over A♣9♦, and you take the pot with your pair of sixes.

Solution to Problem 5

Question 5A: You have the

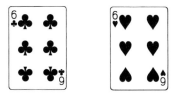

and you're in nice position on the button. The first player just limps, and everyone else gets out of the way. What to do?

A limp in first position at a large table can mean any of several things. From a strong opponent, it most often means a medium pair or a couple of high cards. A strong player with a high pair will usually raise, because he wants to get heads-up rather than face a multi-way pot. And a strong player with a low pair will just throw it away, because limping too often results in throwing the hand away after a raise.

But from a weak player, a limp can mean a lot of different hands. He might limp with a high pair, thinking he's being tricky. Or limp with a small pair, prepared to call a raise. Or limp with suited connectors, because he always limps with suited connectors. So you can't really put a weak player on a hand when he limps. Instead you assume you're against some sort of medium-strength hand and wait for more information.

38 Problem 5

My play here against a good player generally depends on his stack size. If he has a small stack (with an M less than 10), I may raise him with my sixes, hoping to knock out the blinds and isolate against just one opponent, figuring that I'll mostly be a 6-to-5 favorite in a heads-up showdown. If my M is less than 10, I'll raise also, trying to achieve the same result. But if we both have deep stacks, I don't want to get into a position where I can lose a big pot with just a small pair. Instead I'll just call with my sixes, and use my position after the flop to try to win the hand.

In this case you don't know anything about Player A and his M is 28. I'd play small here and just call. Score 3 points for Choice B, calling. Score 1 point for Choice C, making a small raise. No credit for folding or making a big raise.

You call, the small blind folds, and the big blind checks. The pot is $105.

The flop comes

The big blind and Player A both check.

Question 5B: That's not a bad flop for you. The cards are split, and no obvious straights or flushes are possible. It might easily have missed both opponents, and no one has bet, so you should make a stab to try to win it. Score 2 points for Choice B, betting $55, and 1 point for Choice C, betting $80. No credit for checking (too passive) or betting $100 (too much). You want to bet as close to half the pot as possible, so as to give yourself the best possible odds. Remember that if you bet half the pot, you'll break even if your opponents fold just one time in three. If they fold more than that, you make a profit. The bigger your bet, the more often they have to fold for you to emerge ahead. Betting half the pot is usually the sweet spot.

You actually bet $80. The big blind folds, but Player A calls. The pot becomes $265.

The turn is the 3♠. Player A checks.

Question 5C: The trey was a good card for you. It only hurts if Player A was hanging around with a trey, which is unlikely since he called under the gun.

Should you bet now with your pair of sixes? Most players get confused in this situation and spend their energy trying to figure out if Player A really has a king or not. Barring some miraculous read, it's an imponderable question. The right way to think about betting is to ask yourself two simple questions:

Question 1: *If my opponent has a hand that beats me, can my bet get him to fold?*

If your bet makes a hand that would otherwise beat you in a showdown to fold, then you win a pot you would otherwise lose. That's very unlikely here. A player with a pair of kings certainly isn't folding, and someone with a pair of sevens just might fold, but with only one overcard showing he'll probably call. Pairs in between the kings and the sevens will certainly call. The board is just weak enough to keep all the better hands playing.

Question 2: *If my opponent has a hand that I'm beating, will he call my bet?*

If the answer to Question 2 is 'yes,' then you're getting more money in a pot you're winning. That's a good result, but it won't happen often here. The only pairs you can beat are fives, fours, and deuces. The deuces will definitely go away, and the fives and the fours will probably (but not certainly) follow suit. How about two big but unpaired cards, like ace-ten? A good player would fold, because he's about a 6.5-to-1 underdog against any pair, and an even bigger underdog if the pair is bigger than his bottom card. But some weak players might call in that situation. There's one further reason for betting, and that is to prevent weaker hands from drawing out on you. But if those weaker hands don't have much of a chance to improve or aren't likely to be in the pot at this point anyway, that may not be a good enough reason to invest another bet. Here, for instance, the weaker hands fall into two categories: two higher unpaired cards and a smaller pair. The smaller pair has only two outs to beat you; with 44 unseen cards, it's a 21-to-1 underdog to draw out. A hand with two unpaired high cards has six outs on the river, so as just mentioned it's about a 6.5-to-1 underdog to draw out. But that hand should have folded to your bet on the flop. Perhaps it didn't, but at the least you have to downgrade the chance that you're facing that particular hand.

The bottom line: Do you want to invest a bet of perhaps two-thirds of the existing pot to make sure these longshots don't draw out on you? No. The best risk-reward ratio comes from letting those hands draw, but not giving your money to the better hands that you can't beat.

Score 4 points for Choice C, checking your small pair. No credit for betting.

You check. The river comes the T♥. Player A checks.

Question 5D: The arrival of a ten creates a couple of small changes. A hand containing a ten now beats you. In addition, a bet is now somewhat more likely to chase away a pair of sevens, eights, or nines, hands which have now become third pair. It's hard to say whether the net effect is positive or negative. I would still check the hand down and see what happens. Score 2 points for Choice A, checking, no credit for betting.

You check and your opponent shows A♣9♦. Your pair of sixes takes the pot.

Problem 6
Harman Versus Zeidman
— Avoiding the 'Negative Freeroll'

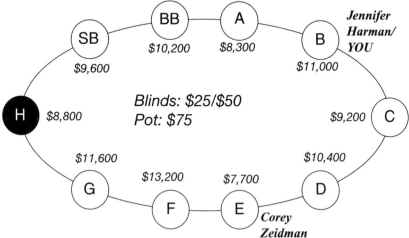

Situation: A little more than an hour into the first round of the 2005 World Series of Poker Main Event. Your playing partner is Jennifer Harman, second to act this hand. Corey Zeidman, three seats to your left, is an experienced player who finished 39th in the Main Event in 2003. You don't know much about the big blind, two seats to your right.

Your hand: Q♦Q♣

Action to you: Player A folds.

Question 6A: *What do you do?*

A.   *Call $50*
B.   *Raise to $150*
C.   *Raise to $200*

41

D. *Raise to $250*
E. *Push all-in*

Action: You actually raise to $200. Players C and D fold. Corey Zeidman calls your $200. All others fold to the big blind, who calls for an additional $150. The pot is now $625, and there are three players.

Flop: Q♥J♦T♠

Action to you: The big blind checks.

Question 6B: *What do you do?*

A. *Check*
B. *Bet $300*
C. *Bet $500*
D. *Bet $800*
E. *Go all-in*

Action: You bet $500, making the pot $1,125. Behind you, Corey Zeidman raises to $2,000, and the big blind folds.

Question 6C: *What do you do?*

A. *Fold*
B. *Call*
C. *Raise to $4,000*
D. *Push all-in*

Action: You actually call for another $1,500, making the pot $4,625. You have $8,800 left in your stack. Zeidman appears to have about $5,500.

Turn: T♦

Question 6D: *You are first to act. What do you do?*

A. *Check*
B. *Bet $1,000*
C. *Bet $2,000*
D. *Bet $4,000*
E. *Push all-in*

Action: You check. Zeidman bets $1,000.

Question 6E: *What do you do?*

A. *Call*
B. *Raise to $3,000*
C. *Push all-in*

Action: You raise to $3,000, and Zeidman calls for another $2,000. The pot now contains $10,625. You have $5,800 left in your stack. Zeidman has about $2,500.

River: 7♦

Question 6F: *You are first to act. What do you do?*

A. *Check*
B. *Push all-in*

Action: You actually push all-in, and Zeidman calls. Zeidman shows 9♦8♦, and his straight flush beats your queens full of tens.

Solution to Problem 6

Jennifer Harman is one of the genuine superstars of the modern poker scene. She's made a seamless transition from "one of the top women players" to "one of the top players, period," with her successes both in tournaments and in the Big Game at the Bellagio. (For more on the Big Game, see Michael Craig's excellent book, *The Professor, the Banker, and the Suicide King*.) Harman's game combines rock-solid technical skills and an acute ability to read her opponents. Mess with her at your peril.

Question 6A: With

in early position, the only question is the right amount to raise. Ideally, I like to make a slightly larger than normal raise with the queens, because I'm hoping to discourage the ace-x hands from coming in against me too cheaply and beating me with an ace on the flop. Jennifer raises to $200, which is four times the big blind. That's an amount I like. It's not too large to discourage all action, but it's large enough to make hands like ace-nine and ace-seven think twice about entering the pot. Score 5 points for Choice C, raising $200.

Score 3 points for Choices B and D, raising $150 and $250. $150 is a little light for queens, allowing drawing hands in too easily, while $250 is a little heavy, potentially discouraging action.

No credit for Choice A, calling. Queens do not play well in a multi-way pot, especially out of position. You don't need lots of players drawing to beat you. Ideally, you'd like to see action from one player or perhaps two, but just taking down the blinds is not a bad result.

Also no credit for Choice E, pushing all-in. This is a beginner's play which, as we showed in *Harrington on Hold 'em:*

Volume I, actually has negative equity. Mostly you will just win the blinds, but when someone behind you wakes up with aces or kings, you'll usually lose your whole stack. Not a good risk-reward ratio.

Corey Zeidman, in fifth position, has 9♦8♦ and elects to call Jennifer's raise. It's a speculative play which I don't really like here. There are two main problems with the call:

1. **Position**. After Zeidman calls, five people will remain to act behind him. A reraise from any one of them will force Zeidman to dump his hand regardless of Jennifer's response.

2. **Implied odds**. The medium suited connectors will only rarely get a flop that enables them to continue with the hand. Even if the pre-flop action ends with Zeidman, most flops will be followed by a bet from Harman and a fold. (Remember, Harman raised in early position, indicating a premium hand. Even a flop like 9♥4♠2♣ could cost Zeidman his whole stack if he proceeds with the hand.) Because the connectors rarely get a flop that allows them to continue with the hand, they need to get a big payoff when they do make a hand. To see how likely that is, you need to look at the cost of entering the pot and the likelihood of the possible payoffs. I like to see a possible payoff of 20-to-30 times my cost when I play with these cards. Here it costs $200 to play, and Zeidman's stack is $7,700. To get the payoff he needs, Zeidman needs to just about double his stack when he hits his hand. That's a tall order.

The ideal time for calling with the suited connectors is in late position, after a series of limpers. There's little chance of a raise behind you, and the large number of opponents plus the small cost of entry means that making 20-to-30 times your bet when you hit isn't an insurmountable obstacle.

The big blind now calls with A♣6♥. It's a tempting play because of the pot odds. (It costs him $150 to call, and there's $475 in the pot, so he's getting better than 3-to-1 odds.) Nonetheless, I would let the hand go. He's in the pot against two players, one a world-class player who raised in early position, the other an experienced player who called the raise from middle position. Either or both players might have a medium-to-high pair or a high ace. Both will have position after the flop. Despite the pot odds, it's a very good time to let the low ace go.

If you're tempted to call with hands like ace-six, ask yourself this question: What flop are you hoping to see? A flop that contains an ace could cost you most of your chips if either player has ace-king or ace-queen, a very likely scenario under the circumstances. How about a flop like king-jack-six? Against a raiser and a caller, and with a king and a jack out on the board, your bottom pair doesn't look too impressive. How about six-five-deuce? Now you have top pair and top kicker, but you're still a big underdog if either player started with a good pair.

The only sort of flops that look really inviting are flops like ace-jack-six, where your two pair are likely to be best, or six-six-x, where your trip sixes will probably pull down a big pot. But that means your chances of hitting a flop that might make you some money are in the 20-to-1 ballpark, too slim to continue play.

I'd be more likely to call with a hand like eight-seven suited, or eight-six suited, or even Zeidman's hand of 9♦8♦. These are hands that are unlikely to be dominated by the presumably big hands that are already in the pot. With these middling hands, you have a chance to hit the flop and actually be the best hand at the table.

Now the flop comes

and the big blind, first to act, checks.

Question 6B: Jennifer Harman has made top set, but on a very dangerous board. If either Zeidman or the big blind called with ace-king, they've made the nut straight. Two other straights are possible: Both king-nine and nine-eight have made a straight as well. Neither holding was likely to have called her pre-flop raise. (Although one, in fact, did.) Plenty of holdings are now drawing to straights or have made two pair. Some possibilities are especially juicy: if either player called with a pair of jacks or tens, they've made a dominated set, and may lose all their money.

The real danger is the ace-king, which is both a very possible holding from the pre-flop action and a hand that she can only beat by drawing a full house. But it's only one possible hand among many, and she's beating most of the others. Now let's evaluate her choices. The pot is $625.

1. **Choice A, check.** No credit for this weak play. Harman likely has the best hand at this point, and wants to get more money in the pot, as well as forcing the possible drawing hands to pay to beat her.

2. **Choice B, bet $300.** One point for this bet. It's the right idea, but any hand drawing to an open-ended straight will be tempted to call, given the 3-to-1 odds and the possibly large implied odds after hitting the hand.

3. **Choice C, bet $500.** Four points for this bet. Something in the range of $500 to $600 feels right here. More money is going in the pot, and the drawing hands are only getting a little better than 2-to-1 express odds. Any hand that can call this bet has to have something.

4. **Choice D, bet $800.** Too big. Remember, you're beating the drawing hands right now, and you want them to stick around and call, as long as they're not getting the odds they need. This nervous bet tries too hard to chase them out of the pot, which is not your idea. Two points if you picked this choice.

5. **Choice E, go all-in.** Uncool. A typical online move, made by players who are afraid to play after the flop. It's not as bad as usual, since there are some hands you can beat that might call here, like the smaller trips. But with a big hand, you want to build the pot gradually. No credit.

Jennifer actually bets $500, making the pot $1,125. Now the action swings to Zeidman, with his 9♦8♦ and a stack of about $7,500.

Zeidman now has an interesting problem. He's flopped a straight, but it's the low end of the straight. Either an ace-king or a king-nine has him beaten. Jennifer's pre-flop raise and post-flop bet are perfectly consistent with an ace-king, although it's almost inconceivable that she would have raised before the flop with a king-nine. If Harman raised with a high pair, she now has either an overpair (if she raised with aces), an overpair with an open-ended straight draw (if she raised with kings), or trips (if she raised with queens, jacks, or tens). Other holdings are much less likely, but would leave her with some combination of two pair, a high pair, and a straight draw.

Zeidman shouldn't be discouraged by the possibility that Harman has the nut straight. There are many other hands that both account for her plays and leave Zeidman in a good position to double up. He needs to put in a big raise here, and in fact he does, raising $2,000. It's a good-sized raise, about at the upper limit of the amount I would want to raise. Nice play. The big blind folds, and the action moves around to Harman. The pot is now $3,125.

Question 6C: It costs Harman another $1,500 to just call, so she's getting 2-to-1 on her money to stick around. It's virtually impossible to fold top set under the circumstances, so no credit if you picked Choice A, folding.

Harman's next job is to consider the possible hands that could be making a raise here. In addition, she may have a read of some sort on Zeidman, but we don't know that. Early in the first round, most players are reluctant to place too much stock in their reads of players that they're seeing for the first time, so it's likely that Harman would emphasize the logic of the situation and the betting so far. Let's look at what hands Zeidman could hold that justify his pre-flop call and his post-flop raise.

- **AK.** This is the big threat. Big Slick both beats her and fits all his plays perfectly. The good news (sort of) is that she has seven immediate outs (three jacks, three tens, and the Q♠), plus ten outs on the river if the turn card comes and misses her.

- **K9.** It takes a very brave man to call a raise in early position from a world-class player with king-nine, so there's only a minimal chance of this holding.

- **98 (probably suited).** Super-aggressive players, like Gus Hansen or Phil Ivey, don't mind calling with this hand in position, figuring they will sometimes be able to take the pot away after the flop if they don't hit their hand. Against most players, I wouldn't assume this was a likely holding if I had opened in early position with a raise. But the big raise after the flop makes this holding a bit more likely.

- **AQ.** A lot of players would call with this hand in middle position, and then raise after the flop with top pair, top kicker. (I wouldn't, because the board combined with Harman's pre-flop raise makes the situation too dangerous.) Harman's in a great situation against this holding, since the only outs are the four kings.

- **KQ.** This holding now has top pair plus an open-ended straight draw. It's less likely that he would have called with this before the flop, but more likely that he would have raised after the flop.

- **JT (probably suited).** Like the nine-eight, this is a possible holding for a super-aggressive player, unlikely for most others. If that's what he has, he's raising with his two pair, but he's drawing almost dead.

- **JJ or TT.** These two pairs match the bets so far, and are drawing almost dead to Harman's queens. These are the hands she really wants to see, since they're usually going to lose all their chips.

- **AA or KK.** Not likely at this point, since an experienced player would reraise with these before the flop. If he has one of these hands, it's probably kings, since the open-ended straight better explains the post-flop raise.

That list pretty much covers the possible hands out there. The most likely hands are ace-king (suited or unsuited), jacks, or tens. All three hands explain both the pre-flop and post-flop action pretty well. Ace-queen and king-queen aren't very likely because they use the last queen in the deck. Aces and kings don't explain the pre-flop call, and the post-flop raise with aces looks optimistic at best. Forget about king-nine; nobody's calling a pre-flop raise with that trash. Jack-ten suited and nine-eight suited are just barely possible given the pre-flop call.

So what should she do? I'd analyze the situation this way: The three most likely hands are ace-king, jacks, and tens. With a jack and a ten on board, there are a lot more ace-king combinations than pairs of jacks or tens. That means it's more likely than not that I'm beaten at this point. But the pot is offering 2-to-1 odds, and I have seven immediate outs even if I am beaten. In addition, I'm beating most of the unlikely hands. So I'm calling, but I'm not raising.

Score 4 points for Choice B, call, and no credit for Choices C or D, raising and pushing all-in.

Harman actually calls for another $1,500, bringing the pot to $4,625. The turn comes a T♦, giving Harman queens full of tens, and giving Zeidman both a flush and a straight flush draw in addition to his straight.

Question 6D: A great card for Harman. Her trips have improved to a full house, so the only possible holding that can be ahead of her now is the hand of the two case tens. She's beaten all the straights, and any flush draws are drawing dead. In the unlikely event that Zeidman is holding precisely the 9♦8♦ (we know he is, of course, but Harman doesn't), he has only one out to a straight flush, since Harman holds the Q♦.

Judging from his large raise last turn, Zeidman has something, and may well be inclined to bet it. Harman has what looks like a virtual lock, so her task is now to extract the most money possible. Since her opponent has indicated his willingness to bet, her best choice is to check, hoping for a bet which she can raise. Score 4 points for Choice A, check.

If you wanted to bet, your bet size should depend on the chip stacks and the pot odds you can offer your opponent. Right now the pot contains $4,625 and your opponent's stack seems to have about $5,500. In these situations, a bet of somewhat less than half the pot offers the best combination of maximizing the money going into that pot while minimizing the chance he will fold. Score 2 points for Choice C, betting $2,000, and only one point for either Choices B or D, betting $1,000 or $4,000. Betting $1,000 gets too little money in, while betting $4,000 is too likely to chase him away. No credit for Choice E, all-in, which has the best chance of being folded.

Harman actually checks.

Now Zeidman has a tough decision. His straight looked very good, and he's picked up in addition both a flush draw (any diamond) and a straight flush draw (the 7♦). (He probably believes that he has an open-ended straight flush draw; he can't know that the Q♦ is already out in Harman's hand.)

But the T♦ was an extremely unpleasant card to arrive on the board. A number of Harman's possible holdings just became quads or full houses. To see just how he stands now, he needs to run through her possible hands and see which he can now beat.

It helps at this point to know something of Harman's style. Like most top players, she plays conservatively in early position, but likes to open up in middle or late position. If I were at a table with Harman, I'd think that an early raise represented only a small subset of hands, perhaps no more than 5 percent of the possible hand holdings. I'd expect to be facing any of the high pairs (aces through tens), or ace-king, with nines, ace-queen, and king-queen as possible but less likely. Did Zeidman know this? We can't tell, but it's a good default assumption when facing any top player. In general, they don't like to fool around from the first two seats when the stacks are deep, because the probability that someone behind them has a real hand is just too great.

With that fact in mind, let's put ourselves in Zeidman's seat and see how Harman's possible opening hands fit the bets we've seen.

- **AA**. This matches the pre-flop raise and the post-flop bet. Whether Harman would call with this hand against the dangerous board and the raise is possible but dubious. Zeidman is winning against this hand.

- **KK**. Also matches the pre-flop raise and the post-flop bet. It's a better match for the call of the raise because of the open-ended straight draw. Zeidman is winning here.

- **QQ**. This matches the pre-flop raise, the post-flop bet, and the post-flop call. It also matches the check on the turn (which is a trap). Zeidman has two possible outs (the Q♦ and 7♦), one of which we know is dead).

- **JJ**. Same as queens. Only two possible outs remain.

- **TT**. Although this hand has made quads rather than a full house, it plays the same as queens and jacks, and leaves the same two possible outs. It is, however, less likely than the other two because only one card holding allows it, rather than the three possible holdings for the queens and the jacks.

- **AK**. Matches Harman's pre-flop raise. It's a partial match for the post-flop bet since Harman would have hit the nuts on the flop with this hand. However, a check would have been very reasonable on her part. But it's not really a match for the call of Zeidman's raise. With a lot of money already in the pot, and the fact that just a call gives away the strength of the hand, ace-king would likely have reraised big and hoped for a call.

- **AQ (less likely)**. The pre-flop raise from early position is possible, as is the post-flop bet with top pair, top kicker on a dangerous board. But the $1,500 call of the raise post-flop is sporting, at best. I wouldn't see that call as very likely.

Combining the loose pre-flop raise with the post-flop call makes this holding very unlikely.

- **KQ (less likely).** The pre-flop raise becomes even less likely with this holding, although the post-flop bet and call now make more sense, as does the check on the turn.

- **99 (less likely).** The pre-flop raise in early position is possible, the post-flop bet into three overcards with an underpair and a straight draw is now very unlikely, and the call of the big raise is impossible in the face of the potentially made straights. This holding has to be eliminated.

Barring some very unusual play on Harman's part, this analysis (from Zeidman's point-of-view) lets us narrow down Harman's potential hands considerably. The ace-queen, king-queen, and nines hands really don't seem possible anymore. Aces and kings are possible. Queens, jacks, and tens are perfect fits for the play so far. Ace-king, the hand that Zeidman now wishes she had, would almost certainly have reraised post-flop.

So the best guess right now is that Harman has a full house, and Zeidman needs to fill his straight flush to win. There's some chance that he's still facing a hand he can beat, but it's not likely enough to make me want to reopen the betting. Zeidman should just check and be glad he's getting a free card.

In fact Zeidman makes a feeler bet of $1,000.

Question 6E: Harman's choices are getting simpler now. She's only losing to one hand, a pair of tens in the hole. Although that hand fits all the bets she's seen, there are so many other hands which she can beat that also fit the betting that she has to put that possibility aside and just concentrate on getting all her opponent's chips in the center.

After his $1,000 bet, he seems to have about $4,500 left in his stack. The right play in this situation is to make your opponent put in a little less than half his remaining stack. A raise of that size will offer him good pot odds, but not the odds he needs to draw out on your monster. When you then put him all-in on the river, he'll be compelled by the odds to call if he has any reasonable hand at all.

Score 4 points for Choice B, raising to $3,000. No credit for the other choices. Many beginners and intermediates would rush to the all-in move here, out of nervousness and a desire to end the hand and "solidify their win." But your goal isn't to solidify the win, but to make the play that, on average, results in winning the most chips. As long as you can make sure your opponent isn't getting the right odds to continue, given what he probably has, you'll make more money by keeping the hand going. That's exactly what Harman is doing here.

Zeidman calls the raise, and the pot becomes $10,625. The river card is the 7♦, which gives Zeidman his straight flush.

Question 6F: Harman now sees that a second possible hand can also beat her, the 9♦8♦. But with the pot over $10,000 and Zeidman having only about $2,500 left in his stack, it's too late to worry. There are plenty of possible hands she's still beating, so she can't back off. Score 4 points for Choice B, pushing all-in. No credit for Choice A, checking. There's too great a danger that Zeidman will just check behind and keep the rest of his stack. (He would, of course, have pushed all-in, but she can't know that.)

Failing to bet here would be an example of what's known in the trade as a *negative freeroll*. If she checks and Zeidman has a hand that beats her, he will bet and she will have to call (because of the pot odds, if nothing else). So she'll lose her money whether she bets or checks. But if Zeidman has a hand that she can beat, she may only get his money if she bets; checking allows him to check and keep the rest of his stack. Allowing a negative freeroll on the river is a serious blunder, which Harman easily avoids.

Harman moves all-in and Zeidman calls, showing the straight flush. He takes down a pot of over $15,000.

A well-played hand on both sides, coupled with some amazing swings of fortune.

Do players really go through reasoning this detailed in the play of the hand? Yes they do, especially when the hand is becoming one in which a player will either get knocked out or doubled up. It's well worth taking a few minutes to run through the possible hands in your mind and see how well they match the betting.

Let's note a couple of other interesting points about this hand. First, as the two players tried to analyze their opponent's possible hands, the menus were almost identical! That's because, for any given board, only a few hands can really synchronize the board and the betting action. As a result, each player is considering the same set of hands as possibilities for his opponent.

Second, notice that conservative, technically correct play, regardless of its merits, actually makes your hand easier to read. When we were looking at the hand from Zeidman's point of view, considering Harman's predilections and bets, we were actually able to narrow Harman's possible hands down to just a couple, one of which was her actual hand. But because Zeidman started with a non-standard play (calling with suited connectors), the analysis from Harman's point of view was never that precise, and in fact she couldn't be sure of what he held until he actually turned over his hand. One of the great strengths of the super-aggressive style is its ability to muddle the reasoning process for your opponents, introducing more confusion and uncertainty into the hand. By keeping their holdings opaque, the aggressive players regain much of the equity lost by starting with inferior-quality hands.

Problem 7
Greg Raymer — All-in
or Suck Bet[1] on the River?

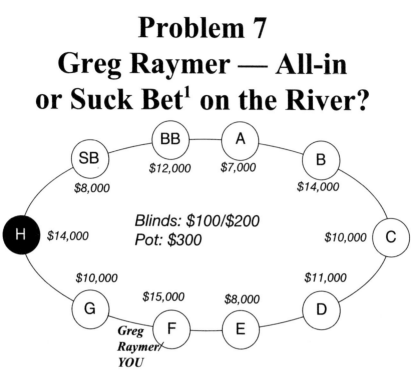

SB $8,000

BB $12,000

A $7,000

B $14,000

H $14,000

C $10,000

Blinds: $100/$200
Pot: $300

G $10,000

F $15,000
Greg Raymer/ YOU

E $8,000

D $11,000

Situation: Third round on the first day of the 2005 World Series of Poker. Your playing partner is the defending champion, Greg Raymer. You've built your stack a bit from your initial $10,000 buy-in. The button is a conservative player who has played well so far. You don't know much about Player B.

Your hand: J♣9♠

Action to you: Player A folds. Player B calls $200. Players C, D, and E all fold.

---

[1] A small bet designed to enlist a call.

58 Problem 7

Question 7A: *What do you do?*

A. *Fold*
B. *Call $200*
C. *Raise to $800*

Action: You call. Player G folds. Player H, on the button, raises to $700. The blinds fold. Player B folds.

Question 7B: *What do you do?*

A. *Fold*
B. *Call $500*
C. *Reraise to $2,000*

Action: You call $500. The pot is now $1,900.

Flop: J♥9♣3♦

Question 7C: *What do you do?*

A. *Check*
B. *Bet $1,000*
C. *Bet $2,000*
D. *Push all-in*

Action: You check. The button bets $1,000. The pot is now $2,900.

Question 7D: *What do you do?*

A. *Call $1,000*
B. *Raise to $3,000*
C. *Push all-in*

Action: You raise to $3,000. The button calls. The pot is now $7,900.

Turn: 9♥

Question 7E: *What do you do?*

A. *Check*
B. *Bet $4,000*
C. *Push all-in*

Action: You check and the button checks.

River: 6♣

Question 7F: *What do you do?*

A. *Check*
B. *Bet $3,000*
C. *Push all-in*

Action: You actually bet $3,000, and the button calls. He shows K♠K♦, and your full house beats his two pair.

Solution to Problem 7

Greg Raymer is a very strong, very aggressive player who burst on the poker scene by winning the 2004 World Series of Poker ahead of a then-record crowd of 2,576 players. Although he was a new face to those who know only the world of television poker, real aficionados of the game had been aware of him for some time. He regularly posted on the Two Plus Two Forums under the name "Fossilman," and it was obvious from reading his posts that this was a player who not only understood the game well, but who had many original ideas for handling complex situations.

Although Raymer is a very dangerous and aggressive player, his personal appearance functions as a sort of camouflage. While players like Gus Hansen and Sammy Farha practically exude danger and menace at the table, Raymer has a cheerful and kindly attitude that suggests you're up against some kind of small-town banker or parish priest. But while he's cheerfully chatting you up, he's also vacuuming all the chips at the table. He's especially dangerous when he's the big stack, which he wields like a mace. You want to confront him early in a tournament, when he's taking chances to build that big stack.

Question 7A: Score 2 points for Choice B, calling, and 2 points for Choice A, folding. There's nothing wrong with folding, especially if you don't see yourself as a strong post-flop player. You don't have a strong hand, your cards aren't suited, and with two players yet to act, you can't be sure that you'll have position after the flop. But it's the sort of hand that strong players don't mind playing in the early stages of big tournaments. An early call from an unknown player doesn't necessarily indicate much strength. Internet players are fond of limping with any two suited cards, and they can often be chased off these hands post-flop.

Aggressive players play a lot of hands like this pre-flop, if they can get in cheaply. If you hit your hand hard, you might be in position to win a big pot and start building your stack. A big stack is a crucial weapon for an aggressive player, and to accumulate a stack on Day 1 of a big tournament, you need to mess around with a few hands like

No credit for raising to $800; you don't have anything yet, and you have a limper in front of you, so don't bother committing a big chunk of your stack. The idea with these hands is to see a bunch of flops cheaply and look for a couple of great situations that will let you accumulate chips. Without the early limper, I would like raising as much as calling.

You call for $200. Player G folds. Player H, on the button, raises to $700. The blinds and Player B fold. The pot is now $1,400, and it costs you another $500 to call.

Question 7B: Not what you wanted to see. The danger of limping with weakish hands is that you'll get an unpleasant raise from someone behind you, so if you call, you'll have both a weak hand and bad position. But it's happened. Now what to do?

The arguments for calling are:

1. Pot odds
2. Post-flop skill

The pot odds are pretty big. You're getting 2.8-to-1, very nice odds indeed. The post-flop skill differential is hard to quantify. Raymer (correctly) assumes that he can outplay most of his opponents after the flop. But do these two factors add up to a call?

In my mind, no. I would let the hand go. Score 3 points for Choice A, folding. If I were in position with the J♣9♠, and I was getting 2.8-to-1 odds, I'd play, but I'd think I was making a close call. Without position, I would let the hand go without too much thought. Raymer obviously feels differently, and he's had a lot of success playing his way, so score 1 point for Choice B, calling. (Hey, it's my book.) It's a Gus Hansen type move, but Raymer and Gus actually have many similarities in their style. No credit for Choice C, reraising, which could get you in a lot of trouble. If your opponent pushes all-in, are you going to call?

You actually call the raise. The pot is now $1,900. The flop comes

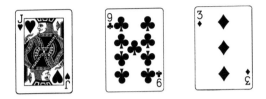

Question 7C: Jackpot! You've hit a big hand, and it's so far completely concealed. Based on your pre-flop action, your opponent probably figures you for a small-to-medium pair, or something like ace-queen or ace-jack. Now comes the real work. In order to play hands like jack-nine pre-flop, you need to be able to win some big pots when you actually hit your hand to balance all the times when you're out of position with nothing after the flop.

Top two pair is a prime candidate for slow-playing, so score 3 points for Choice A, checking. Since your opponent raised before the flop, you should be able to get him to commit some money by checking. If he started with a high pair, he still believes he has the best hand, and he's hoping you hit the flop in some way so you can play with him. No credit for betting any amount here.

You check. The button bets $1,000. The pot is now $2,900.

Question 7D: Time to build the pot. Simply calling here (1 point) isn't good enough. It reveals that you have some sort of a hand, but doesn't get any extra money in the pot. You want to raise, and raising to $3,000 is a good amount. It gets another $2,000 in the pot, while still giving your opponent reasonable calling odds. From the point of view of the button, he'll be looking at a pot of almost $6,000 and calling will cost him just another $2,000. The 3-to-1 odds should look very good. If he has an overpair to the board or top pair, he'll have to call. Even if he has a hand like ace-king, he might believe you're trying to buy the pot and call anyway, giving you a chance to give up on fourth street. Score 3 points for Choice B, raising to $3,000.

No credit for moving all-in. You're announcing you have a big hand and forcing your opponent to make a single all-or-nothing decision. Continue massaging the pot while keeping your opponent involved. You'll have a chance to win all his chips at the end of the hand.

You raise to $3,000 and your opponent calls. The pot is now $7,900. The turn comes 9♥.

Question 7E: The turn gives you a full house and locks up the hand. Now let's think about your opponent. He raised two limpers before the flop and got one call from an opponent he must regard as dangerous. He bet after the flop and got check-raised by the same dangerous opponent, and he just called. What possible hands can we put him on?

• **An overpair (AA, KK, QQ).** These are the most likely hands right now. The pre-flop raise and the bet on the flop make sense. If he thought he was facing a lower pair, then the call of the check-raise also makes sense. He wasn't ready to throw the hand away, especially with good odds, but he was afraid that you had played with jacks or nines and made trips. He also thinks you may be bluffing, or playing aggressively with top pair, but he's not ready to make a decision for most of his chips yet.

• **A pair of jacks.** This is the nightmare scenario. It's unlikely, since he has to have the last two jacks in the deck, but it matches all his bets so far, and his call of your check-raise is just a trap. He's going to double up, and you're going to lose most of your chips, and your only out is the last nine in the deck.

- **AK or AQ.** These are possible hands (though ace-queen is just barely possible), provided he thinks you're bluffing with the check-raise. They match the other bets reasonably well. To win more money, you'll need to make him think you were bluffing on the flop but now have cold feet.

The right play now is a check. If he's holding ace-king or one of the overpairs, a check signals that you've been bluffing or you've realized your top pair may not be good enough. A check might set up another profitable bet on the river. Score 2 points for Choice A, checking, 1 point for Choice B, betting $4,000 (it might work, and if it works you'll probably get all his chips), and no credit for Choice C, the hasty all-in.

You actually check, and he checks behind you. The pot remains at $7,900. The river card is the 6♣.

Question 7F: The 6♣ couldn't have helped him, so you're going to win the hand unless he has precisely the last two jacks. With almost the nuts, you can't check. There's too much danger that he'll just check behind you, as he did on the turn. Players will sometimes check on the river to induce a bluff if they think their opponent's hand is very weak, and he may believe that he can only win the hand by bluffing. That's not the case here; your opponent has something, but he's not convinced it's best. He'll probably be happy to just check the hand and find out. So you have to bet. No credit for checking.

Right now the remaining stack sizes are

- You: $11,300
- Him: $10,300.

Should you make a modest bet like $3,000, which is likely but not certain to be called, or push all-in, betting in essence $10,300, which is unlikely to be called (but not impossible)? If you think the $3,000 bet is 80 percent to be called, but the $10,300 bet is only 20 percent to be called, then the $3,000 bet has a slightly higher expectation ($2,400 to $2,060), and it's the better bet. The key number is the ratio between the profit from the all-in bet and the profit from the "suck bet." Here that ratio is $10,300-to-$3,000 or about 3.5-to-1, so if you think the suck bet is, say 70 percent to be called, but the all-in is 20 percent, (a 3.5-to-1 ratio) then the bets are essentially equivalent.

In practice, I think players don't move all-in on the river often enough with a lock hand. Oddly enough, the bigger the discrepancy between the plausible suck bet and the all-in move, the more likely it is that the all-in bet is correct, since the payoff for getting called all-in is so huge. Remember, there's always some chance the all-in will be called, and there's always some chance the suck bet will be folded.

We're just guessing in this case, but I would say from the way the hand was played that the $3,000 bet will mostly be called, and the all-in will mostly be folded, so the two bets are probably about equivalent. Score 2 points for Choice B, betting $3,000, and 1 point for Choice C, pushing all-in. The more aggressively you like to play, the more you want to push all-in. Because you're seen as aggressive, your bet is more likely to be called, and you need the big stack more than a conservative player, given the way you play.

Problem 8
Calling with Good Odds

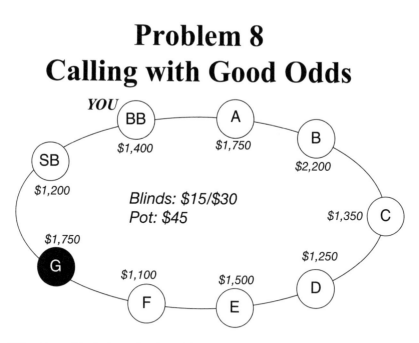

Situation: Early in a single-table online tournament. Player B has several times limped and called a raise pre-flop. The same is true for Player D. You don't know much about the small blind.

Your hand: K♣Q♠

Action to you: Player A folds. Player B calls. Player C folds. Player D calls. Players E and F fold. The button calls. The small blind calls.

Question 8A: *What do you do?*

A. *Check*
B. *Raise to $90*
C. *Raise to $200*

Action: You actually check. The pot is now $150.

Flop: A♦K♥T♠

Action: The small blind checks.

Question 8B: *What do you do?*

A. *Check*
B. *Bet $75*
C. *Bet $150*

Action: You actually bet $75. Player B folds. Player D calls. The button and the small blind fold. The pot is now $300.

Turn: 2♣

Question 8C: *What do you do?*

A. *Check*
B. *Bet $150*

Action: You actually check. Player D bets $100. The pot is now $400.

Question 8D: *What do you do?*

A. *Fold*
B. *Call*
C. *Raise to $300*

Action: You actually call. The pot is now $500.

River: A♣

Question 8E: *What do you do?*

A. *Check*
B. *Bet $250*

Action: You check. Player D bets $200. The pot is now $700.

Question 8F: *What do you do?*

A. *Fold*
B. *Call*
C. *Raise $500*

Action: You actually call. Player D shows A♥7♦ and takes the pot.

Solution to Problem 8

Question 8A: You're in the big blind with the

and four players have limped in front of you. The temptation in this position is to make a big raise and try to take the pot down. After all, if everyone limped, they must be weak, right?

It's a clever little play, and one of the first moves everyone learns to make when playing single-table tournaments. But I won't do it without a solid hand. I want to be holding ace-king, ace-queen, or a pair of tens or better. (At a weak table, I might make the move with nines or even eights.)

Here's the problem. At a strong table, not everyone will be limping with queen-five suited or similar junk. Players might limp with ace-king under the gun, or a pair of nines in late position. Not all of these hands are going away when you make your move. At a weak table, players will play lots of junk, but some of those junk players will call anyway, to show they "can't be pushed around."

If I'm in doubt about whether to raise or not, I look to see if I know anything about the *first limper*. If I know that he will limp and then fold, I'm more inclined to make a move. If I'm pretty sure he will call my raise, then I'll just check and see a flop. Why is the first limper so crucial? Because all the other limpers had a chance to raise, but didn't. Unless they're very tricky, that means they're not interested in playing the hand for a lot of money before the flop. But if the first limper calls, then the other players are getting successively better pot odds to stick around. A call can induce a chain of calls, and then I'm in a big pot out of position against several players — not a great situation.

Incidentally, David Sklansky and T.J. Cloutier like to make an unusual play after an early limper. With a premium pair, aces or kings, and some aggressive players yet to act, they'll just call with the premium pair. Once the action starts, they can move all-in, and can often get someone to go all the way with them. It's a tricky and unexpected move. The big wins more than compensate for the occasions when no one raises and their big pair gets in trouble after the flop.

King-queen offsuit doesn't meet my standards for raising, especially since Player B has already been seen to limp and call a raise. Score 3 points for Choice A, checking. Score 1 point for Choice C, raising $200, which isn't terrible, although I wouldn't do it. No credit for Choice B, the small raise.

You actually call. The pot is $150. The flop comes

The small blind checks.

Question 8B: You've flopped a pair of kings and an inside straight draw, but that's not a good flop for you. With four other players in the pot, the presence of the ace is very worrisome.

You've got two ways to play the hand. You can just check, and hope the hand is checked around, or you can bet half the pot, and see if you encounter resistance. At a very passive table I would be inclined to bet. At an active or unknown table, my preference is for checking.

When you do check, you can learn something from who bets and who doesn't. For example, if I checked and Player B, the initial limper, bet, I'd just go away. He's betting with two players yet to act, so he's probably happy with his hand. But if everyone checked and the button bet, I would stick around. He might well just be trying to steal. By the way, if the small blind had bet in front of me instead of checking, I would have thrown the hand away in a second.

Score 2 points for Choice A, checking, and 1 point for Choice B, betting $75. No credit for Choice C, betting $150. That's too much given the number of players yet to act and the weakness of your hand.

You actually bet $75. Player D calls, but the other players all fold. The pot now has $300.

The turn card is the 2♣.

Question 8C: Your bet cleaned out most of the field. Player D's call gave you two pieces of information:

1.   He liked his hand enough to call.

2.   He didn't like his hand enough to raise.

Since an ace with a good kicker (king, queen, jack, or ten) would probably have raised on the spot, his most likely hand at this point is an ace with a weak kicker. There are other possibilities, of course. He might have a king with a weaker kicker than you, or a pair of tens, or he might have a queen-jack and be slow-playing a straight.

You're probably beaten, but you may not be. No need to put more money in the pot now. Just check and see what he does. Score 2 points for Choice A, checking, no credit for other plays.

You check, and he bets $100. The pot contains $400.

Question 8D: You're getting 4-to-1 odds. Your opponent doesn't seem to want to chase you away, which is a bad sign. On the other hand, you might have as many as nine outs (four jacks, three queens, and two kings), which is just about the right price even if you only get to see the next card. Call, and see what happens.

Score 3 points for Choice B, calling. No credit for the other choices.

You call, and the pot is $500. The river card is the A♣.

Question 8E: That's actually a good card for you. Not only because he's less likely to have an ace (he either has one or he doesn't at this point), but also because if he has king-ten he's now losing to you, since his pair of tens just went away. However, that's not enough to make you want to bet. You'd be delighted to check the hand down and see if your kings are good. Score 2 points for Choice A, checking, no credit for betting.

You check, and he bets $200. The pot is now $700.

Question 8F: You don't like it, and you're probably beaten, but the 3.5-to-1 pot odds make for a call. Score 2 points for Choice B, calling, no credit for folding or raising.

You call, and he shows A♥7♦ to take the pot with three aces.

He indeed had the hand that was his most likely hand as soon as he called on the flop. You were drawn into the hand because of your reasonable holding (second pair and gut-shot straight draw) and the good pot odds. Those things happen in poker.

Problem 9
Phil Hellmuth —
Calculating the Proper Bet Size

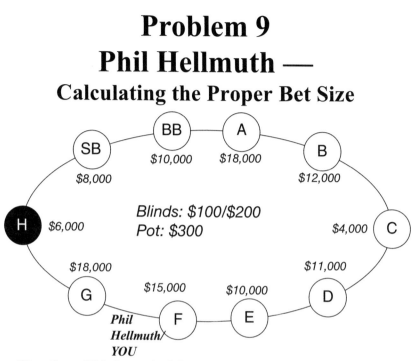

Situation: Third round of the 2005 World Series of Poker. Your playing partner is Phil Hellmuth, winner of 9 World Series of Poker Bracelets. Most of the players at the table seem inexperienced in live play. We're seeing a lot of limping with suited cards, connectors, and weak aces. You have no particular read on Player G, sitting right behind you.

Your hand: 3♦3♣

Action to you: Player A limps for $200. Player B limps for $200. Player C folds. Player D limps for $200. Player E folds. The pot is now $900.

73

74 Problem 8

Question 9A: *What do you do?*

A. *Fold*
B. *Call $200*
C. *Raise to $1,000*

Action: You call for $200. Player G raises to $1,100. The button and the small blinds fold. The three limpers in front of you fold. The pot is now $2,200

Question 9B: *What do you do?*

A. *Fold*
B. *Call $900*
C. *Reraise $3,000*

Action: You actually call $900. The pot is now $3,100.

Flop: K♦7♣6♣

Question 9C: *What do you do?*

A. *Check*
B. *Bet $1,500*
C. *Bet $3,000*

Action: You check. Player F checks behind you.

Turn: 6♠

Question 9D: *What do you do?*

A. *Check*
B. *Bet $550*

C.   *Bet $1,100*
D.   *Bet $2,200*

Action: You bet $550. Player F calls. The pot is now $4,200.

River: J♥

Question 9E: *What do you do?*

A.   *Check*
B.   *Bet $2,000*
C.   *Bet $4,000*

Action: You check. Player F bets $2,500. The pot is now $6,700.

Question 9F: *What do you do?*

A.   *Fold*
B.   *Call $2,500*
C.   *Raise all-in*

Action: You fold.

Solution to Problem 9

One problem that internet players have when they first move to live tournaments is limping with too many hands. The rationale for limping is usually articulated as "It's just a tiny percentage of my stack" and "I just want to see a flop." But three problems arise:

1.   Those "tiny" percentages add up, as the hours roll by, to big percentages as you keep missing flops.

2. In many hands you never get to see a flop when players in late position attack you with big raises.

3. Mediocre starting hands can develop into middle pair or bottom pair hands after the flop, which can then draw you in even further. Unless you're a highly skilled post-flop player, you can find yourself chasing good hands and losing lots of money.

Here Player A limps in first position with ace-trey suited. It's too weak a hand even to limp. If several players limp as well and no one raises (almost a best-case scenario), then hitting the ace may well cost you a pile of chips with your weak kicker, while the straight and flush possibilities are extreme long shots. Save the $200 for another time.

Player B limps with a pair of fives, a defensible play, particularly after a limper. Limping tends to cause a cascade effect, pulling other limpers along with weak hands. If no one sticks in a raise, the fives will get close to the express odds they need to call, and large implied odds to boot.

Player D limps with eight-five suited. Again the hand is too weak even for limping. Part of the problem is selective memory. We remember the times when we played a couple of low suited cards and hit a flush to win, because that's an exciting memory. We forget all the boring hands where we limped with two low suited cards, missed the flush, and threw the hand away.

Question 9A: Hellmuth has a small pair plus position on the three limpers so far. In addition, the pot has risen to $900, so he getting expressed odds of 4.5-to-1 for his call. Although he's 7.5-to-1 against hitting trips on the flop, his express odds are creeping into the ballpark of what he needs, and his implied odds make the call pretty easy.

Score 3 points for Choice B, calling $200. No credit for folding or raising.

Player G, directly behind Hellmuth, picks up ace-king offsuit and raises to $1,100. It's an excellent play. In the cutoff seat, he's very likely to have position on anyone who calls for the rest of the hand, so I like both his raise and the amount (5.5 times the big blind). If he were seated a couple of positions earlier, say in fifth position, he should raise even more, perhaps seven to eight times the big blind, to try to drive out any players behind him. Remember that the pot is now large enough so that you'd really like to win it right now, but if someone does want to play against you, he'll have to pay a high price and be out of position besides.

The button folds, as do the blinds. The three limpers in front of Hellmuth fold. The pot is now $2,200.

Question 9B: Hellmuth has a small pair and is now getting 2.5-to-1 odds. In addition, Hellmuth will be out of position for the rest of the hand. The odds might be about right against a somewhat loose opponent. In this situation, your previous observations are very important. Could this player have made a raise with an ace-jack or a king-queen in addition to all the higher pairs? If the answer is "yes," then there are enough non-pairs in the mix for you to call. If the answer is "no," and you're pretty sure he's only raising with a high pair or ace-king or ace-queen (or maybe just ace-king, if the guy's a rock), then you should let the hand go.

Hellmuth, of course, knows that unless he hits a trey, he won't really know where he stands in the rest of the hand. But he probably assumes that against an unknown player, he'll be able to smell danger coming and avoid the worst. So he's willing to gamble a little.

The counter-argument, of course, is that you might have to get 10 to 20 percent of your stack involved in this pot, with just a pair of treys. If the flop comes with three medium cards, and you check, and he fires a pot-sized bet at you, are you just going to fold? Most pros would hope that they could get some kind of sense from the player as to what the bet meant, and play accordingly. On the other hand, if you check, and he checks behind you, you're probably a favorite to have the best hand.

Score 3 points for Choice B, calling, and 2 points for Choice A, folding. Don't call in situations like this (small pair, out of position) if you have reason to believe that your opponent plays better than you do.

You actually call. The pot is now $3,100. The flop comes

Question 9C: Your first thought should be that ace-king and king-queen just made a pair of kings, so the only hands you may be a favorite against now are ace-queen and (less likely) ace-jack. On the bright side, the pairs below kings now have to be afraid of the king on board.

Your first step is to check and see what your opponent does. You don't have anything, and you don't know what this flop has done for your opponent, so check and get some information. Score 3 points for Choice A, checking, no credit for betting.

Player G, now with a pair of kings, checks as well. This is another good move, denying Hellmuth any information and, as we say, "leaving him out in the air." Player G's hand is almost certainly good, and if Hellmuth called with some sort of pair, he has only a couple of outs. So Player G is trying to make some money later in the hand.

The turn comes the 6♠.

Question 9D: You now have to assess the significance of both your opponent's check and the appearance of another six. Assessing the check is difficult. Against a top player, you really couldn't draw any conclusions from the check. It might indicate a weak hand, or it might indicate a strong hand that was exploiting position and denying you information. Against an inexperienced player, the check most likely indicates weakness. Inexperienced players are usually nervous with a good hand and eager to finish the hand quickly. They have a low tolerance for the inevitable uncertainty that comes with playing a good, but not nut, hand down to the river. An inexperienced player would probably make a big bet here with any high pair. So if you don't know much about your opponent, the value of your treys has risen a bit.

The 6♠ was a good card for you, because it didn't improve the board. If you had the best hand on the flop, you still have the best hand. However, if a card now comes that pairs the board, your treys will be counterfeited. So you've got to do something to get Player G out of the pot. That means you're going to bet. But how much?

Consider these two points:

1. **If you have the best hand right now,** it's because your opponent has something like ace-queen or ace-jack. In that case, he probably believes he doesn't have the best hand, but he has outs. If he believes that you have a lower pair, he thinks he has six outs. If he thinks it's possible that the king paired you, then he may only have three outs. Even if he thinks he has six outs, he's more than a 6-to-1 underdog in the hand. (In reality he would have more outs because of the cards that could counterfeit your treys; but he can't know that.) You need to bet enough so that he's at least denied the right calling odds. With the pot currently at $3,100, a bet over $500 would be enough.

2. **If you have the worst hand right now,** a larger bet probably won't chase him away. If you have the worst hand because he has a pair of kings, he's sticking around to the end. If he has a pair lower than kings, you can scare him with a bet, but

he'll probably grit his teeth and call. Unless you've really seen him play like Casper Milquetoast, you can't assume that a pair of queens or jacks or tens will fold to a single overcard on board. In that case, the bigger your bet, the more you rate to lose.

Hellmuth bets $550, a perfect bet if he's in fact facing two unpaired high cards, and a bet designed to lose the minimum if he's beaten. Score 5 points for that bet (Choice B), 2 points for Choice C, betting $1,100, and no credit for the other choices.

Player F, with his pair of kings still looking good, calls the $550 very quickly. He's showing great patience, and trying to squeeze as much money from the hand as possible.

The pot is now $4,200. The river comes a J♥.

Question 9E: Three bad pieces of news just arrived. Player F called your bet, and he called it quickly, and a jack arrived. The quick call indicates he knew his hand was strong enough to call and he didn't have to ponder the significance of your bet or calculate pot odds. The arrival of the jack eliminated ace-jack as a hand you could potentially beat.

The message is pretty clear: You're beaten, and you probably can't chase him away. Take your loss and don't put any more money in the pot. Score 3 points for Choice A, checking, and no credit for any bet.

You check, and Player F bets $2,500. The pot is now $6,700.

Question 9F: His bet was big enough so you don't have to consider calling. Score 3 points for Choice A, folding, no credit for anything else.

Final Note: An apparently innocuous little hand which, upon closer examination, contained a number of interesting decisions.

Another point worth noting here. Phil Hellmuth is one of the strongest no-limit hold 'em players around, particularly adept at the kind of post-flop hand analysis that we're spotlighting in this volume. To many players, particularly those who've been introduced to the game via television, his skills have been overshadowed by his table behavior, which draws the constant attention of the cameras. However, beneath the "poker brat" image lies an extremely strong player, well-versed in all the technical skills of the game. For most of the 1990s, Hellmuth was very likely the best no-limit hold 'em tournament player in the world.

Problem 10
Phil Ivey —
Maneuvering with Nothing

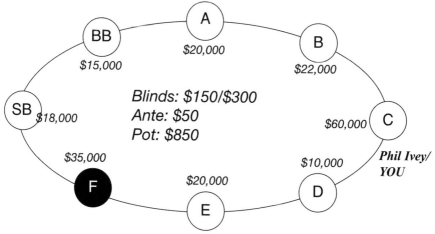

Situation: In the middle of the Monte Carlo Millions tournament in 2004. Your playing partner is Phil Ivey, third to act this hand. The table has been generally tight and passive, except for Player F, who has been aggressive. Many of the players seem a little intimidated by your presence and big stack. You're looking to steal pots when possible.

Your hand: 9♠3♦

Action to you: Player A limps in for $300. Player B folds.

Question 10A: *What do you do?*

A. *Fold*
B. *Call $300*
C. *Raise to $1,200*

Action: You actually call $300. Player D folds. Players E and F, on the cutoff seat and the button, both limp for $300. The small blind folds. The big blind checks. The pot is now $2,050.

Flop: Q♣8♣6♦

Action: The big blind checks. Player A checks.

Question 10B: *What do you do?*

A. *Check*
B. *Bet $1,000*   .
C. *Bet $2,000*

Action: You actually bet $2,000. Players E and F fold. The big blind folds. Player A calls $2,000. The pot is now $6,050.

Turn: 4♦

Action: Player A checks.

Question 10C: *What do you do?*

A. *Check*
B. *Bet $4,000*
C. *Bet $7,000*

Action: You actually bet $7,000, and Player A folds.

Solution to Problem 10

Phil Ivey is considered by many, if not most, to be the best no-limit hold 'em tournament player in the world right now. He's won many tournaments, reached six final tables on the World Poker Tour (through the end of season 3), and finished 10th in the World Series of Poker Main Event in 2003 and 20th in 2005. His style puts relentless pressure on his opponents, and few really enjoy facing him during a tournament.

We've included a number of Phil Ivey hands in this book, both so you can see how he plays, and so you can see how to adapt parts of his style to your own game. Here's our first hand, from the Monte Carlo tournament of a couple of years ago.

Question 10A: Player A limps and Player B folds. You might have guessed that we didn't include this hand so you could watch Ivey fold the

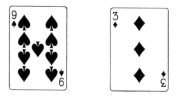

and you'd be right!

Ivey actually calls. Score 3 points for Choice A, folding, no credit for Choice B, calling, and one point for Choice C, raising. There's obviously nothing wrong with folding, because your hand is very weak and you're not in good position. But Ivey wants to limp in. Why?

Part of the reason is that Ivey already has a big stack. (In fact, he's leading the tournament at this point, with about one-third of the players already eliminated.) When an aggressive player has a big stack, the other players at the table get cautious. They're acutely aware that the aggressive player can take them out at any time, and they're more likely to fold, rather than play, marginal hands when the big stack is still around. Ivey knows this, of course, so he's looking to get involved in cheap pots where he can feel out his opponents, see if there are any good hands floating around, and then lower the hammer when he smells weakness.

Another part of the reason is that Ivey, after several hours, probably has some reads on the other players at the table, and thinks his reads can give him a little extra edge when he has to evaluate what the other players are doing. Ivey is an excellent observer, very good at getting a sense of what sort of hands may be out against him. We can't duplicate his reading ability here; instead we'll just focus on the betting patterns of the hand. But be aware that reading ability plays a role in these sorts of hands. Right now, for example, Ivey might be pretty sure that two or three players behind him will be throwing their hands away, which would improve his position considerably.

Despite these considerations, a hand like nine-trey should just be folded. When you're a strong, aggressive player, and you're playing well, and the cards are running right, and the table is intimidated, it's easy to start believing that you can do almost anything at all. Any hand is a potential winner; any opponent can be pushed around. Good players start crossing that thin line between weak but playable situations and genuinely bad situations. And when you cross that line, you may get punished.

I don't mind getting involved with weaker hands when I'm at a table that looks like the players can be run over. But I need a hand that has some potential, say a ten-nine offsuit. With a nine-trey, you have to rely almost completely on your ability to push the other players out. Unless you flop two pair or trips or a full house, your cards won't be able to help you.

If you really, really want to make a move here, at least raise. Now you're representing a big hand and you may be able to chase away some of the potential limpers. Although just calling commits fewer chips, each extra player you allow in the pot substantially reduces your odds of winning. Raising with a weak hand is actually a higher-equity play than just calling.

Now Player D folds, but Players E and F limp in. Once players start to limp, the pot odds become a big inducement for other players to limp in with marginal hands. (Player E, in fact, has a jack-four suited, while Player F has jack-ten offsuit.) By the time Player F called, the pot had $1,750 and it cost him only $300 to call, so he was getting almost 6-to-1 odds and he had position as well. The small blind folds, and the big blind just checks.

From Ivey's point of view, this was not such a good result, as there are now a lot of players that might catch a piece of the flop. On the bright side, the pot has grown to $2,050, so there's now some money worth winning. Also, no one has yet shown any strength by raising, which is a useful piece of knowledge. Players like Phil Ivey and Gus Hansen like to attack players who haven't shown real strength. It's very hard for a player with a medium to smallish stack, who's already invested a lot of time and money, to put his whole tournament at risk with middle pair or a draw. Aggressive players know that and ruthlessly exploit it. Ivey doesn't know exactly what he's up against, but it's probably a motley collection of suited cards, ace-x hands, and perhaps a small pair somewhere.

The flop comes

The big blind and Player A check.

Question 10B: Some good news for Ivey. The flop was better than average for him, given that he didn't hit his hand. (With a hand like nine-trey offsuit, note that "hitting the hand" isn't crucial anymore. A flop like A♥Q♣9♦, for instance, would be much worse, even though Ivey would have a piece of it.) No ace on board, so the players who called with ace-x are unhappy. Someone may have a club draw, and with four opponents, there's likely to be at least a pair of eights or a pair of sixes somewhere. The real question is: Does anybody have a queen with a decent kicker?

Now the two players in front of Ivey check. Although either could be trapping, that's more good news. Ivey is looking to attack weakness, and so far no one has shown any strength.

Ivey now bets the pot, $2,000. Score 4 points for Choice C. No credit for Choice A, checking. You didn't invest $300 in this hand to check if you missed the flop. Also no credit for Choice B, betting only $1,000. The idea is to bulldoze your opponents out of the hand. If anyone has some good cards, you need to find out right now, before investing any more money. By betting the pot, you're giving a very strong hand a chance to raise you, after which you can let the hand go. If no one raises, the hand is winnable.

The two checkers in front of you have also allowed you to put a squeeze play on the two players behind you. Look at the poor fellow in the cutoff seat. He has to worry not only about you, but also about the button behind him, and the two players who have checked but are still alive in the hand. Even someone with a holding like queen-jack would have to be worried, and might well toss it. If he folds, the same logic applies to Player F on the button. These players are under such pressure that if either of them sticks around or raises, you're done with the hand.

In fact, both Players E and F fold. The big blind also folds (holding ace-eight, actually the best hand right now). Player A, however, calls $2,000.

Two more clues now appear. The one caller was the only player who wasn't squeezed. He knew that he could see the next card for $2,000. And he only called — he didn't raise. So he has something. But unless he's trapping, he probably doesn't have a queen. The most likely candidates are something like middle pair, or maybe a straight draw or a flush draw. Of course he could have a pair of eights or sixes in the hole, and be trapping you with a set. But these hands are far less likely.

The turn now comes a 4♦, and Player A checks.

Question 10C: Whatever he was playing, the 4♦ didn't help it. And he checked again, still not indicating strength. Ivey now bets a little more than the pot, $7,000. Score 4 points for Choice C. No credit for the other plays.

Player A folds. (He actually had 9♦8♦, and hit middle pair on the flop.)

Three more observations:

1. This hand was played at a televised table, and no one likes to look foolish on television by calling off all his chips with a medium-strength holding against a top player who's practically screaming that he has a big hand. Ivey knows this, and he uses that knowledge ruthlessly.

2. Playing very aggressively will either get you knocked out of a tournament early, or allow you to collect a big pile of chips. The very aggressive players like Ivey, Gus Hansen, Greg Raymer, and Eric Lindgren, think that aggressive play represents a good use of their time. If they're playing after the first day, they're playing with a real chance to win, rather than just trying to survive.

3. This style doesn't work as well online because players have less time and money invested in the tournaments. It's much easier to look someone up when you have to click a mouse button, than when you actually have to shove your chips in the table with dozens of folks watching.

Super-aggressive play looks easy when it works, but it's a real test of nerves and observational power. In this problem, Ivey got carried away, but saved the day with good betting and sheer force of will.

Problem 11
Ivey Versus Guoga
— Betting a Good Hand

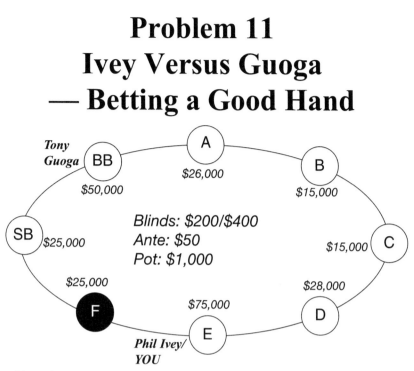

Situation: One round later in the same tournament as the last problem. Your playing partner, Phil Ivey, has continued to accumulate chips. Tony Guoga, (also known as "Tony G") in the big blind is a skilled player with an apparently flamboyant, but basically tight, style. The table remains generally cautious, although a couple of new players have recently appeared.

Your hand: 4♠4♦

Action to you: Player A folds. Player B calls $400. Players C and D fold.

Question 11A: *What do you do?*

A.   *Fold*
B.   *Call $400*
C.   *Raise $1,500*

Action: You actually call $400. Player F, on the button, calls $400. The small blind calls $200. Tony G in the big blind raises $2,700. Player B folds.

Question 11B: *What do you do?*

A.   *Fold*
B.   *Call $2,700*

Action: You actually call. The button and the small blind fold. The pot is now $7,800.

Flop: A♥5♦4♣

Action: The big blind checks.

Question 11C: *What do you do?*

A.   *Check*
B.   *Bet $5,000*
C.   *Push all-in*

Action: You actually bet $5,000. The big blind check-raises to $15,000.

Question 11D: *What do you do?*

A.   *Fold*
B.   *Call $10,000*

C. *Reraise to $30,000*
D. *Reraise all-in*

Action: You actually call $10,000. The pot is now $37,800.

Turn: Q♣

Action: The big blind checks.

Question 11E: *What do you do?*

A. *Check*
B. *Bet $10,000*
C. *Push all-in*

Action: You actually bet $10,000. The big blind goes all-in for his last $32,000. The pot is now $79,800.

Question 11F: *What do you do?*

A. *Fold*
B. *Call $22,000*

Action: You call and the big blind shows A♦K♥, for a pair of aces. You win with your trip fours.

Solution to Problem 11

In front of you Player A folds and Player B calls. Players C and D fold.

Question 11A: A small pair is a good hand for getting in cheap, especially in position against several opponents. You're looking to flop a set, after which you may make a big score. If you don't flop a set, your position may let you take down the hand. Two points for Choice B, calling. No credit for Choice A, folding (too tight). Also no credit for Choice C, raising. Since someone has already limped, showing some strength, you have no first-in vigorish. Merely the presence of a single limper has reduced your winning chances quite a bit.

You call, as do the button and the small blind. But the big blind raises $2,700, making the pot $5,100. Player B now folds.

Question 11B: The big blind might be raising with a big pair, but he might also have a hand like ace-king or ace-queen, and simply be pounding on the limpers. He might even have a much weaker hand, and just be making a play, attacking the limpers. You have position and a pair, and the pot is offering almost 2-to-1 odds. Score 4 points for Choice B, calling. No credit for folding.

You call, and the pot becomes $7,800.

The flop is

The big blind checks.

Question 11C: You hit your set on the flop, and you now have a huge hand. Only the two higher sets can beat you, and it's unlikely, from his pre-flop raise, that your opponent holds a pair of fives. He could have aces, but sets don't come along very often in tournaments, so you're going to assume he doesn't, and play as if your hand is best.

Many players would check here, setting a trap for their opponents later in the hand, hoping they catch up a little more so they'll be willing to call a big bet on the end. That's the standard way of handling a set after the flop.

But if you're Phil Ivey, you don't want to play that way. If you're going to bet aggressively when you don't have anything (as in the last hand), you have to make those bets credible by betting strongly when you have a big hand as well. If you start checking your big hands, players will quickly figure out that strong means weak and weak means strong, and you'll be easy to read. So lead out strongly with your set and see what happens. Score 4 points for Choice B, betting $5,000. 2 points for Choice A, checking. No credit for Choice C, going all-in, which isn't really aggressive at all. Going all-in shuts down the action and will probably prevent your opponent from losing any more chips.

You bet $5,000, and the big blind check-raises you to $15,000.

Question 11D: Your opponent probably has ace-king or ace-queen and is pushing his top pair, top kicker combination. Those hands explain both the big raise before the flop and the check-raise. He probably doesn't have any other high pair, because he'd be nervous about the ace out there.

There are two ways to try to get more money in the pot: call now and bet or raise on the turn, or raise now. Of the two, calling now is better. If you've read his hand properly and he has something like ace-king or ace-queen, there's a chance he can pair one of his cards on the turn. If he pairs the ace he improves to trips, but you improve to a full house. If he pairs the other card, his two pair are losing to your trips. In either case, you're more likely to get the rest of his chips than if you raise now.

Score 4 points for Choice B, calling. No credit for folding, obviously. Two points for Choice C, reraising to $30,000. No credit for Choice D, moving all-in, which is too precipitous. The right way to get all his chips is to get them in the center in stages, so that by the end, there are so many chips in the middle that he has wonderful pot odds for betting the rest.

You call. The pot is now $37,800. The turn comes the Q♣. The big blind checks.

Question 11E: That's a good card for you, except in the very unlikely case where he has queens in his hand. He may have just made two pair. You want to keep betting, to keep money moving toward the center. Score 3 points for Choice B, betting $10,000. No credit for checking or moving all-in. He's shown he's willing to play, so keep betting until either all his chips are involved, or he folds.

You bet $10,000. He check-raises all-in for his last $32,000.

Question 11F: Finally a no-brainer. Call and see what happens. Three points for Choice B, calling, no credit for Choice A, folding.

You call. He shows A♦K♥ for a pair of aces. You win with your set.

The turning point of the hand was the check-raise on the flop, and Phil Ivey's call. As we saw in the previous hand, he likes to steal pots when players show they're weak. Once he sees strength, he backs off unless he has a real hand. Here the big blind showed strength twice, raising with a pot-sized bet pre-flop, then check-raising on the flop. Neither bet took Ivey out of the hand.

At that point, as Ivey's opponent, you need to stop and say "He has something real, what could it be?" Your betting has pretty much announced that you have something like top pair and top kicker. What could he reasonably have? Probably the weakest hand that fits his bets is something like ace-five or ace-four, where he called before the flop with an ace (aggressive, to be sure), then hit two pair on the flop. Would a good player stick around with something like a pair of nines or tens in the face of a pre-flop raise, an ace on the flop, and now another big raise? Not likely. If you still wanted to push the hand a little, bet out on the turn and see what happens, but if that bet doesn't win, you should be thinking about living to fight another day.

Problem 12
A Weak Hand
in a Multi-Player Pot

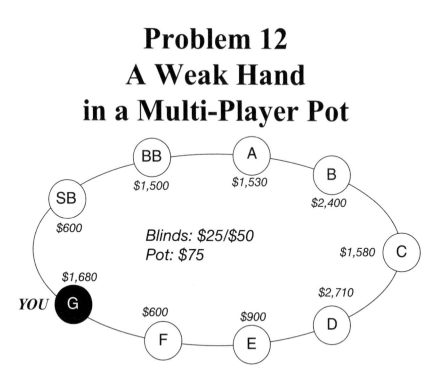

Situation: Single-table online tournament. Everyone started with $1,500 in chips. We are now into the third round. Players D and E are very loose, playing more than half the pots. Player F has played good, solid poker but has been unlucky so far. You're on the button, and you've projected a tight image at the table. The small blind has been loose and aggressive, but has lost most of his chips pushing weak hands.

Your hand: K♠9♣

Action to you: Players A, B, C, D, and E all fold. Player F calls from the cutoff seat.

Question 12A: *What do you do?*

A. *Call $50*
B. *Raise to $100*
C. *Raise to $200*
D. *Fold*

Action: You actually call. The blinds call and check behind you. There is now $200 in the pot, and you have position on all the other players.

Flop: 7♥6♠6♣

Action: The blinds and Player F check to you.

Question 12B: *What do you do?*

A. *Check*
B. *Bet $100*
C. *Bet $200*

Action: You actually check.

Turn: 5♣

Action: The blinds and Player F check to you.

Question 12C: *What do you do?*

A. *Check*
B. *Bet $100*
C. *Bet $200*

Action: You actually check.

River: K♦

Action: The blinds check. Player F bets $100.

Question 12D: What do you do?

A.   Fold
B.   Call $100
C.   Raise to $400
D.   Raise all-in

Solution to Problem 12

It's a fairly tight online sit-and-go. We're already into the third round of blinds and antes, and we still have our original nine players. My caution flag is already up a little; the players may be a bit more skilled than average.

Question 12A: I'm obviously not thrilled about my

but in front of me five players fold, including the two loose players, and the solid player right in front of me only calls. There's no real harm in folding this hand, of course, so give yourself 2 points for the super-solid Choice D, fold. But this is a situation where I don't mind doing a little speculating. The flop is cheap, and I'm in position with a couple of moderately high cards. Score 3 points for Choice A, calling. If either of the blinds raises, of course, I'm throwing the hand away.

What about the raising plays? Yes, a raise might steal the small pot that's out there, but it might not, and right now our hand isn't very good. I much prefer playing the hand cheaply and seeing if our position can make some money. Score 1 point for Choice C, raising $200, which might steal the pot, but no credit for Choice B, raising just $100, which offers such great pot odds that your opponent will be compelled to call. As an aside, note that I would be much more enthusiastic about raising if Player F had previously shown that he liked to call with weak hands. If I had some hard observational data to that effect, a raise would be routine.

We call and the blinds call also. The pot is now $200. The flop comes

All three players in front of us check.

Question 12B: We have nothing, but everyone checked in front of us. They're saying they have nothing as well. Should we make a stab at it?

A lot of players might routinely toss out a bet here, but I'm a little uncomfortable. We're against three opponents, and the more opponents we have, the less I want to try speculative stealing plays. In addition, the flop isn't as innocuous as it might look. We had three calls before the flop but no raises, which to me indicates that the players probably don't have high cards, but are more likely to have medium-to-low cards or suited connectors. If that's right, then this flop could have hit somebody or at least be giving someone a draw to a good hand. Of course I could be wrong, but do I want to invest $100 or $200 to try a steal against three opponents? I think not. I'll take a free card and see if something good happens. If a nothing card like a deuce or a trey comes on the turn, perhaps I'll make a play for the pot.

Score 3 points for Choice A, checking. Score 1 point for Choice B, betting $100, a cheap way of trying to steal. No credit for Choice C, betting $200.

We check. The turn comes the 5♣. Again, all three players check.

Question 12C: Once again, we have nothing and everyone else has checked. Now what?

The same analysis applies as on the flop, only more so. If I was worried that a 7-6-6 could have connected with someone's hand, now I'm really worried that a 7-6-6-5 actually has connected. I would have folded quickly if anyone had bet, but even in the absence of a bet I'm basically done with the hand.

Score 3 points for Choice A, checking, but no credit now for either bet. The situation smells bad.

We check. The river comes the K♦, giving us top pair. The two blinds check and Player F bets $100.

Question 12D: Just when we decided we're pretty much done, the poker gods deal us top pair and Player F finally makes a small bet.

I don't really think we have the best hand here, and if we call, we'll have to fold to a raise from either of the blinds. But it's possible no one has anything, or Player F is just making a stab, or Player F has ace-seven and thinks it's good. Since we're getting odds of 3-to-1 on our money, we're being well-compensated for calling. Score 4 points for Choice B, calling. No credit for any other play.

We call and the blinds fold. Player F shows 8♦6♥ and wins with trips.

As we feared, there were some low cards floating around out there and the flop didn't miss all of them. Remember that cutting your losses in dubious situations is just as good as winning a nice pot.

Problem 13
Pot Odds Dictate

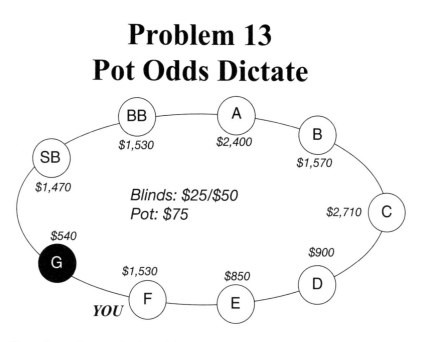

Situation: Same single-table tournament as the last hand, one hand later. You're now in the cutoff seat. You have no particular information on Player B. Players C, D, and G are the loose players. The player directly to your right, Player E, is tight, solid, and dangerous. Your table image is tight.

Your hand: A♣T♠

Action to you: Player A folds. Player B calls $50. Players C, D, and E all fold.

Question 13A: *What do you do?*

A. *Fold*
B. *Call*
C. *Raise to $200*

Action: You actually call for $50. The button and the small blind fold. The big blind checks. The pot is now $175, and you have position on the other two players.

Flop: A♥J♥5♦

Action: The big blind checks and Player B bets $100.

Question 13B: *What do you do?*

A. *Fold*
B. *Call*
C. *Raise to $300*

Action: You actually call $100. The big blind folds. The pot is now $375.

Turn: 9♥

Action: Player B bets $150.

Question 13C: *What do you do?*

A. *Fold*
B. *Call*
C. *Raise to $500*

Action: You actually call $150. The pot is now $675.

River: T♦

Action: Player B bets $250.

Question 13D: *What do you do?*

A. *Fold*
B. *Call*
C. *Raise to $700*
D. *Raise all-in*

Action: You actually called on the end for another $250, and Player B showed T♥8♥, a flush. He collects $1,175 from the pot.

Solution to Problem 13

After your loss in the previous hand, you're back to an average stack, but in good position on the cutoff seat. You pick up

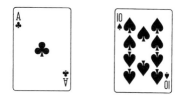

Question 13A: You get one limper, the player in second position, about whom you know very little. All the other players fold, including the two loose players and the solid player right in front of you. You hold ace-ten offsuit, not a bad hand but not a great hand either.

Score 4 points for Choice B, call. The combination of good position and a medium-strength hand argues for playing the hand small, not big. Good players don't like to get involved in big pots with mediocre hands. Try to play big pots with big hands and small pots with small hands, and you'll stay out of a lot of trouble.

Under slightly different circumstances, I would have put in a raise here. If my ace were just a little stronger, say ace-jack instead of ace-ten, I would like a raise. In that case there's one more ace I can beat, and one less ace that beats me. Increasing the ratio of "aces I can beat" to "aces I can't beat" improves my holding by a lot, and even that slight improvement makes me want to get more aggressive with the hand. Another possible improvement is the location of the limper. A player limping in second position makes me more cautious than, say, a player limping in fifth position. If just the one player right in front of me had limped, I would certainly raise here, since there's less of a chance he has some ace, and more of a chance he has suited connectors or some such middling hand.

Score one point only for Choice C, raising. No credit for Choice A, folding, which is too mousy. You certainly want to see a flop with a reasonable hand and position.

You actually call for $50. The loose player on the button folds, which you're glad to see. The small blind also folds, and the big blind checks to see a free flop. The pot is now $175, and you have position on two other players.

The flop comes

The big blind checks, and Player B bets $100, a little over half the pot.

Question 13B: We've paired our ace, which is nice, but our opponent is betting out despite the ace on board, so he may have a pair of aces as well. There's also the matter of two hearts on board, which might or might not be significant.

So how much do we like our hand? Right now I'd say we probably have the best hand, but it's not that strong, and certainly not strong enough that I want to get involved in a raising war. The most likely scenario right now is that our opponent has an ace and is betting his pair of aces. If he has an ace, there are four aces that beat us (AK, AQ, AJ, and A5), and seven aces that are losing to us (A9, A8, A7, A6, A4, A3, and A2). That 7-to-4 ratio might look good, but the smaller his kicker, the less likely that he played it before the flop and bet it after the flop, so all aces aren't equally likely.

(As an aside, notice that we're happier with this flop than if the flop had come, say, A-7-5. We don't really care that the jack on board is higher than our ten, since ace-jack would beat us anyway, whether a jack appears or not. Two undercards to our ten creates two more aces that are beating us, which we don't like at all.)

What about the two hearts on board? Won't a raise by us chase away a heart flush draw? It well might, but we have more serious problems to worry about. Remember, too, that the big blind isn't out of the hand yet, so he could be sitting behind us with something. All in all, I'm just not in a raising mood here. Score 3 points for Choice B, calling. No credit for Choice A, folding, of course, but also no credit for Choice C, raising.

You actually call for $100. The big blind folds. The pot is $375. The turn comes the 9♥, and Player B bets $150.

Question 13C: That's not a good card for us. The nine moves another ace from the winning column to the losing column, as ace-nine now beats us. And the third heart makes the danger of a heart flush a little more real. But we might still be winning, and the cheap $150 bet gives us better than 3-to-1 calling odds, so we have to stick around. No credit for folding or raising, and score 3 points for Choice B, calling.

You call for $150. The pot is now $675. The river comes a T♦, and Player B bets $250.

Question 13D: The good news is we're now beating ace-king and ace-queen, as well as ace-nine and ace-five. King-queen just made a straight (as did eight-seven), but those were unlikely holdings at best. Our opponent is undeterred, and his bet gives us 3.5-to-1 odds to call, so he's not exactly encouraging us to go away. My instincts say we're losing, but 3.5-to-1 is a nice price to find out for sure. Score 3 points for Choice B, calling, and no credit for raising or folding.

You call for $250, and Player B shows T♥8♥, for a winning flush.

In retrospect we can now see that Player B made a loose pre-flop call from early position, and then a sort of semi-bluff on the flop. After that he hit his flush and was just trying to milk us on the turn and the river. Our hand was just strong enough throughout to allow us to be milked.

A results-oriented player would now probably say "If only you raised aggressively on the flop, you could have won the hand!" True enough, we could have, had we known his hand. But there were other dangers lurking around besides the flush draw, and we had to attend to those as well. Good play means threading a course between a multitude of different threats. In this case our hand felt good enough to keep hanging around, but not good enough to push aggressively. The bad news is we lost $550, one-third of our stack. The good news is we still have $980, and we're alive and kicking.

Problem 14
Playing a Hand
that Can Win on Its Own

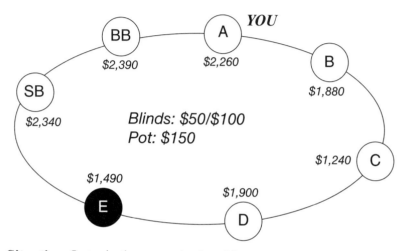

Situation: Later in the same single-table tournament. You've had a run of luck and more than doubled up to $2,260 in chips. A couple of the loose players have busted out. Of the players that remain, the small blind is loose, and the big blind is a tight, good player who tends to check medium-strength hands.

Your hand: A♣T♠

Action to you: You're first to act.

Question 14A: *What should you do?*

A. *Fold*
B. *Call $100*
C. *Raise to $300*

110 Problem 14

Action: You actually raise to $300. Everyone folds around to the solid player in the big blind, who calls for another $200. The pot is now $650.

Flop: 9♣7♠5♦

Action: The big blind checks.

Question 14B: *What do you do?*

A. *Check*
B. *Bet $300*
C. *Bet $600*

Action: You actually check. The pot remains at $650.

Turn: 5♣

Action: The big blind checks.

Question 14C: *What do you do?*

A. *Check*
B. *Bet $300*
C. *Bet $600*

Action: You actually check. The pot remains at $650.

River: K♣

Action: The big blind checks.

Question 14D: *What do you do?*

A. *Check*

B. *Bet $300*
C. *Bet $600*

Action: You actually check. The big blind turns over A♠J♣, and his jack kicker beats your ten.

Solution to Problem 14

You're moving up in the tournament, now effectively tied for the lead with two others. The good, solid player remains right in front of you.

Question 14A: The table has now shrunk to seven players, and

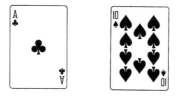

is a marginal hand for opening in first position at a seven-player table. You're one of the chip leaders, so you're certainly entitled to push a little with otherwise marginal hands. Score 4 points for Choice C, raising to $300 (three times the big blind). Score 2 points for Choice B, just calling. It's a little too tight for my taste in this situation, but not unreasonable. No credit for Choice A, folding.

You actually raise, and everyone folds except for the solid strong player in the big blind, who calls. The flop comes

He checks to you.

Question 14B: Right now we know three important facts:

1. He's a good, solid player, so he's not playing out of position with trash.

2. He called someone who opened under the gun.

3. He didn't raise.

Put these three facts together and his most likely holdings are two high cards, ace-x, or a low to medium pair.

If he has two high cards, he might be ahead of us or we might be ahead of him. We're beating KQ and KJ, but we're losing to AK, AQ, and AJ.

If he has ace-x, we're beating A2, A3, A4, A6, and A8. We're losing or tied with the other seven ace-x holdings. As in the last hand, the lower the kicker, the less likely is a call with the hand. So we're not doing well if he started with ace-x.

If he played a low to medium pair, three of the possible pairs just became trips, and the others are still beating us.

So right now we probably don't have the best hand. Next question: Are there any hands that are currently beating us that we can make lay down? Note that if we bet, and a hand that we can already beat lays down, we haven't gained all that much. But forcing a hand that would beat us on a showdown to lay down is a big accomplishment. The candidate hands here are AQ, AJ, and AT (which currently splits the pot with us). These hands will probably (not certainly) fold to a bet, which is a gain. But the other hands that are beating us will call, which means we've put more money into a pot we're losing.

Let's keep the pot small and see what happens. Perhaps our position will continue to work for us. Score 3 points for Choice A, checking. No credit for either of the two betting plays.

You actually check, and the turn comes 5♣, pairing the board. The big blind checks again.

Question 14C: The five was an authentically neutral card. Any hand that beat us before is still beating us, but no new hands are beating us. Again, we can't assume that we're the favorite, and the arguments are the same as before. Score 3 points for Choice A, checking. No credit for either of the two betting plays.

You actually check. The river is the K♣. The big blind checks once again.

Question 14D: The K♣ is actually a bad card, turning some hands we used to be beating, like king-queen and king-jack, into winners. There's also the distant possibility of a club flush, so again we're happy to just see the showdown for free. Score 3 points for Choice A, checking, and no credit for either of the betting plays. Heads-up, there's little need to bet a hand only moderately strong, but still good enough to win the pot on its own. Checks like this provide a good counter-balance if you tend to make continuation-type bets, since they provide disguise and show you don't always bet with medium or weak hands.

You check and your opponent shows A♠J♣. His jack kicker beats your ten.

Somewhat sheepishly you notice that he held one of the few hands that you could have driven out with a bet! That's poker.

One more thought before we leave this hand. Our quiet play was partly predicated on the fact that our opponent was a solid, conservative player. *We would have played the hand quite differently against an aggressive player.* If we were sitting down against Sam Farha, for example, instead of Player B, we couldn't have checked on the flop. In that case, Sam would have seen our check as weakness and come out firing on the turn regardless of his hand. Our defense then would be to call his bet with a certain percentage of our hands, just to prevent ourselves from being pushed off the table.

A better strategy against an aggressive player like Sam is to bet on the flop after his check. We might win the pot right there, but if he elects to call, he'll probably check to us on the turn, where we can check again if we choose. Roughly the same amount of money will go in the pot in either case, but our bet on the flop will have bought an extra chance to win a small pot, plus some control of the hand going forward.

A good general rule is that against passive players you can afford to check a middling-to-weak hand, but against aggressive players you often have to bet those hands, just to hold your own at the table.

Problem 15
Reading Your Opponent

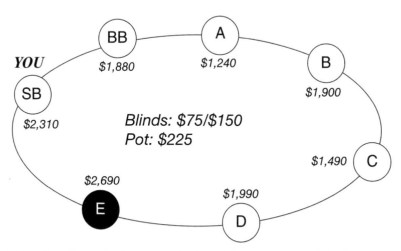

Situation: Later in the same single-table tournament. You're now in second place with $2,310 in chips, and in the small blind. Your nemesis, the solid player on your right, is now on the button. The big blind is known to be loose. Your table image is tight and conservative.

Your hand: K♥6♠

Action to you: Players A, B, C, and D all fold. Player E, on the button calls $150.

Question 15A: *What do you do?*

A.   *Fold*
B.   *Call $75*
C.   *Raise to $450*

116 Problem 15

Action: You actually call $75. The big blind checks. The pot is now $450.

Flop: 6♦2♦2♣

Question 15B: *What do you do?*

A. *Check*
B. *Bet $300*
C. *Bet $450*

Action: You actually bet $300. The big blind folds, but Player E calls. The pot is now $1,050. You have $1,850 left in your stack, while Player E has $2,240.

Turn: 3♣

Question 15C: *What do you do?*

A. *Check*
B. *Bet $700*
C. *Bet $1,000*
D. *Push all-in*

Action: You actually check. Player E checks behind you.

River: 3♦

Question 15D: *What do you do?*

A. *Check*
B. *Bet $700*
C. *Bet $1,000*
D. *Push all-in*

Action: You actually check. Player E bets $300. The pot is now $1,350.

Question 15E: *What do you do?*

A. *Fold*
B. *Call*
C. *Raise $1,000*
D. *Push all-in*

Action: You actually call, and Player E shows Q♦T♦ for a flush.

Solution to Problem 15

Solution to Problem 15: The blinds are up to $75/$150, and you're now firmly in second place. The solid player on your right, however, remains in first place.

Question 15A: The pot is $375, and it costs you an additional $75 to play. Your hand of

certainly isn't much, and you'll be out of position to boot. But the 5-to-1 odds are just a little too good to turn down with a king in your hand and no one showing strength yet. Score 3 points for Choice B, calling. Score 1 point for Choice A, folding. A little too prudent for even my taste, but not a serious error. No credit for Choice C, raising, which is way too optimistic, even if no one has yet shown any real interest.

You actually call $75, and the big blind checks. The pot is now $450. The flop comes

Question 15B: That's a pretty good flop for you. You now have top pair with a good kicker, and given the absence of pre-flop raising, it's unlikely that anyone is holding a pair higher than yours. Could anyone have a deuce? The button almost certainly doesn't unless it's ace-deuce or a pair of deuces. A tight, solid player doesn't like to put money in the pot with x-deuce, even if he is on the button. But the big blind could have anything, so if a deuce is out there, he's the one to have it.

Your best move now is to bet out and see what happens. If someone has a deuce, they'll let you know soon enough. Score 4 points for Choice B, betting $300, two-thirds of the pot. Score 2 points for Choice C, betting the pot. If no one has anything, your smaller bet should get the job done. No credit for checking. You have a hand, and it's time to make someone pay to beat you.

You actually bet $300, and the big blind folds. Player E calls $300. The pot is now $1,050. The turn comes a 3♣.

Question 15C: You're happy to see the big blind fold, since he was the player most likely to have a deuce. But the solid player on the button called, so he must have something. What is he most likely to have?

Since he has something, and a high pair isn't consistent with the betting so far, the best guess is that he has two over cards, both diamonds. Since your table image is conservative, it's dangerous for him to assume that you're bluffing with nothing. If you have something, then two high cards without a flush draw only give him six outs, not enough reason to call a bet of two-thirds the pot. But two high cards with a diamond draw fit his play perfectly. He could call before the flop, relying on his position, and call after the flop with 15 outs (9 diamonds plus the 6 remaining high cards).

Some other possibilities remain, however. He might have called with something like ace-deuce or king-deuce, and now be trapping you with his trip deuces. Or he might have only called with a small to medium pair, let's say something like 77, 55, 44, or 33, and be trapping you with that. The flush draw is more likely because it's more straightforward, and this is a player who has played his cards in a straightforward manner. But you always have to be aware of the potential for disaster.

So now what? One of the hands you could have beaten (a pair of treys) is now beating you. What began as a simple little hand has become a genuinely difficult problem, complicated by the fact that the pot is becoming large relative to the stack sizes. Let's look carefully at your possible options:

- **If you bet $700** (40 percent of your stack), the pot will contain $1,750 and it will cost Player E $700 to call. He's being offered odds of 2.5-to-1. If he has what we think is his most likely hand, two high cards with a diamond draw, you haven't even denied him the express odds he needs to play. You will chase him away if he just has two high cards or if he thinks your original bet was just a stab to win the pot.

- **If you bet $1,000** (60 percent of your stack), the pot will contain $2,050 and it will cost Player E $1,000 to call. Now his pot odds are down to 2-to-1 and you've denied him his express odds. But he may figure that if he hits his hand and bets on the end, he'll get the last $850 in your stack, in which case his odds, if you call, are $2,900-to-$1,000, or almost 3-to-1. In that case you still haven't been able to deny him the odds he needs, even by committing 60 percent of your stack.

- **If you push all-in**, his calculation changes. The pot contains $2,900 and it costs him $1,850 to call, so his odds drop to 1.5-to-1. Now he's definitely supposed to throw away the drawing hands. But if he's been trapping, you're going to be out of the tournament. Do you really want to jeopardize your whole tournament on a lousy pair of sixes?

A tough dilemma. Here's how I would score the choices:

- No credit for Choice C, betting $1,000, which risks a lot without accomplishing its goal.

- One point for Choice D, the all-in move, which will chase the draws away, but at the potential cost of your entire stack if you've read the situation wrong.

- Three points for Choice B, betting $700. Denying the proper calling odds isn't the only goal of your bet. This bet will chase away the hands that wondered if you were bluffing, while fattening the pot in the cases where he continues to draw and misses. But it's also a defensive bet, which may prevent him from pushing all-in, which forces you to a difficult decision. At the same time, you have a chance to keep some of your chips if things go wrong.

- Three points for Choice A, checking, which is not a bad play with such a modest hand.

You actually check, and Player E checks behind you. The river comes the 3♦. The pot is still $1,050.

Question 15D: The third diamond arrives, which is bad news. Your best guess is that you're probably beaten now. Score 2 points for Choice A, checking; no credit for any other play.
    You check, and Player E bets $300. The pot is now $1,350.

Question 15E: It certainly feels like you're beaten, and the $300 bet smells strongly of a suck bet. But you're being offered 4.5-to-1 odds, which is worth a little pain. Call and see what happens. Score 3 points for Choice B, calling, no credit for Choice A, folding, and certainly no credit for any raise.

You call and he shows Q♦T♦ for a flush.

He had the hand that matched all his bets, but you held your losses to a relative minimum.

Problem 16
Chris Ferguson — Playing Aces

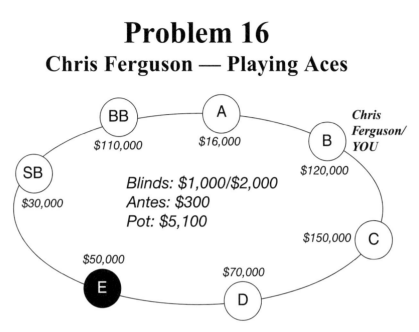

Situation: About halfway through the 2004 Monte Carlo Millions tournament. Your playing partner is Chris Ferguson, second to act at this 7-player table. Ferguson won the World Series of Poker in 2000, and is now regarded as one of the very best players on the circuit. His trademark long hair and cowboy hat disguise the shrewd mathematical mind underneath: He has a PhD in computer science. The big blind has been active throughout this session, and likes to stick in a lot of small raises during a pot. The small raises don't indicate anything about the strength of his hand.

Your hand: A♠A♣

Action to you: Player A folds.

Question 16A: *What do you do?*

A.   Call $2,000
B.   Raise to $6,000
C.   Push all-in

Action: You actually raise to $6,000. Players C, D, E, and the small blind all fold. The big blind reraises to $12,000.

Question 16B: *What do you do?*

A.   Call $6,000
B.   Reraise to $30,000
C.   Push all-in

Action: You actually call $6,000. The pot is now $27,100.

Flop: K♠J♣6♦

Action: The big blind bets $12,000.

Question 16C: *What do you do?*

A.   Fold
B.   Call $12,000
C.   Raise to $30,000
D.   Push all-in

Action: You actually call. The pot is now $51,100.

Turn: 7♥

Action: The big blind checks.

Question 16D: *What do you do?*

A. *Check*
B. *Bet $20,000*
C. *Bet $50,000*
D. *Push all-in*

Action: You actually bet $20,000. The big blind raises to $40,000.

Question 16E: *What do you do?*

A. *Call*
B. *Push all-in*

Action: You actually call. The pot is now $131,100. You have about $56,000 left in your stack. The big blind has about $46,000.

River: 2♥

Action: The big blind checks.

Question 16F: *What do you do?*

A. *Check*
B. *Bet $20,000*
C. *Push all-in*

Action: You actually bet $20,000. The big blind folds.

Solution to Problem 16

Question 16A: Score 3 points for Choice B, raising to $6,000. Score 2 points for Choice A, just calling, which is a common mistake at a full table, but a reasonable way to diversify your play at a small table.

In general, a high pair plays best against a single opponent. Being in a pot with multiple opponents carries too great a risk that one of the hands will draw out on you. Since a limp at a full table in early position encourages other players to limp in, it's usually a mistake to limp there with a high pair. As the table gets smaller, the odds that a bunch of players will limp in against you also gets smaller. In addition, an opponent with a low M might decide that your limp means weakness and move all-in. While I don't like limping with aces at a full table, it's a reasonable move once in a while as the table shrinks.

No credit for the beginner's play of pushing all-in. You want to make some money with your hand, not just chase everyone away.

You raise to $6,000, and everyone folds except the big blind, who mini-reraises to $12,000. The pot is now $21,100.

Question 16B: The mini-reraise from the big blind puts you in an interesting position. First, note that the reraise itself is a very odd play. You're now being offered 3.5-to-1 odds to call, and you'll be in position on the big blind after the flop. Any hand that could have legitimately raised from early position is literally being forced to at least call. In addition, you've got another chance to raise and either drive your opponent away or build a bigger pot.

Many players, when faced with an unusual play, just dismiss it by thinking something like "Humph — dumb play" or "I sure wouldn't have done that," and then proceed to play the hand. Even if you're sure a play can't be technically "correct," remember that your opponent made the play for a reason. If you can figure out the reason, you may get a big clue as to your opponent's actual hand. So what hands could the big blind hold that would make the mini-raise seem like a good idea?

One possibility is a high pair, like kings or queens. Now the big blind might think, "My opponent probably raised with two high cards or a pair lower than mine. I want to get more money in the pot, which I can do by offering good pot odds. In addition, I might get my opponent to think I'm weak and try to bully me out of the pot. By giving him a chance to reraise, I could get his whole stack in pre-flop."

The other possibility is a medium pair, like nines or eights. Now the big blind might think, "I'm happy to play against two high cards, but I need to find out quickly if I'm up against a higher pair. Our stacks are both deep. If the flop comes with three low cards, I could lose a lot of chips to a higher pair if that's what he has. I'll mini-raise now. If he sticks in a big reraise, he must have a high pair, and I can let the hand go relatively cheaply."

I wouldn't make the mini-raise myself, so I don't think any of these arguments are "correct." But the lesson to be learned here is simple and important: Your opponents might make incorrect moves, but *they make them for reasons that seem valid in the heat of battle.* By trying to figure out why the move might have seemed correct, you can often narrow down your opponent's possible hands considerably.

Having said all that, what should we now do with our aces? We could of course reraise; we're a big favorite against any hand our opponent actually has. Score 2 points for Choice B, reraising to $30,000. But notice that our arguments against trapping with aces aren't valid any longer. We're now guaranteed to be against a single opponent, so trapping is now a valid option. Score 4 points for Choice A, just calling. It's a misleading move, and seems to imply we led off with something like ace-queen, ace-jack, or a medium pair. Our goal now is to win a very big pot with some good play after the flop. Two points for just pushing all-in. It may chase away a lot of the hands we're looking to crush, but it might also get called, which makes the hand very easy to play.

You actually call. The pot is $27,100. The flop comes

The big blind bets $12,000.

Question 16C: Not the best possible flop. Two of the hands that might have stood up to us — kings and jacks — just became trips. A pretty unlikely but possible hand — king-jack — has become two pair. It's unlikely that a pair of sixes stuck in a mini-raise pre-flop, so that's a catalog of the hands that are beating us right now. Against everything else, we're still winning handily.

Our opponent made a bet of a little less than half the pot. A lot of hands might have made that bet to see if the pot was immediately winnable. If we had a pair of tens or a pair of nines, for example, we'd be hard-pressed to call with the two overcards on board. I wouldn't try to read too much into the bet. The big blind is out of position and needs to do something, even if the flop missed.

My feeling about the pot now is that we're probably ahead, but I'm not so confident that I want to stick in a raise and possibly receive a very unpleasant surprise. We still have position, so let's just call and encourage our opponent to keep on betting. It's working so far.

Score 3 points for Choice B, calling. No credit for the other plays.

You actually call. The pot is now $51,100. The turn comes 7♥. The big blind checks.

Question 16D: The turn card was harmless, and the check was more good news. Time to keep massaging the pot. Score 3 points for Choice B, betting $20,000. It's a good amount, about 40 percent of the pot, and it should keep the ball rolling. No credit for Choice A, checking. There's no reason yet to assume we're beaten. It's possible, but it's much more likely that we're still ahead. As long as you think you're in the lead, keep building the pot. No credit for the big bets either. You don't want someone with just a pair of kings or jacks to slip away.

You actually bet $20,000. The big blind raises to $40,000. The pot is now $111,100.

Question 16E: We get check-raised, but the pot is offering us 5.5-to-1 to call. That's a very peculiar check-raise. Of course, the mini-raise before the flop was peculiar as well. Now what?

You certainly can't fold your overpair with 5.5-to-1 odds and position besides. The simplest explanation might just be that our opponent likes mini-bets (we've seen them before) and therefore we can't conclude anything about the strength of the hand. We can still beat most cards that played before the flop, and the odds are fine, so let's keep going.

Score 2 points for Choice A, just calling, which is reasonable, but 4 points for the better play of pushing all-in. Here's why.

If you just call, the pot will be $131,100, and you will have $56,000 left in your stack, and your opponent will have $46,000. Given the size of the blinds and antes at this stage of the tournament, you're both essentially pot-committed. You probably have the best hand at this point. It's most likely that you're up against a pair of kings or jacks, in which case your opponent just has a couple of outs on the river. If you are up against trip kings or trip jacks, that's unfortunate, but you're going to lose your whole stack on the river anyway.

It's also possible that your opponent is on some sort of a draw, with a hand like ace-queen or queen-ten. In that case you may get called now, but you may not get called on the river. Either way, there's very little reason to wait now. The pot has grown large enough, and your hand is strong enough, to just get your chips in now and see what happens.

You actually call. The pot is $131,100. The river is a 2♥. The big blind checks.

Question 16F: More good news. No straights got made (flushes were already impossible) and the big blind checked on the river, a potentially costly move if he was sitting there with trips. The preponderance of evidence is that we have the best hand, so we'll bet. How much?

With the huge pot and the relatively tiny stacks, the right play is again to push all-in. Score 5 points for that play (Choice C). It's tempting to bet a smaller amount on the theory that it will be easier for your opponent to call, but that's an illusion. If you bet $20,000, your opponent is being offered 7.5-to-1 odds to call. If you push all-in, your opponent is being offered about 4.5-to-1 to call. Are there hands that will fold to the big bet but call the small bet? At this point in the hand and the tournament, probably not. So go all-in.

Score just 2 points for Choice B, betting $20,000, and no credit for Choice A, checking.

You actually bet $20,000, and the big blind folds. (The big blind was holding the A♥Q♣.)

Problem 17
Attacking Limpers

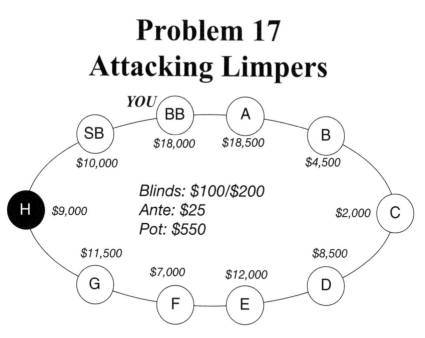

Situation: Large multi-table online tournament. You have just been switched to this table and don't have any reliable information, except that some number of players have been limping into pots.

Your hand: J♦J♠

Action to you: Player A limps for $200. Players B and C fold. Players D and E also limp for $200. Players F and G fold. The button limps. The small blind calls. The pot is now $1,450.

Question 17A: *What do you do?*

A. *Check*
B. *Raise to $600*
C. *Raise to $1,400*
D. *Raise to $2,500*

Action: You actually raise to $1,400. Player A calls $1,200. All the other players fold. The pot is now $3,850.

Flop: 6♣5♥2♥

Question 17B: *What do you do?*

A. *Check*
B. *Bet $2,000*
C. *Bet $3,500*
D. *Push all-in*

Action: You bet $3,500. Player A calls. The pot is now $10,850.

Turn: 8♥

Question 17C: *What do you do?*

A. *Check*
B. *Bet $5,000*
C. *Push all-in ($13,100)*

Action: You actually push all-in. After a long time, Player A calls and shows the A♥K♠. The river is a 4♠, and you win the pot.

Solution to Problem 17

Question 17A: Your

is a nice hand, but it must be played aggressively before the flop. It's a terrible hand against several opponents, all of whom stay to see the flop, since any overcard may be beating you.

Here you're last to act, and you have five limpers. It's unlikely that there's an overpair to your jacks lurking out there. A high pair likes to be against a single opponent with a weaker hand, not against a bunch of opponents. Any high pair should have raised before the flop, so you most likely have the best hand right now. Fortunately, you have a big stack, so you have the resources to put pressure on your opponents.

You need to bet enough so that you chase away at least four of the five limpers. If you chase everybody away, you're not unhappy, because there's already a fair amount of money out there. But you wouldn't mind facing a single opponent, especially if they're holding a middle pair.

No credit for Choice A, checking, which is absolutely the wrong idea.

Also, no credit for Choice B, raising to $600, which is actually worse than checking. This would be a fine bet at the $100/$200 level when you're first in the pot, but here the bet functions only as a pot-sweetner. Player A would need to put in $400 more to see a pot of $1,850. He's getting 4.5-to-1, better odds than he got on his original limp, so he'll probably stick around. Each succeeding player will get better odds yet, so the likelihood is that all the players will call. You'll have the same situation as Choice A, but you'll have more of your money in the pot.

Score 2 points for Choice C, raising to $1,400. It's a big enough raise that it will chase at least some players away, but once a single brave player calls, those behind him will be getting good odds to stick around. Even a pot-sized bet isn't big enough here.

Score 4 points for Choice D, raising to $2,500. The right range is between 150 and 200 percent of the existing pot. It should chase almost all the players away, leaving you either heads-up against one opponent or winning the already-large pot, which is a fine result.

You actually raise to $1,400. Player A calls $1,200, and the other players all fold. The pot is now $3,850.

The flop comes

Question 17B: That's a good flop for you, but a flop that will be hard to let go. If your opponent is playing with a medium pair (tens, nines, eights, or sevens), you just became about an 89 percent favorite if he doesn't have a heart, and about an 85 percent favorite if he does. If he called with something like ace-king or ace-queen, things are a bit more interesting, depending on just how many hearts he has in his hand. If he has no hearts, you're about 75 percent; one heart, and you're about 72 percent; two hearts, and you're an underdog at about 45 percent!

The crucial question is: Could he have called with a really low pair (sixes through deuces), since three of those five pairs just became trips? A good player, facing a big raise and with four other players yet to act, would have thrown those pairs away quickly. But online, weak players have trouble letting those hands go. Since you're new to the table, you haven't formed an opinion about Player A yet. Consider the trips an unlikely but possible threat.

Sight unseen, my guess at the table would be that I'm facing a medium pair or ace-king (with some number of hearts). Both hands fit the pre-flop limp and the subsequent call (although the call gets shakier as the pair gets weaker).

It should be clear to bet here, so no credit for Choice A, checking. I'd bet a sizeable amount, so that hands like ace-king with one heart aren't getting the odds they need to call. (You can't chase away the A♥K♥, and the medium pairs are such big underdogs that they shouldn't call any reasonable bet if they knew what you had.) Score 4 points for Choice C, betting $3,500, close to the size of the pot, and 2 points for the smaller bet of $2,000. No credit for Choice D, pushing all-in, which might only be called by the hands that are beating you!

You bet $3,500, and Player A calls. The pot is now $10,850. You have about $13,100 left in your stack, and Player A has a little more.

The turn comes the 8♥.

Question 17C: We're not delighted to see the 8♥. If Player A was holding the A♥K♥, or the A♥Q♥, or a pair of eights, all possible hands, he just took the lead. So what should we do?

Score 2 points for Choice C, checking, and 2 points for Choice B, making the smaller bet, not unreasonable plays. Score 5 points for Choice C, pushing all-in! It looks bold, even a little goofy, since our situation just got worse, but it's really the best play under the circumstances. Here's why:

1. I'm going to ignore the possibility that we're up against trip sixes, fives, or deuces. It's almost impossible to call with small pairs pre-flop in a big pot with a lot of players left to act. If Player A made that call, he's got me, but I don't think he did.

2. Although a couple of the possible hands we could be facing just hit the jackpot, we're still beating the others, and there are many more of them.

Now let's ask the two crucial questions for making a big bet late in the hand.

1. Are there hands that are beating me that will fold?

2. Are there hands I'm beating that will call?

Always ask yourself these two questions when you're contemplating a big bet on the turn or the river! If the answer to both is 'yes,' you've got a great betting opportunity. If the answer to both is 'no,' then just check. If one answer is 'yes' and the other is 'no,' then you need to look closely at how many hands are in each group, and the likelihood that they will, in fact, call or fold.

Here the answer to Question 1 is 'no.' The hands that are beating you are A♥K♥ or A♥Q♥, which just made a flush, and a pair of eights which just became trips. They aren't folding. But fortunately, there aren't very many of these hands.

The answer to Question 2 is 'yes.' Ace-king or ace-queen with a single heart might call you, on the theory that you may be bluffing, and they have outs even if you're not. A pair of tens or nines or sevens might call because you could be playing a lower pair, or bluffing with two high cards, and if the pair has a heart, then they have even more outs (11) if they're wrong. Betting only $5,000 gives these medium pairs with a heart the correct odds to call. This category (the hands you're beating that will call) actually contains a lot of hands.

So there's plenty of hands that can call and lose, and your all-in move denies the hands with a single heart the proper pot odds to call if they knew what you had. You're probably still the favorite in the hand, and if you hold on and win, your stack will grow to almost $40,000 in chips.

At some point in big tournaments, you have to gamble to get a big stack when the odds appear to be in your favor. Online, most players are actually much too willing to gamble without closely analyzing the situation. But if you've analyzed well, make sure you have the heart to put your chips in the middle. These aggressive, volatile plays are the plays that help you win tournaments when they work.

A footnote to this hand: There's a strategy for handling ace-king in early position that's employed by many top players as an alternative to simply raising. The move goes as follows:

- Limp in early position.

- Some limpers enter the pot behind you (as in this hand), looking to see a cheap flop with a motley assortment of holdings.

- One of the blinds picks up a reasonable hand and counters with a big raise, looking to scoop the pot from all the limpers (as in this hand).

- You then counter with a very big (or perhaps all-in) reraise, representing a slow-played pair of aces.

- The limpers run for cover.

- The blind reluctantly folds, and you scoop a big pot.

Note that unless the blind happened to pick up aces or kings, you're still in great shape even if you're called, with lots of dead money in a big pot. It's a clever play and one worth adding to your repertoire.

Problem 18
Evaluating a Weak Hand

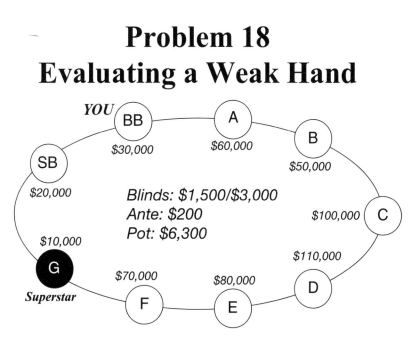

Situation: The Bay 101 Tournament in San Jose, toward the end of the second day. At this tournament, several top players are designated 'Stars' and a bounty of $5,000 is placed on each. It's real money, paid right on the spot in cash. One such star remains at your table and is now on the button. You are the big blind.

Your hand: 6♠5♦

Action to you: Players A through F all fold. The button moves all-in for his last $10,000.

Question 18: *What do you do?*

A. *Fold*
B. *Call $7,000*

Action: You actually fold, and the button takes the pot.

Solution to Problem 18

Score 5 points for Choice B, calling, but no credit for the serious blunder of folding.

All-in situations toward the end of tournaments are largely decided by pot odds rather than cards. The pot contains $6,300 from the blinds and antes, plus $10,000 from the button, plus (don't forget!) the $5,000 bonus if you knock out the superstar. That's a total of $21,300 in the pot, and you only have to pay $7,000 to call. Your pot odds are better than 3-to-1. Your

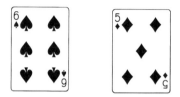

offsuit may look puny, but it's a pretty good hand against his possible holdings. Consider some of these percentages:

Suppose he pushed with any two cards (which is his correct strategy on the button with an M of 2); in that case your winning chances are 40 percent. You're only a 3-to-2 underdog.

Suppose he was a little conservative, since he won't have to post the blinds for several more hands; let's say he was willing to push with roughly the top 60 percent of his hands — all pairs, aces, kings, most of the queens, and jacks, and a few others like ten-nine, ten-eight, and nine-eight, suited or unsuited. Every hand he plays will be a favorite against you, but your chances are still about 36 percent. You're not even a 2-to-1 underdog.

Suppose he was a very conservative old-school player, who never even bothered to read *Harrington on Hold 'em, Volume II.* (Shocking!) He'll only push with a pair of fours or better, ace-seven suited or better, ace-nine offsuit or better, and king-jack suited or better. Your winning chances shrink to 30 percent. You're now a 2.3-to-1 underdog. Still an easy call.

Even if you knew he was an absolute rock, and his pushing range was just tens or better and ace-king, your chances would still be about 25 percent, so your decision would be a toss-up. That's clearly an unrealistic assumption, so you must call.

Problem 19
Harrington Versus Hansen
— Playing a Medium Pair

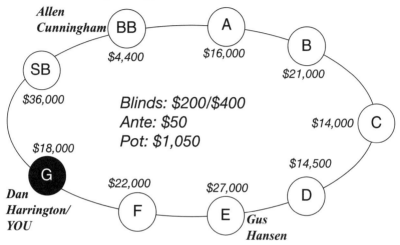

Allen Cunningham BB $4,400

A $16,000

B $21,000

SB $36,000

$14,000 C

Blinds: $200/$400
Ante: $50
Pot: $1,050

$18,000

$14,500

G

$22,000

F

$27,000

E *Gus Hansen*

D

Dan Harrington/ YOU

Situation: Late in the first day of a major tournament. Allen Cunningham in the big blind has a tiny stack with an M of 4. Gus Hansen is the big stack at the table and has been his usual aggressive self. I'm your playing partner, and I'm on the button with a moderate stack and an M of 16.

Your hand: 7♥7♠

Action to you: Players A, B, C, and D all fold. Gus raises to $1,300. Player F folds.

Question 19A: *What should you do?*

A.   Fold
B.   Call

143

C.   *Raise to $4,000*
D.   *Raise all-in*

Action: You actually call $1,300. The small blind folds. Allen Cunningham pushes all-in for his last $4,000. Gus Hansen calls $2,700. The pot is now $10,350.

Question 19B: *What do you do?*

A.   *Fold*
B.   *Call $2,700*
C.   *Raise all-in*

Action: You actually call for $2,700. The pot is now $13,050.

Flop: K♥5♠4♦

Action: Gus bets $3,200. The pot is now $16,250.

Question 19C: *What do you do?*

A.   *Fold*
B.   *Call $3,200*
C.   *Reraise all-in*

Action: You actually fold. Gus shows 7♦5♣, for a pair of fives, and Cunningham shows a pair of queens. The turn and the river are a ten and a seven, and Gus wins the pot with two pair, sevens and fives.

Solution to Problem 19

Question 19A: I'm not folding the

against a raise from an aggressive player. With that possibility eliminated, my choice becomes calling or raising, and if I raise, how much?

The simple argument for raising is that Gus may be bluffing and I could take the pot down right here. Balanced against that reason are four arguments for just calling:

1. **My M**. Right now my M is 16; not huge, but not tiny either. A raise to something like $4,000 gets almost a quarter of my chips committed with a pair of sevens. If my M were 9 or 10, I'd certainly be planning on raising here and probably going all the way with the hand. Against a known aggressive player, you must be prepared to gamble with hands like small pairs and a shrinking M. But with a good, solid M of 16, I'm inclined to be a little more cautious.

2. **My position**. I have position on Gus throughout the hand. I can play some small-ball and let my position do some of the work for me.

3. **The big stack**. The big stack is sitting right behind me in the small blind. I'd like to see what he does before I make a decision for a lot of chips. If he gets in the hand, I'm less

enthused about playing, and by calling I can get that information cheaply.

4. **The small stack**. Allen Cunningham is in the big blind with the smallest stack, and his M is only about 4. He'll be looking to get involved with a wide variety of hands. If he moves all-in, I can see what Gus does before I have to act.

That's a lot of good reasons for just calling. Score 3 points for Choice B, calling. Score 1 point for Choice C, raising to $4,000. It's still a reasonable move against an aggressive player. No credit for folding or pushing all-in.

By the way, sevens and eights are the only pairs that really give me trouble in this situation. With any pair better than eights I'm certainly raising. With any pair less than sevens I'm just calling.

You actually call. The small blind folds. Allen Cunningham moves all-in for his last $4,000 from the big blind. Gus Hansen calls $2,700. The pot is now $10,350.

Question 19B: It costs me just $2,700 to call, and the pot is almost four times as big, so there's no question I have the odds to call. No credit for folding in this situation. The real question is — can I do anything better?

The key here is that Gus called but didn't raise. Usually when both players have deep stacks, and one player just calls in a position like this, it means he's playing with a medium-strength hand. That's a good situational tell, more reliable than most. A very strong hand would raise because of the possibility of winning a huge pot, and a merely good hand would also raise, because of the possibility of *losing* a huge pot. (If a good hand raises and doesn't win the pot, they're probably beaten and can get out quickly, whereas calling and seeing a flop can get them locked into a second-best hand.) But just calling without raising indicates a medium-strength hand, one that's happy to see a flop. Probably

Gus has a jack-nine or eight-six type hand, or a weak ace like ace-four or ace-trey, a hand that can really benefit from a good flop. And since I called but didn't reraise the first time around, and since my reputation is conservative, Gus probably believes that I have a low pair, or perhaps a king-queen or queen-jack suited type hand.

A complicating factor, of course, is Allen Cunningham. Note that although his M is low, he still didn't have to be desperate this hand. Next hand he's in the small blind, and after that he moves to the button and has seven more hands before he has to dip into his stack for some serious money. I'm expecting to see him show down a pretty good hand — something in the ace-jack, king-queen or better range. Still, eliminating Gus from the hand will greatly increase my chance of pulling down the pot.

No credit for Choice B, just calling. The pot odds look great, but after the flop Gus will be able to put a lot of pressure on me. Score 4 points for Choice C, pushing all-in, which should get rid of Gus and leave you heads-up against Allen where you might be a slight favorite to win, with a lot of dead money from Gus in the pot.

You actually just call. The pot is now $13,050. The flop comes

Gus bets $3,200, creating a side pot.

Question 19C: I actually liked this flop, with two cards below my sevens, but as soon as Gus bet I understood just how big a blunder I had made on my last turn.

My problem is pretty simple. I may well still be beating Gus (assuming I was beating him to start), but how am I doing against Allen? If he went all-in with a higher pair than mine I'm still losing, and if he went all-in with a couple of picture cards, several of those combinations just beat me as well. If I call against Gus, I may be only playing to win the money in the side pot, since the main pot may be out of reach (unless I can spike a seven on one of the next two streets.)

What's really happened here is that Gus and I are, in effect, locked in a game of "chicken," and whoever bets first wins by putting the opponent in an untenable position. Assuming Gus and I are playing roughly the same type of hands, there's no advantage any longer to acting second. In fact, the advantage goes to the player who can act first, leaving his opponent a Hobson's choice.[2]

Did Gus realize all this when he merely called on the flop? I can't be sure, but I wouldn't be surprised. While some players dismiss Gus as just wildly aggressive and lucky, the truth is that he's one of the most astute tacticians around, and he's worked out many original ideas in his private laboratory.

Score 3 points for Choice A, folding. No credit for calling, and no credit for reraising all-in.

---

[2] A choice between two evils.

Problem 20
Learning From Past Mistakes

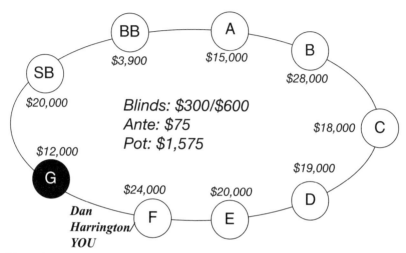

Situation: Early in the second day of the 2005 Bellagio tournament. I'm at a new table, in relatively the same position as last hand, with an M of 16. Player E is a competent player with some good results. The big blind is on the short stack with an M of only 2.

Your hand: K♣Q♣

Action to you: Players A, B, C, and D all fold. Player E raises to $1,800. The pot is now $3,575.

Question 20A: *What do you do?*

A. *Fold*
B. *Call $1,800*
C. *Reraise to $5,000*

Action: You call $1,800. Player G, on the button, folds. The small blind calls $1,500. The big blind goes all-in for $3,300, raising $2,100. Player E folds. The pot is now $10,175.

Question 20B: *What do you do?*

A. *Fold*
B. *Call*
C. *Reraise to $7,000*
D. *Reraise all-in*

Action: You reraise to $7,000. The small blind folds. You take back $4,900 of your reraise, leaving a pot of $12,275. The big blind turns over K♠6♠. The flop came K♥7♣2♦, and the small blind yells "I folded deuces!" The turn and the river were blanks. You collect a big pot with a lot of dead money.

Solution to Problem 20

This hand occurred on the day after the previous problem. Sometimes in poker you get a chance to make a mistake, survive, and learn from it!

Question 20A: A tight player has raised in the fifth seat. My

is strong enough to play with position, but not strong enough to reraise. I'm happy to call and see what happens. Score 3 points for Choice B, calling. No credit for Choice A, folding, which is super-tight under the circumstances, and no credit for Choice C, reraising, which is too loose for my taste.

After my call, the button folds, the small blind just calls, but the big blind goes all-in for his last $3,300. Now Player E folds.

Question 20B: Now I'm in almost the same situation as the previous problem. I'm not concerned with the big blind, whose M was so small that he was almost forced in with any reasonable hand. I'm focused instead on the small blind, who only called the first time around. A strong hand would have raised to nullify some of the effects of being out of position. I'm pretty sure he's got a small pair or a couple of low connectors, and he wants to see a relatively cheap flop. If I'm right, I want to get rid of him and go heads-up against the big blind, who could have almost anything.

Note that the pot right now contains plenty of dead money. There's $1,800 contributed by Player E, and another $1,800 from the small blind, if I can chase him away. That dead money is a big payoff for an aggressive move.

Score 5 points for Choice C, raising to $7,000. It's the right move and the right amount. Score 2 points for Choice D, going all-in. It's the right move, but the wrong amount. Raising to $7,000 gets the job done if I've read the situation correctly, but lets me get away with most of my stack if the small blind has been trapping with some huge hand (very unlikely, to be sure). No credit for calling (the same mistake as last hand) or folding.

Problem 21
Calling With a Low M

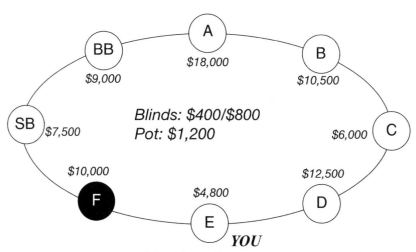

Situation: Large multi-table online tournament. 400 players started, 50 remain, 40 get paid. Player A has been playing generally tight. In the last three rounds, he has only raised one hand.

Your hand: A♠Q♥

Action to you: Player A raises to $2,500. Players B, C, and D all fold.

Question 21: *What do you do?*

A. *Fold*
B. *Call $2,500*
C. *Raise all-in*

153

Action: You actually fold, as do Players F and the blinds. Player A takes the pot.

Solution to Problem 21

As the end of a tournament approaches, a key component of betting assumes greater and greater importance. It's what we, in *Harrington on Hold 'em: Volume II,* called *first-in vigorish*, also know as *folding equity*. Whenever you push all your chips at a pot, you have two ways to win: your opponent may fold, or he might call but you could win the showdown. When you call a bet for all your chips, however, you only have one way to win: by showing the best hand when all the cards are dealt. First-in vigorish is a hugely important part of strategy in the endgame of tournaments.

Some players, however, fall in love with the idea of first-in vigorish so much that they're willing to throw away perfectly playable hands just because their opponent has bet, rather than them. This problem is a case in point. Player A, with a tight reputation, made the first bet at the pot, and Player E threw away his

rather than play the hand without the edge of being first in the pot. He made a bad mistake. Let's see why.

First, let's notice that Player E's stack, $4,800, gives him an M of just 4. That's well within the Red Zone, so he's looking to push all his chips in the pot with any reasonable hand, as long as he's first to act. An ace-queen is a much stronger hand than he needs to make the first move. He would cheerfully push all-in from first position with this hand, and in fact Player E was well aware of this.

Player E also correctly realized that moving all-in after Player A bet $2,500 had essentially no chance of winning the pot by itself. The pot would be $8,500.

$$\$8,500 = \$1,200 \text{ (blinds)} + \$2,500 \text{ (Player A's bet)}$$
$$+ \$4,800 \text{ (Player D's bet)}$$

Player A would need only $2,300 to call and the pot odds would be about 3.7-to-1. If Player A had a pair and were certain you had an overpair, he would be wrong by only a little bit to call, so he has to call your bet regardless of what he holds. (If one of the other players calls your all-in and Player A was bluffing, he could fold, but that won't help you.)

So if you push all-in, Player A will call and you might even get a call from someone behind you if they have a really strong hand. Your A♠Q♥ will be required to win a showdown. Is it adequate for the task?

Player E thought the answer was 'no.' He decided that since Player A had been playing tight, he would only have bet with a pair of tens or better, or ace-king or ace-queen. Player E did some mental arithmetic, decided he was between 30 and 40 percent to win against that range, and realized that even if he had a 40 percent chance to win a pot of $10,800, his equity was only $4,320.

$$\$4,320 = (0.40)(\$10,800)$$

which was less than his equity if he just folded and kept his current stack of $4,800. So he threw in his cards.

Let's commend Player E for his arithmetic skills. The *Pokerstove* program reveals that his chances against that precise range of hands were actually 34.4 percent, so his estimate was right on the money. His reasoning was undone by a different problem: his estimate of Player A's range of hands was much too tight.

At the latter stages of tournaments, you simply can't assume that players are waiting for premium-quality hands for betting or raising, even in early position. This is obviously true for the short stacks, who are desperate to get their chips in the pot, but it's also true for the big stacks, who usually understand that they're supposed to be using their chips to push around the short stacks. The fact that Player A hasn't played any hands for a couple of rounds doesn't necessarily mean much. Player A might not have picked up any playable hands (Has that ever happened to you?) or might have picked up a middling-strength hand only to see someone open the pot with a big bet. As the big stack at the table, I might consider raising with any of the following hands: a pair of eights or better, ace-king, ace-queen, ace-jack, or even king-queen, suited or unsuited.

At the table, I wouldn't do any real calculations with a hand like A♠Q♥ in Player E's position. My M of only 4 tells me all I need to know. I'm pushing if I'm first to act, and I'm calling (or pushing) if someone comes in ahead of me. In my mind, the only reason for not playing an ace-queen is if I really, really need the money that comes with finishing 40th, and I'm content to just sit on my hands and try to sneak into the money. But if I came to play, I'm playing with any ace-queen.

As an exercise, however, let's do the math and verify that pushing is the correct play. I'm going to make these assumptions:

1. After I push, the button, small blind, and big blind will only play if they pick up aces, kings, or queens, in which case they will push also and Player A will fold.

2. If the button and the blinds all fold, Player A will always call.

3. Player A bet for value 90 percent of the time, with the hand range that I outlined above: 88 or better and AK, AQ, AJ, and KQ, suited or unsuited.

4. Player A bluffed 10 percent of the time — believe it or not, bluffing happens — with a hand something like nine-eight suited, where I'm a 60-to-40 favorite.

Let's see what happens.

How often does someone pick up one of the top three pairs? Since I hold an ace and a queen, there are only three ways to pick up a pair of aces and the same three ways to pick up a pair of queens. There are still six ways to pick up a pair of kings. That's a total of 12 possible top pairs, out of 1,225 possible hands, so the chance of a top pair is about 1 percent. With three players left to act, there's about a 3 percent chance that someone has a top pair. To calculate the pot in this case, I'll assume that the push comes from the small blind, and the final pot is $12,900.

$$\$12,900 = \$1,200 + \$2,500 + \$4,800 + \$4,400$$

With that calculation settled, the breakdown of hands looks like this:

- 3 percent of the time, I'm up against a top pair in the small blind, and I'm 23.5 percent to win a pot of $12,900. (The reason my winning percentage is that high — I'm most often against a pair of kings, where I'm not dominated.) My equity here is $91.

$$\$91 = (.03)(.235)(\$12,900)$$

- 87 percent of the time, I'm against Player A's range of hands, where I'm 46.5 percent to win, and the pot is $10,800. My equity is $4,369.

$$\$4,369 = (.87)(.465)(\$10,800)$$

- 10 percent of the time, I'm against one of Player A's bluffs, which I'm representing as nine-eight suited to make the calculations easier. I'm 60 percent to win and the pot is $10,800. My equity is $648.

$$\$648 = (.10)(.60)(\$10,800)$$

My total equity in the hand is the sum of these three numbers or $5,108.

$$\$5,108 = \$91 + \$4,369 + \$648$$

That's about $300 better than just folding, so pushing is indeed a better play.

If I didn't allow the possibility of a bluff, pushing would still be right, but the gain from pushing would only be about half as big. But allowing for a bluff, even if the chance is small, is crucial to playing these hands well. Players do bluff, and they bluff more when they think the table is tight and chips are easy to steal. Don't fall into the trap of "putting your opponent on a hand," and then ignoring all the other hands he might be holding. Once in a while, at the end of a hand where you've picked up a lot of clues, you can narrow your opponent's possible holdings down to just a couple of hands. But pre-flop? It's almost impossible to be that precise.

Score 5 points for Choice C, pushing all-in. No credit for folding. Score 5 points for calling if your intention is to then push all-in after the flop. This allows your opponent to (incorrectly) fold some hands that he would have routinely called preflop.

Problem 22
Hennigan Versus
Nguyen — Slow-Playing

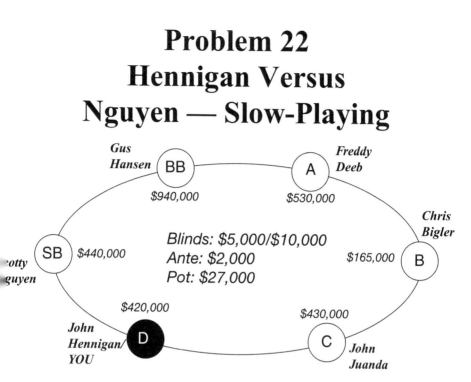

Gus Hansen **BB** $940,000

Freddy Deeb **A** $530,000

Chris Bigler

SB $440,000

$165,000 **B**

Blinds: $5,000/$10,000
Ante: $2,000
Pot: $27,000

Scotty Nguyen

$420,000

$430,000

John Hennigan/ YOU **D**

C John Juanda

Situation: Final table of the 2002 Bellagio Five-Diamond Classic. Your playing partner on the button is John Hennigan, one of the most dangerous and courageous pros in poker.

Your hand: 8♦7♠

Action to you: Deeb, Bigler, and Juanda all fold.

Question 22A: *What do you do?*

A. *Fold*
B. *Call $10,000*
C. *Raise to $30,000*

Action: You actually call $10,000. Nguyen in the small blind calls $5,000, and Hansen checks. The pot is now $42,000.

Flop: 8♥8♣5♦

Action: Nguyen bets $20,000 and Gus Hansen folds.

Question 22B: *What do you do?*

A. *Call $20,000*
B. *Raise to $40,000*
C. *Raise to $60,000*
D. *Push all-in*

Action: You actually raise to $40,000. Nguyen puts in $70,000 more, raising you $50,000. The pot is now $172,000. You have $370,000 left in your stack, Nguyen about $390,000.

Question 22C: *What do you do?*

A. *Fold*
B. *Call $50,000*
C. *Put in $150,000, raising Nguyen $100,000*
D. *Push all-in*

Action: You actually call $50,000, making the pot $222,000.

Turn: K♣

Action: Nguyen bets $120,000. The pot is now $342,000.

Question 22D: *What do you do?*

A. *Fold*
B. *Call $120,000*

C. Push all-in

Action: You actually call. The pot is now $462,000.

River: A♦

Action: Nguyen checks. You have $200,000 left in your stack, Nguyen about $220,000.

Question 22E: *What do you do?*

A. Check
B. Bet $100,000
C. Push all-in

Action: You actually push all-in. Nguyen folds and shows the A♥5♥. You take the pot.

Solution to Problem 22

Question 22A: There is no really wrong play in this situation. Your hand is weak enough that you can just fold it and let the blinds fight. Raising is plausible and might work. However, the two players behind you, Scotty Nguyen and Gus Hansen, are both aggressive and don't mind a good fight, so raising from the button is not going to win the hand as often as you like. Calling is a quiet little play which keeps you in the hand cheaply with your positional advantage active. I like that play a little more than the others.

Score 2 points for Choice B, calling, 1 point each for folding or raising.

Scotty Nguyen calls from the small blind and Gus checks in the big blind.

The flop comes

Scotty Nguyen bets $20,000 and Gus folds.

Question 22B: A great flop. It's very unlikely that Scotty has the case eight, so you should be a big favorite in the hand. The first problem, however, is not so easy. How do you respond to Scotty's bet?

The two obvious choices are to call or to make a small raise. Calling represents a draw, or perhaps an underpair to the board, or a five, or maybe two overcards, which might be good if we thought Scotty was bluffing. A small raise represents the same hands but a more aggressive attitude. Maybe we don't have much, but we think Scotty is bluffing and we want to move him off the hand. (A big raise is screaming "I have an eight or an overpair!" Scotty might not believe us, but we'd be very unhappy if he did.)

To decide between the call or the small raise, we have to know something about Scotty Nguyen and how he plays. He's very aggressive, of course, but a little less respectful of apparent strength than players like Phil Ivey or Gus Hansen. Both Phil and Gus will attack weakness relentlessly, but will pull back if resistance appears and they have nothing. Scotty will push a little harder against resistance. If he thinks he can push you off a hand, he'll keep trying to do so. It's a higher risk and higher reward approach than Phil's or Gus's.

With that profile, the small raise looks slightly better than the straight call. It gets more money in the pot immediately and offers great calling odds if Nguyen has anything at all. Score 3 points for Choice B, raising to $40,000, and 2 points for Choice A, just calling. No credit for either of the big raises, which could end the hand right here.

You actually raise to $40,000, and Nguyen puts in $70,000, raising you an additional $50,000.

Question 22C: Nguyen raises you, which was a little unexpected. But he only raises a little bit; the pot has $172,000 and you need $50,000 to call, so you're being offered 3.5-to-1. Those are big odds, and coupled with your reputation (Hennigan is notoriously hard to push off a hand if he has something), Nguyen must expect you to call unless you're on a complete bluff.

Score 3 points for Choice B, calling, no credit for raising or folding. The pot odds are so good that you're not really letting the cat out of the bag by calling. You might be calling with an underpair or a five or a draw, although the only plausible draw right now is the open-ended straight if you have precisely a seven-six. Hopefully that's enough possibilities to keep your opponent guessing.

What about Nguyen's hand? You really don't know what he has, although in truth you don't care much. You're beating all Nguyen's hands except for a pair of fives or the case eight with a better kicker than your seven, or eight-five. At this stage of the tournament, with four players clustered together, all with Ms between 15 and 20, this hand is your chance to double up and contend for first. The chance of your being beaten is so unlikely that you're simply going to pay it off.

You call, and the pot becomes $222,000. The turn is the K♣. Nguyen bets $120,000.

Question 22D: There's now a club flush draw on board, but that's another long shot that you can't worry about. Whatever Nguyen has, it's probably not a draw, so there's no need to rush the betting. Just call, and try to get the rest of your money in on the river, where the pot will be so large that Nguyen may have to call.

Score 3 points for Choice B, calling, 1 point for Choice C, raising, no credit for Choice A, folding. You actually call, and the pot becomes $462,000. The river is an A♦.

Nguyen checks.

Question 22E: No more room here for finesse. Just shove the rest of your money in the pot (you can affect a hangdog look if you want, but Hennigan doesn't bother with such trifles) and see what happens. Score 4 points for Choice C, pushing all-in, no credit for the $100,000 teaser bet (if $100,000 will get called, so will $200,000), and no credit for checking.

You actually push all-in and Nguyen astutely (and somewhat surprisingly) folds, despite hitting his ace on the river.

Problem 23
Ivey Versus Lederer —
Defending Against a Probe Bet

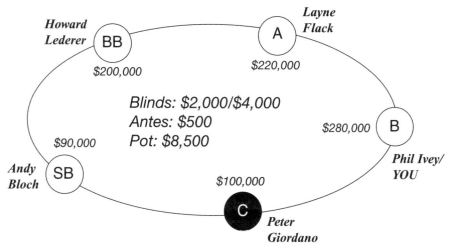

Situation: Final table of 2003 Foxwoods Tournament on Season 1 of the World Poker Tour. Your playing partner is Phil Ivey, who needs no introduction and who currently has the big stack. Howard Lederer is a very strong, solid player, who is quite capable of laying down a hand if he thinks he's beaten.

Your hand: Q♦6♦

Action to you: Layne Flack calls $4,000.

Question 23A: *What do you do?*

A. Fold
B. Call $4,000
C. Raise to $12,000

Action: You actually call $4,000. Giordano folds, but Bloch calls $2,000 and Howard Lederer checks. The pot is now $18,500.

Flop: K♥T♥3♣

Action: Andy Bloch checks. Lederer bets $8,000. Flack folds.

Question 23B: *What do you do?*

A. *Fold*
B. *Call*
C. *Raise to $25,000*

Action: You actually raise to $25,000. Bloch folds and Lederer folds. You win the pot.

Solution to Problem 23

Question 23A: Not an atrocious call at a five-handed table. You have a little bit of a hand, you're getting 3-to-1 pot odds, and you'll have position after the flop on every player but the button (who may not enter the hand). It's a little risky, but aggressive players often make calls with less.

Score 2 points for Choice B, calling. Score 1 point for Choice A, folding, certainly a conservative and reasonable play. No credit for raising with a limper in ahead of you. The idea here is to see a flop and then wield your positional advantage. Raising would be reasonable at a five-handed table if no one had entered ahead of you.

You actually call $4,000. Giordano folds, but Bloch and Lederer call. The pot is $18,500. The flop comes

Bloch checks and Lederer bets $8,000. Flack folds. The pot is now $26,500.

Question 23B: No one showed strength before the flop. Bloch only checks, showing no real interest in the hand. Lederer makes a bet of less than half the pot, a probe-type bet. He might have something; he might just want everybody to go away so he can take a small pot. Flack, in fact, goes away.

Ivey, although the flop missed him completely, smells weakness at the table and makes a big raise. He's basically thinking that if Lederer had a strong hand like a king with a good kicker, he would have either bet more or checked, and with a monster like trips or two pair, he might not have bet at all with two aggressive players like Flack and Ivey next to act. If Ivey is right, Lederer doesn't have a big hand; the best Lederer might have is a king with a weak kicker. Ivey also knows that Lederer is capable of going away with a small loss if he thinks he's likely beaten. Put all these facts together, and a strong raise looks like a positive equity play. It's also a standard defense against a player who likes to make small probe bets to win pots where no one has anything. Just come over the top strongly, letting him know that approach won't work at this table.

Ivey actually raises to $25,000, and Lederer lays down K♣4♣. Score 3 points for Choice C, raising. Score 1 point for Choice A, folding, which isn't a bad play, but which doesn't take advantage of the situation. No credit for just calling, which shows weakness when you are, in fact, weak — usually a bad idea.

One footnote to this problem: This hand was played in 2002, and might play out differently today. Before the television era in poker, players weren't aware of just how many moves other players were making. The general assumption was "I might make an occasional move, but my opponents pretty much have the hands they're representing." No one believes that anymore, so more hands are contested.

Problem 24
Ivey Versus Williams —
Playing a Small Pair Out of Position

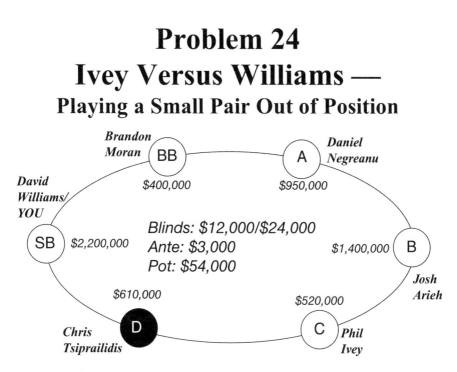

Situation: Final table of the 2004 Borgata Tournament. Your playing partner is David Williams. Williams, Josh Arieh, and Phil Ivey are all known to be very aggressive. Daniel Negreanu prefers small-ball. Brandon Moran and Chris Tsiprailidis are solid.

Your hand: 5♠5♥

Action to you: Negreanu and Arieh fold. Ivey raises to $70,000. Tsiprailidis folds.

Question 24A: *What do you do?*

A. Fold
B. Call $58,000
C. Raise to $200,000
D. Raise all-in

Action: You actually call $58,000. Moran folds. The pot is $182,000.

Flop: T♦4♣2♦

Question 24B: *What do you do?*

A. *Check*
B. *Bet $90,000*
C. *Bet $180,000*

Action: You actually check. Ivey bets $105,000. The pot is now $287,000. Ivey has about $345,000 left.

Question 24C: *What do you do?*

A. *Fold*
B. *Call $105,000*
C. *Raise to $250,000*
D. *Push all-in*

Action: You actually push all-in. Ivey folds. You win the pot.

Solution to Problem 24

Negreanu and Arieh both fold. Negreanu folds the J♠6♥, Arieh the J♥5♣. Although both are aggressive players, neither likes to be aggressive with these hands. When aggressive players attack the pot with weaker hands, they like to use hands like seven-five rather than something like queen-five, even though queen-five is an objectively stronger hand.

The reason is not what you might think. Most players, when they see a pro making a move with a hand like seven-five offsuit think that the reason must be the straight possibilities of the two cards. Actually, the possible straights play a relatively minor role. The real reasons are disguise and domination.

Suppose you make a move at the pot with a hand like queen-five, and get called. The flop, let's say, comes queen-nine-deuce, hitting your hand nicely. If you now get involved, your opponent thinks "He has a queen." If you get action, the action will come from someone with a queen and a better kicker, or a hand that beats the queen.

But if you play seven-five and the flop comes with three low cards, your hand is beautifully disguised. You may be able to win some decent money from an opponent with ace-king, who thinks you have two high cards also. The straight possibilities with the two low cards are an added bonus, but the real reason for attacking with these hands comes from the element of disguise.

In addition, these hands are unlikely to be dominated. The great danger of playing a hand like queen-five is that you may be facing king-queen or queen-jack, and your hand is dominated by the queen with the better kicker. In a battle of non-pair versus non-pair, your chances are much better when you can avoid domination.

Ivey picks up A♣3♦, and he now raises $70,000. With one of the two short stacks and just four players left in the hand, Ivey figures that any ace is a good enough reason to attack. Ivey is very aggressive, but even a conservative player in Ivey's situation would make the same play.

Tsiprailidis folds the 9♥6♥.

Question 24A: Williams, in the small blind, has an interesting hand, a little pair:

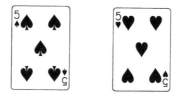

He's not folding. His real question is: call, raise, or move all-in? It's a tough problem.

As we attack this problem, let's make two simplifying assumptions. First, let's ignore the small stack sitting in the big blind. Given the action from Ivey and Williams, he's probably going to fold unless he picks up a very strong hand, something in the top 5 percent or so of all hands. That's a small enough calling frequency that whatever play we decide is correct for the two-player case will almost certainly be right overall. We'll also ignore, for now, the play of just raising and focus on calling versus pushing. Later we'll revisit the ordinary raise and see if it might be right. But for now, we'll look at calling versus pushing.

Intuitively, it seems that pushing all-in should show a nice profit. Ivey will fold many of the hands that he used for raising, and our fives will be a small favorite against some of his calling hands. Let's make some reasonable assumptions and see if this works.

With three players left in the hand, plus a short stack, I'll estimate that Ivey would raise with

- Any pair (73 possible hands; remember that since we have two fives, there's only one way he can hold a pair of fives, not six ways.)

- Any ace (184 possible hands; as before, since we hold two fives, there are just eight possible ace-five hands, not 16.)

- Any two cards 10 or higher — KQ, KJ, KT, QJ, QT, JT (96 possible hands).

This is probably a conservative list. I wouldn't be astonished if Ivey had moved at the pot with a nine-eight, for example. But the more hands he could use, the better a play pushing becomes, since he has more hands to fold. So whatever we get for an answer will represent a conservative estimate for the strength of pushing.

Our three categories gave us a total of 353 hands that Ivey might be holding. If we push, with how many of these hands will he call? There's no way to be sure. After folding, his M will be a little less than 9, still not low enough to be really desperate. I'd call with tens or better, plus ace-king and ace-queen. Ivey is very aggressive when he hasn't seen any strength at the table, but when he has to show down a hand, it's usually a hand that fits the circumstances pretty well. Let's supplement my list with nines and ace-jack. That makes a total of 84 calling hands, about 25 percent of the hands he might have raised with. For an aggressive player, that percentage seems about right. Of his calling hands, 43 percent are the high pairs, and 57 percent are the strong ace-x hands where we're a favorite.

How much money is at stake? There are three possible results of our push:

1. If Ivey folds, we win what's currently in the pot — $124,000.

2. If Ivey calls and we lose, our loss is the $58,000 it took to call Ivey's bet (remember, we were the small blind, so we already had $12,000 out there) plus the $450,000 that covered the rest of Ivey's stack — a total of $508,000.

3. If Ivey calls and we win, we get the current pot plus the rest of Ivey's stack — $124,000 plus $450,000, or $574,000.

174 Problem 24

Our last job is to figure out how often we win if we push and Ivey calls. We know he calls about 25 percent of the time, and of those, he has a high pair 43 percent of the time, and two high cards 57 percent. So

• High pairs = 25 percent times 43 percent or about 11 percent.

• Two high cards = 25 percent times 57 percent or about 14 percent.

We win 20 percent against the high pairs, and about 54 percent against the two high cards, which means

• when Ivey calls, we win about 2.2 percent plus 7.5 percent or about 10 percent

• and we lose the rest, about 15 percent

Almost done now. Here's the last calculation.

• 75 percent of the time, Ivey folds and we make $124,000. Our equity is 0.75 times $124,000 or $93,000.

• 10 percent of the time, Ivey calls and we win. Our equity is 0.10 times $574,000 or $57,400.

• 15 percent of the time, Ivey calls and we lose. Our equity is 0.15 times -$508,000 or -$76,200.

Our total equity is $74,200.

$$\$74,200 = \$93,000 + \$57,400 - \$76,200$$

As we suspected, pushing all-in has a substantial positive expectation.

Assigning an evaluation to calling is a little more difficult. So many permutations exist after the flop that we need to rely on some general, common-sense observations. If we call, the pot contains $182,000, we have a pair of fives, and we're out of position. One time in eight, we hit a third five and we'll almost certainly win the pot, although we can't tell how big the pot will be. If the flop misses Ivey, we may not make any extra money. The rest of the time, seven times out of eight, we'll miss the flop and be out of position with our small pair. One, two, or three cards higher than our fives will be on board. Ivey will know if he hit his hand or not. We won't. And we act first.

Under this scenario, is there any reason to think our equity will be 40 percent or more of the pot? No. At best, we might be breaking even, but I doubt we could do better than that in the long run. So pushing dominates calling by a wide margin.

Could making a more modest raise be the right play? It's almost certainly better than calling, because it will force Ivey to lay down a bunch of hands. But when it doesn't win the pot, we're in the same situation as before — out of position with a low pair, and now against a very good hand. Once again, I'd rather have pushed than have to play the low pair out of position after the flop.

One final consideration needs to be mentioned. Phil Ivey is currently the short stack, with just 25 percent of your chip stack. You have a chance to knock out the most dangerous player at the table at relatively small cost. Take it.

Score 5 points for Choice D, raising all-in. Score 2 points for Choice C, raising $200,000. Score 1 point for Choice B, calling, and no credit for Choice A, folding.

Williams actually calls, and Moran folds his K♦3♣. The pot is $182,000.

The flop comes

Question 24B: That's an excellent flop for you. Two cards lower than your fives, plus a ten. If Ivey was playing two high cards, you very likely have the best hand. We know from our previous hands that Ivey likes to take the lead when he sees weakness, and so far all he's seen from you is a pre-flop call. If you check, he'll have no reason not to bet. Then you can raise and hopefully win a larger pot. Score 3 points for Choice A, checking. No credit for either bet, which might just chase Ivey away.

You check. Ivey, having seen nothing that indicates he's up against a hand, bets $105,000.

Question 24C: Time to lower the hammer and push all-in. Score 3 points (Choice D). No credit for the smaller bet. If Ivey reraises you, the pot odds would compel you to call anyway, so you might as well get the chips in first. Also no credit for folding or calling.

You push all-in, and Ivey folds.

One final comment: In this book I'm emphasizing how to play well after the flop. But in this hand I advocated making a big pre-flop all-in raise to end the play quickly. Contradiction?

Not really. Small pairs don't play well after the flop. They're usually the best hand before the flop, but they're often not the best hand after the flop. In order to play from a position of strength, you have to play small pairs pre-flop as fast as possible, especially out of position. Often that requires the beginner's play: the quick all-in move to end the hand. Regardless of your post-flop skill, the mathematics dominates your strategy here.

Problem 25
Negreanu Versus
Arieh — Playing a Small Pair

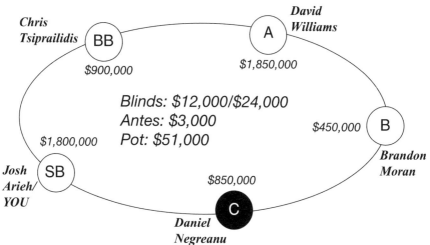

Situation: Final table of the 2004 Borgata tournament. Your playing partner is Josh Arieh. Arieh is a courageous attacking player and one of the bright young lights on the poker scene.

Your hand: 5♥5♣

Action to you: David Williams and Brandon Moran fold. Daniel Negreanu, on the button, raises to $60,000. The pot is now $111,000.

Question 25A: *What do you do?*

A. *Fold*
B. *Call $48,000*
C. *Reraise to $200,000*

Action: You actually call $48,000. Chris Tsiprallidis folds. The pot is now $159,000.

Flop: 9♦9♣7♠

Question 25B: *What do you do?*

A.   Check
B.   Bet $80,000
C.   Bet $120,000

Action: You actually check. Daniel Negreanu bets $120,000. The pot is now $279,000.

Question 25C: *What do you do?*

A.   Fold
B.   Call $120,000
C.   Raise to $240,000

Action: You actually call $120,000. The pot is now $399,000.

Turn: 8♦

Question 25D: *What do you do?*

A.   Check
B.   Bet $100,000
C.   Bet $230,000

Action: You actually bet $230,000. Daniel Negreanu calls. The pot is now $859,000.

River: 9♥

Question 25E: *What do you do?*

A.   *Check*
B.   *Bet $400,000*

Action: You actually check. Daniel Negreanu bets $360,000. The pot is now $1,219,000.

Question 25F: *What do you do?*

A.   *Fold*
B.   *Call $360,000*
C.   *Reraise all-in*

Action: You actually fold.

Solution to Problem 25

Question 25A: Even at a short table, a small pair out of position is a difficult and treacherous hand. Pre-flop, there's an excellent chance that the small pair is the best hand. Post-flop, the hand breaks down into a number of different cases. Here are the important ones:

- You hit your set. Obviously the best possible case, and you rate to win a big pot if your opponent has something. Unfortunately, this case only occurs one time in eight.

- The board shows a higher card and two lower cards. This is the second most-favorable case. It probably missed your opponent, so if he has two higher cards, you still have the best hand. But at some point you'll have to bet to find out.

- The board shows a pair, plus a higher card. This is the third most-favorable case. If your opponent started with two higher cards than you, odds are he didn't hit this flop. As before, at some point you'll have to bet to find out.

- The board shows two higher cards and a lower card. You probably still have the lead over two high cards, but you're not comfortable.

- The board shows three higher cards. The worst case. If the cards are all high-to medium (ace-queen-jack or jack-ten-eight type flops), you're very likely beaten, and may not even call a bet.

Other cases, like flopping three of a kind on board or three lower cards, happen so rarely you don't need to think about them much, although they're generally favorable for you.

When you have a low pair out of position, you will at some point need to make a move at the pot. Unless you flop a set, the value of your hand will deteriorate the further into the hand you go, since the chance that someone has flopped a card that beats you is steadily rising. But the earlier you make your move, the less information you have about your opponents. Hence the inherent difficulty in playing small pairs out of position, especially for small-ball players. Your best chance of having the best hand at the table comes pre-flop, but that's when you have the least information on your opponents.

Here you have a small pair, the

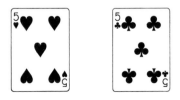

in the small blind, and Negreanu, an aggressive player, has raised from the button. By itself, this doesn't tell you much, and your small pair rates to be best right now.

Score 3 points for Choice C, reraising to $200,000. Out of position, it's slightly the best of a bad set of choices. The idea is to decide the hand right now, from a position of relative strength. If you take down the pot, great. If you get reraised, throw your hand away. If you get called, reevaluate after you see the flop, but you're probably done with the hand unless something favorable happens.

Score 2 points for Choice B, calling. Most pros would agree with this play, which is the classic small-ball method of handling this holding. You don't get overly involved before the flop with a weak hand. While the play looks conservative, it comes with its own set of risks, as we shall see.

No credit for Choice A, folding. You have a pair, only five people remain, therefore you have to play somehow.

You actually call. Chris T in the big blind folds. The pot is now $159,000.

The flop comes

Question 25B: As we explained in the last section, that's a pretty good flop for you. You can't be sure, because Daniel is very capable of betting from the button with almost anything. But as flops go, this one is generally good for the small pair.

Now what? You have two choices, checking or betting. Let's see how each is likely to play.

- If you check, Daniel will most likely bet, whether he hit this flop or not. Since he may have nothing, and you certainly have something, you will call, unless the bet is huge.

- If you bet, Daniel can fold, call, or raise. If he folds you take the pot, and if he raises you're probably beaten and can throw the hand away. If he calls you're in roughly the same position as if you had checked first, and he bet, and you called.

Under the circumstances, betting out is clearly better. You may win the hand right away, which is good. If you're raised, you ascertain that you're probably beaten, throw the hand away, and limit your loss to that one bet. Even if you're called, you've at least determined that your opponent was willing to call into your show of strength, which gives you a better picture of his hand than if he had bet after you checked.

Score 3 points for Choice B, betting $80,000. Score 1 point for Choice C, betting $120,000, which is a little too big under the circumstances. Either bet can win if your opponent has nothing, but a call on his part is a bad sign, and you don't want to spend more money than necessary. No credit for Choice A, checking.

You check. Negreanu bets $120,000. The pot is $279,000.

Question 25C: The pot is offering more than 2-to-1 odds, and your pair of fives may still be good. You might be beaten, but your call before the flop and your check after the flop has almost forced a bet from Negreanu, so you have to call. Score 2 points for Choice B, calling, no credit for other plays.

You call, bringing the pot to $399,000. The turn comes the 8♦.

Question 25D: That's a very bad card for you. There are now straight and flush draws on board, in addition to the possibility of an already-made straight. In addition, any card that pairs the board beats you, and any overpair beats you.

If a weak card had come, say a four or trey or deuce, I would be inclined to lead out and make a try to win the pot, with the idea that if I didn't win the pot I was done with the hand. With a turn card this dangerous, however, I would regrettably let the hand go and just check, with the intention of folding if Negreanu bet. Might I be laying down the winning hand? Sure. But my opponent bet both before the flop and on the flop, the board is dangerous, my fives don't look good anymore, and if he bets again, I'm not going to be making a heroic stand for half my chips. I'm going to exit quietly, stage left.

Score 3 points for Choice A, checking. No credit for either bet.

You actually bet $230,000, and Negreanu called. The pot became $859,000. The river card is the 9♥.

Question 25E: Although you now have a full house, nines full of fives, it's actually a relatively weak hand. Your opponent beats you if he has the case nine, an eight, a seven, or any pair higher than your fives. Reviewing the betting, he raised pre-flop (on the button), he bet on the flop (after your check), and he called your big bet on the turn. The first two bets could have been made with a couple of random high cards like ace-king or queen-ten, just on the possibility that you didn't have much. It's the call of your bet on the turn that's especially troublesome.

Your best-case scenario right now is that he has a hand like ace-ten, king-ten, or queen-ten. In that case he bet pre-flop with two high cards (perfectly reasonable), then bet on the flop with two overcards to the board (again reasonable, after your check), and finally called on the turn with an open-ended straight draw plus two overcards. He might have thought that he had as many as 14 outs: all sixes, all jacks, plus three tens and three aces. In that case he would have been a 2.3-to-1 underdog to make his hand, but his pot odds for calling on the turn were 2.7-to-1: easily enough to justify a call even without implied odds.

But that's the best-case scenario. In order to call on the river, you have to balance the odds of that scenario against all the other scenarios where he's simply betting with a made hand, all of which beat you. Conclusion? You're probably beaten. Try to check the hand down. Score 3 points for Choice A, checking. No credit for other plays.

You check, and Negreanu bets $360,000.

Question 25F: The $360,000 bet takes the pot up to $1,219,000. You're now getting almost 3.4-to-1 on your call. That's a good price, but your opponent has now bet or called on all four rounds. Give him the pot. If he's been bluffing the whole way, pat him on the back.

Score 3 points for Choice A, folding. No credit for calling or raising.

You actually fold. Negreanu's hole cards were the Q♦Q♥, and he had been betting for value the entire hand.

Problem 26
Hellmuth Versus
Matusow — Reading the Table

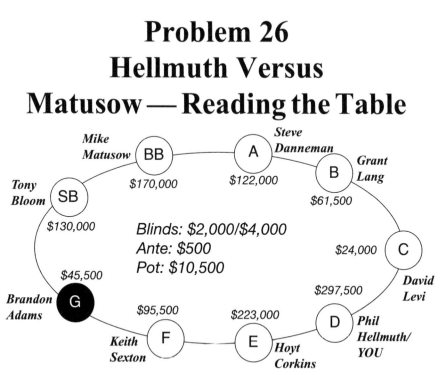

Situation: Final table of the ESPN Superstars II Competition. Your playing partner is Phil Hellmuth. You are the chip leader at this point.

Your hand: J♥T♥

Action to you: Steve Danneman folds. Lang and Levi fold.

Question 26A: *What do you do?*

A. *Fold*
B. *Call $4,000*
C. *Raise to $12,000*

Action: You actually raise to $12,000. Hoyt Corkins calls $12,000. Sexton, Adams, and Lang all fold. Matusow calls $8,000. The pot is now $42,500.

Flop: A♥5♥5♦

Action: Matusow checks.

Question 26B: *What do you do?*

A. *Check*
B. *Bet $18,000*

Action: You actually check. Hoyt Corkins checks behind you. The pot remains at $42,500.

Turn: 8♦

Action: Matusow bets $18,000. The pot is now $60,500.

Question 26C: *What do you do?*

A. *Fold*
B. *Call $18,000*
C. *Raise to $50,000*

Action: You actually call $18,000. Corkins folds. The pot is now $78,500.

River: K♦

Action: Matusow checks.

Question 26D: *What do you do?*

A.   *Check*
B.   *Bet $40,000*
C.   *Bet $80,000*

Action: You actually check. Matusow shows 6♦5♠ for trip fives and wins the pot.

Solution to Problem 26

Question 26A: In middle position at a 9-player table,

is definitely a playable hand. In *Harrington on Hold 'em: Volume I,* I recommended playing that hand with a mixture of 50 percent raises and 50 percent calls, and that was as part of a *conservative* strategy. Hellmuth is an aggressive player pre-flop, so he raises to $12,000 with the hand. Score 2 points for Choices B and C, either calling or raising with the hand. No credit for folding.

Behind Hellmuth, Corkins picks up the Q♠Q♣ and elects to just call. It's a tricky play, but I'm not enthusiastic about it after a raise from Hellmuth. Let's explain why.

Hellmuth is aggressive in a slightly different way from a player like, say, Phil Ivey. Both will bet plenty of hands before the flop. Ivey, as we have seen, will bet almost any hand if he likes the situation and feels he can make some money. Hellmuth is more circumspect. He likes to attack with paint, and you'll see him on camera make plenty of pre-flop raises with hands like queen-ten, king-jack, queen-jack, in addition to all the stronger hands.

After the flop, the two players are very different. Ivey will continue attacking until he encounters real strength, at which point he'll back off if he has nothing. Hellmuth is much more cautious. With a weakish hand, he'll check or use small probe bets to see where he stands, but he'll try not to lose a lot of chips in unclear situations.

Now let's look at Corkins' call again. Of course he could raise, but he's trapping to try and win money from Hellmuth after the flop. But if you're playing against someone who's careful after the flop, your best chance for making money is before the flop. Of course, Hellmuth may throw the hand away anyway after your raise. But even so, you've also prevented players behind you from calling with good odds and perhaps drawing out on the flop. I think Corkins should have raised here.

After three more folds, action passes to Matusow in the big blind. He looks down to see 6♦5♠ and calls anyway. On the tape, he announced that he was "calling in the dark" as soon as Hellmuth raised, so he may have felt he needed to back his claim for psychological reasons. But after Corkins' call, the pot is $34,000 and he only needs $8,000 to call, so he's getting more than 4-to-1 odds. Even out of position with a weak hand, it's a defensible play.

With $42,500 in the pot, the flop comes

Matusow, first to act, has hit the jackpot and checks. He wants to see if either of the other two players will take the lead in the betting.

Question 26B: Hellmuth now has a draw to a heart flush. If he hits the hand, he'll almost certainly be winning. Only king-x of hearts or queen-x of hearts will dominate him, and those hands aren't likely from the pre-flop betting.

Hellmuth has no interest in trying some kind of semi-bluff bet here. What, after all, did Corkins have when he called? If he has a pair or an ace then Hellmuth is beaten right now, and those are the most likely calling hands. So he checks, looking for a free card. The ace on board was a bad card for Hellmuth, but with three players in the hand, he might get lucky and sneak through without a big bet. Score 4 points for Choice A, checking, no credit for Choice B, betting.

Corkins didn't like the ace on the flop, but he still has a pair of queens. Should he bet or check? Many players would bet here, to find out where they stand. If their bet wins the pot, great, and if it doesn't and they get raised, they just throw the queens away. Corkins takes a different approach. He probably reasoned, "If I have the best hand now, the only card I'm afraid of on the turn is a king, or perhaps a third heart. If I don't have the best hand, I can save some money by keeping my powder dry. Someone in front of me might be trapping with an ace right now."

I have a slight preference for betting in Corkins' position, but don't mind his play. If he's been aggressive throughout the session (which is certainly his style) then this is a good, cheap way of varying his play. *Notice that Corkins' queens are strong enough to check, since only one overcard (kings) now hurts him.* If Corkins had a lesser hand, like jacks, tens, or nines, he has to bet, to protect his weaker hand from the more numerous overcards.

So Corkins checks, and the pot remains at $42,500.

The turn comes the 8♦, putting a second diamond on board.

Matusow now bets $18,000. Since no one bet on the flop, there may not be an ace out there. If neither Hellmuth nor Corkins has an ace, the action will dry up for this hand, and there are now two possible flush draws. Matusow wisely decides to take the pot down now. The pot goes to $60,500.

Question 26C: Hellmuth has a flush draw which he thinks will win. The pot is now offering him 3.3-to-1. He needs a little more than 4-to-1 to call based on expressed odds alone, but Matusow bet into two players, so he must have something, probably an ace. It's reasonable to assume that Hellmuth, if he hits his flush, can win a little more on the river, so the implied odds look all right.

The wild card here is Corkins. If he were to stick in a big raise, Hellmuth's calculations collapse. But he only called before the flop and checked after two checks to him, so he probably doesn't have much. Hellmuth figures he can leave Corkins out of his calculations, and calls.

Score 4 points for Choice B, calling. No credit for raising or folding.

Now the action switches to Corkins. If he had seen a check from Matusow and a bet from Hellmuth, he might think that no one had anything and Hellmuth was just on a steal. But since Matusow initiated the action with two players yet to act, including the pre-flop raiser and a caller, he must have something, and with an ace on board, any "something" beats Corkins' queens. So Corkins folds. The pot is now $78,500.

The river comes a K♦, putting the third diamond on board.

Matusow sees the third diamond and checks. He thinks he probably has the best hand, but he's not sure if weaker hands than his will call a bet. Against Hellmuth, he's probably right. Hellmuth has a reputation for making great (and sometimes not-so-great) laydowns. Against a weak player, I think Matusow would bet, since many players would call on the end with just a pair of aces, and certainly with ace-king. You'll lose money to the diamond flush, but that came through the back door and should be a long shot, not something that would stop you from betting.

Question 26D: You've missed your hand and Matusow showed real strength on the turn, so don't lose all your chips trying to bluff him. Just show down the hand and take your lumps. Score 3 points for Choice A, checking, no credit for any of the betting plays.

Problem 27
Hansen Versus Hennigan
— Smelling the Threat

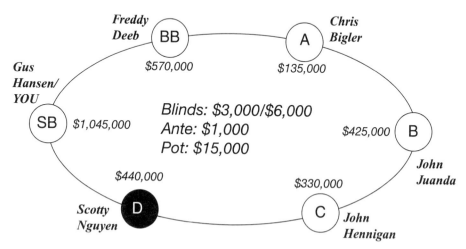

Situation: Final table of the 2002 Bellagio Five-Diamond Classic. Your playing partner in the small blind is Gus Hansen, in the process of winning his first major WPT event.

Your hand: K♥8♥

Action to you: Chris Bigler and John Juanda both fold. John Hennigan raises to $15,000. Scotty Nguyen folds.

Question 27A: *What do you do?*

A. *Fold*
B. *Call $12,000*
C. *Raise to $40,000*

Action: You actually call for $12,000. Freddy Deeb calls for $9,000. The pot is now $51,000.

Flop: K♦Q♠7♥

Question 27B: *What do you do?*

A. *Check*
B. *Bet $25,000*
C. *Bet $50,000*

Action: You actually bet $25,000. Freddy Deeb folds. John Hennigan calls. The pot is now $101,000.

Turn: 6♣

Question 27C: *What do you do?*

A. *Check*
B. *Bet $40,000*
C. *Bet $80,000*

Action: You actually bet $40,000. Hennigan calls. The pot is now $181,000.

River: A♥

Question 27D: *What do you do?*

A. *Check*
B. *Bet $90,000*
C. *Bet $150,000*

Action: You actually check. Hennigan bets $50,000. The pot is now $231,000.

Question 27E: *What do you do?*

A. *Fold*
B. *Call $50,000*
C. *Raise to $150,000*

Action: You actually fold. Hennigan had 7♣7♦ in the hole, for a set of sevens.

Solution to Problem 27

Question 27A: The pot contains $30,000 after Hennigan's bet, and it costs only $12,000 to call, so Gus is getting 2.5-to-1 odds. However, he's out of position on the raiser with the

which is not especially strong. Gus likes to play pots, and, unlike most other top pros, his approach to the game doesn't emphasize position as much. I'm not surprised that he called with this hand at a short table, but it wouldn't be my preference, even with the advantage of a big chip stack.

Score 1 point for Choice B, calling, 2 points for Choice A, folding. Definitely no credit for Choice C, raising, which is the only clear error with this medium-to-weak hand.

Gus actually calls and Deeb calls behind him in the big blind. The pot becomes $51,000 before the flop.

Deeb's call brings in another player with position on Gus. The pot odds were much more favorable for Deeb than they were for Gus; he was getting over 4.5-to-1 odds on his call and his position was even better once he knew the small blind was playing. He actually called with the T♥9♣, a play I like under the circumstances, but he might reasonably have called with less. It's another reason to be cautious with Gus' hand.

With three players in the hand, the flop comes

Question 27B: That's a good flop for Gus. He now has top pair, albeit with a weakish kicker. Top pair is a good holding, but with two other players in the hand, one of whom raised pre-flop, it's not a hand for slow-playing. Gus correctly leads out for $25,000, half the pot. Score 3 points for that play (Choice B). Score 1 point for Choice C, betting the pot. You're committing more money than should be necessary for your purpose. If no one has a pair, your bet should win the hand. One point for Choice A, checking; it's slightly inferior, but not outrageously so.

Gus bet $25,000, Deeb folds, and Hennigan calls $25,000. The pot is now $101,000.

The turn comes the 6♣.

Question 27C: Gus's bet on the flop eliminated one opponent, but not the pre-flop raiser. Now Gus needs to start thinking about what Hennigan might reasonably have. Since Gus is known to be aggressive and to fire at many pots without necessarily having a hand, Hennigan probably didn't need a strong holding to call.

So what might he have? Here's a list of five possibilities:

1. **A King**. If Hennigan has a king, Gus is in serious trouble, since most kings beat Gus's hand. AK, KJ, KT, and K9 give Hennigan kings with a higher kicker, while KQ, K7, and K6

give him two pair, and K8 ties. Gus is only beating K5 through K2, and those are the least likely kings for Henningan to have played pre-flop.

2. **Trip Queens, trip sevens, or trip sixes**. (Trip kings are very unlikely since two kings are accounted for.) A pair of queens or a pair of sevens in the hole would account for the pre-flop raise and the call, since Hennigan is now trapping. A pair of sixes would have raised pre-flop and might have called on the flop, but that's less likely.

3. **Other pairs**. Hennigan might have raised pre-flop with a queen plus a good kicker, an ace or jack. He'd certainly be calling with middle pair against a player like Gus who might have anything. Lower pairs are possible for the same reason.

4. **An ace**. Hennigan could have raised with ace-jack, ace-ten, or ace-nine, and now calls, thinking the ace might be good.

5. **Drawing hands**. There are no flush draws available, but Hennigan could have played a hand like jack-ten or perhaps even jack-nine. Unless he has exactly jack-ten, however, the call based on a straight draw looks unlikely.

That's a pretty exhaustive list. Gus is losing to most of the kings and the trips, but beating all the other hands for now. Gus's loose reputation and willingness to fire at pots may make him some money if Hennigan is calling with the weaker hands.

Gus now bets $40,000. That's a good amount, so score 3 points for Choice B. The hand is far from a lock, so score only 1 point for betting the larger amount, $80,000 (Choice C). Gus isn't trying to make a fortune from this hand; he's just betting when his analysis indicates he's in a favorable position. Since he's beating most of the hands that Hennigan might reasonably have, he doesn't have to stop pushing yet. He also has to bet with his good hands, since his style depends on betting with many of his bad hands. No credit for Choice A, checking.

Hennigan calls the $40,000 bet, making the pot $181,000.

The river comes the A♥.

Question 27D: Oops. Hennigan called again, and now a bad card came. The call on the turn pretty much eliminated the straight draws as possibilities, as well as the lowest pairs. The ace on the river made all the aces into winners. If Hennigan has been playing with something like queen-jack, will he call a bet now with the ace and king on board? Probably not.

Gus can't bet at this point. There aren't many hands left on Gus's list that he can beat, and almost none of those would call a bet at this point. He has to check and hope Hennigan checks behind him, after which he just might win a showdown.

Score 4 points for Choice A, checking. No credit for any betting play.

Gus in fact checks and Hennigan bets $50,000. The pot is now $231,000.

Question 27E: The pot is offering Gus 4.6-to-1 to call. Of course, Hennigan knew that when he bet, so he's expecting to get called.

Gus folds, a wise decision. Despite the huge pot odds, there's little chance any more that Hennigan has been playing a hand that Gus could beat. The ace eliminated most of the hands that Gus had been hoping Hennigan held, and the small suck bet, fishing for a call, showed that Hennigan probably isn't pushing a hand that couldn't win a showdown. Score 4 points for Choice A, folding, and no credit for calling or raising.

In fact Hennigan had the 7♣7♦ in the hole. He played the hand well and consistently throughout, and probably won as much as he could have. The ace on the river was an extraordinarily bad card for him; almost any other card would have allowed Gus to bet or call a bet on the end, but the ace eliminated the biggest class of hands that Gus could beat.

Problem 28
Flack Versus Giordano
— Bet or Check on the River?

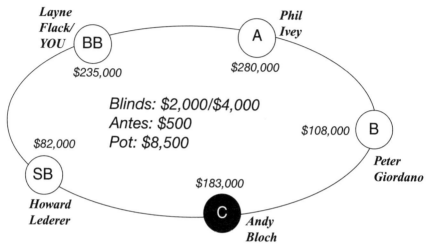

Layne Flack/ YOU — BB — $235,000

Phil Ivey — A — $280,000

Blinds: $2,000/$4,000
Antes: $500
Pot: $8,500

$108,000 — B — Peter Giordano

$82,000 — SB — Howard Lederer

$183,000 — C — Andy Bloch

Situation: Final table of 2003 Foxwoods Tournament on Season 1 of the World Poker Tour. Five players remain. Your playing partner is Layne Flack, also known as 'back to back' Flack, one of the most aggressive of the younger players. In my view, his style most closely resembles that of the late Stu Ungar. Giordano has been playing tight so far, mostly playing only high cards.

Your hand: 7♦6♦

Action to you: Phil Ivey folds. Giordano raises to $15,500. Bloch folds. Lederer folds. The pot is $24,000.

Question 28A: *What do you do?*

A. *Fold*
B. *Call $11,500*
C. *Raise to $30,000*

Action: You actually call $11,500. The pot is now $35,500.

Flop: 9♥7♠2♠

Question 28B: *What do you do?*

A. *Check*
B. *Bet $14,000*
C. *Bet $30,000*

Action: You actually check. Giordano checks.

Turn: 9♠

Question 28C: *What do you do?*

A. *Check*
B. *Bet $14,000*

Action: You actually bet $14,000. Giordano calls. The pot is now $63,500.

River: 9♣

Question 28D: *What do you do?*

A. *Check*
B. *Bet $40,000*

Action: You actually check. Giordano checks behind you. He held Q♦J♠, and your full house wins the pot.

Solution to Problem 28

Question 28A: You're out of position, with a relatively weak

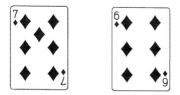

But the pot is offering 2-to-1 odds, and you're against a relatively tight player who may have reason to fear your aggressive reputation. Folding is the conservative play, but a call isn't unreasonable. Score 2 points for Choice B, calling and 2 points for Choice A, folding. No credit for Choice C, raising.

You actually call. The pot becomes $35,500. The flop comes

Question 28B: You've hit middle pair, a little bit of a hand. Your opponent is a conservative player, and hence likely to play high cards. Your best guess right now is that the flop missed him, but he may have raised with an overpair. Either betting a little, to feel out your opponent, or checking, to get some free information, are reasonable plays. I have a slight preference for checking. Score 2 points for Choice A, checking, 1 point for Choice B, betting the smaller amount. No credit for a big bet. Right now you don't know enough to commit a lot of money.

You actually check. Giordano checks behind you. The pot remains $35,500.

The turn comes the 9♠.

Question 28C: You gave your opponent a chance to bet, and he declined. The nine is a good card for you, since it cut down on the chance he was slow-playing top pair (a little unlikely in any case, as a conservative player would bet it.) The third spade is a little worrisome, but it's a long shot that he has two spades in the hole. He might have semi-bluffed on the flop with two high spades.

You're probably ahead right now. If your opponent has a single spade, you need to bet. Score 3 points for Choice B, betting $14,000. No credit for checking.

You actually bet $14,000. Giordano calls. The pot is now $63,500.

The river comes the 9♣.

Question 28D: The nine on the river completes your full house, but leaves you paralyzed. You're beaten by overpairs to your sevens or hands containing the case nine. You're winning against everything else. Overall, you're favored to have the winning hand here, but that doesn't tell you if you should bet or check. Too see what action you should take, you need to understand how your opponent will behave with different holdings. Remember that at this point, the pot is $63,500, you have $205,000 left in your stack, and your opponent has $78,000.

- **Case 1a: He is strong and you check**. If you check and he has a strong hand, he will certainly bet. Exactly how much he bets is a matter of his style on the river. Most players don't like to push all-in on the river with a very strong hand for fear their opponents will fold a losing hand. An average bet is probably about half his existing stack, or around $40,000.

Since he might be bluffing and the pot odds are good, you call, losing $40,000.

- **Case 1b: He is strong and you bet $40,000.** He will reraise all-in. You can probably throw your hand away despite the pot odds. His leverage on the bet is so little that it's hard to credit him with bluffing in this spot. You lose the amount of your bet, $40,000.

- **Case 2a: He is weak and you check.** He checks behind you. We've postulated his style is tight, and this isn't a situation where a tight player wants to bluff.

- **Case 2b: He is weak and you bet $40,000.** He sometimes calls, depending on how he assesses the hand and the pot odds.

If he is strong, you lose about the same whether you check or bet. But if he is weak, you make more money by betting, since he might not fold. Score 4 points for Choice B, betting $40,000, no credit for Choice A, checking.

You actually check and he checks behind you. His hole cards were Q♦J♠, and your full house wins.

Problem 29
Ivey Versus Helppi 1

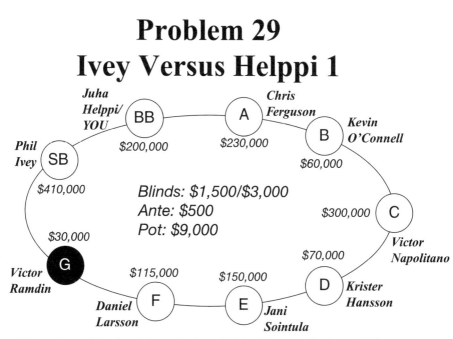

Situation: Final table of the 2004 Monte Carlo Millions tournament. You're in the big blind. Your playing partner is the Finnish star Juha Helppi, winner of the Ultimate Poker Classic in season 1 of the World Poker Tour. Helppi is known to be somewhat tight, but very dangerous. Phil Ivey has been playing well and has accumulated the big stack at the table. The rest of the table is a mixture of Americans, Swedes, and Finns, plus the Englishman Kevin O'Connell.

Your hand: K♥9♥

Action to you: The first seven players all fold. Phil Ivey raises to $11,000.

Question 29A: *What do you do?*

A. *Fold*
B. *Call $8,000*
C. *Raise to $25,000*

Action: You actually call $8,000, and the pot becomes $26,500.

Flop: Q♦T♥2♦

Action: Phil Ivey bets $16,000.

Question 29B: *What do you do?*

A. *Fold*
B. *Call $16,000*
C. *Raise to $50,000*

Action: You actually call. The pot is now $58,500.

Turn: 8♥

Action: Phil Ivey bets $35,000.

Question 29C: *What do you do?*

A. *Fold*
B. *Call $35,000*
C. *Raise to $70,000*
D. *Raise all-in ($173,000)*

Action: You actually raise all-in. Phil Ivey folds. You take the pot.

Solution to Problem 29

Some tournaments are decided by a struggle between two key players, long before the heads-up session is reached. These next four hands are taken from the 2004 Monte Carlo Millions tournament, and feature a series of battles between Phil Ivey and Juha Helppi. Ivey is famous as one of the most aggressive and probably the overall best no-limit player today. If Helppi is to have a chance in the tournament, he will have to figure out how to survive the inevitable Ivey onslaught. Let's peek over his shoulder and see how he does.

Question 29A: Seven folds, then Ivey raises to $11,000 from the small blind. By itself, Ivey's raise doesn't mean much. He's very aggressive and there's just one player left to push out of the hand, so he's probably willing to raise with a large number of hands. Your hand,

is much better than average and probably better than most of the hands Ivey would use to raise. Without question, you can at least call. Score 3 points for Choice B, calling and no credit for Choice A, folding.

If your hand is better than Ivey's average raising hand, should you raise? It's not a bad play, but it wouldn't be my choice. While king-nine suited is a good hand (in the top 20 percent of all hands on our heads-up chart in *Harrington on Hold 'em: Volume II*), it's not a great hand. Before I get involved in a big pot, I'd like to have something a little more substantial than just a king with a medium kicker. You'll have position in the hand, so keep the pot small for now and let the position work for you. Score 1 point for Choice C, raising.

You call, the pot becomes $26,500, and the flop comes

Ivey fires out a bet of $16,000.

Question 29B: The flop missed you, although you did pick up an inside straight draw plus a backdoor flush draw. Did the flop miss Ivey? Probably, since most flops miss most hands, but there's no way to tell for sure, since an aggressive player can bet whether he hit the flop or not.

You should call the bet, for four reasons:

1. Your king-high may be the best hand right now.

2. If you don't have the best hand, you have some draws that will probably give you the best hand. A jack will almost certainly put you on top, and a king will probably work as well. There's also the possibility of hitting running hearts for a flush.

3. If Ivey doesn't have a queen, your call will be scary, and you may be able to take the pot away on the turn.

4. The available pot odds are now 2.6-to-1, which are good enough given the situation.

Score 3 points for Choice B, calling. No credit for Choice A, folding. Also no credit for Choice C, raising. You still don't have a clear enough picture of where you stand to raise the pot.

You call, and the pot becomes $58,500. The turn is the 8♥. Ivey bets $35,000. The pot is now $93,500.

Question 29C: The arrival of the 8♥ clarifies your position considerably. You now have a heart flush draw as well as the inside straight draw, for a total of 12 pretty sure outs (nine hearts plus the three jacks which are not hearts). In addition, the three remaining kings may be outs. The remaining nines might even be outs if Ivey has been betting with a hand like ace-six. So if you don't have the best hand right now, you very likely have 12 outs, with perhaps as many as 15, and even possibly 18.

Ivey has continued to bet at the pot, representing a strong hand. Rather than continuing to call, however, this is the perfect time to execute a semi-bluff raise. You should move all-in! This can win in a number of ways:

- Ivey can fold right now. If he has nothing, he will fold. If he's been playing with middle pair, he probably will fold as well, rather than risk an enormous pile of chips. This is the most likely result of the hand.

- Ivey could call with top pair, but if he does, you will have many outs to beat him.

- Ivey will almost certainly call with a hand better than top pair, like two pair or trips, but even so you will have 12 outs to win.

Notice what has happened by waiting until the turn to make a move at the pot. By calling his bet on the flop, you indicated that you had something. Since Ivey may have been betting with nothing, you raised the possibility that he was beaten already. This made your bet on the turn even more credible. But by waiting until the turn, you made an aggressive player put three bets in the pot, for a total of $61,000. When you push all your chips, you want a pot big enough to compensate for your risk. Waiting until the turn enabled you to get an ample pot.

Score 4 points for Choice D, pushing all-in. Score 2 points for Choice C, the smaller raise, which might induce your opponent to call with a hand that, at this point, beats you. 1 point for Choice B, calling. No credit for Choice A, folding.

This particular move, calling on the flop and raising on the turn, is a very effective move against an aggressive player when you're in position. Not only will you be a favorite to win this particular pot, but you have indicated that you're a player who can't be pushed around, so you should be able to slow him down in the future. Be careful not to overuse the play; as he slows down, his betting hands will get, on average, stronger, after which the play becomes less effective.

Notice also the power of making a move on a large stack. A player with a large stack likes to push around smaller stacks with pot-stealing bets. He doesn't like to be put in a do-or-die situation for 60 percent of his stack. After all, he may have spent the whole tournament building that big stack, and you're threatening to stick him back in the pack with what may be a monster hand. Most players try to figure out how to avoid confrontations with big stacks knowing that the big stacks have the power to knock them out. But as long as your stack is decent-sized, you have a threat as well: the threat of nullifying all their good play to this point. Use it.

Problem 30
Ivey Versus Helppi 2

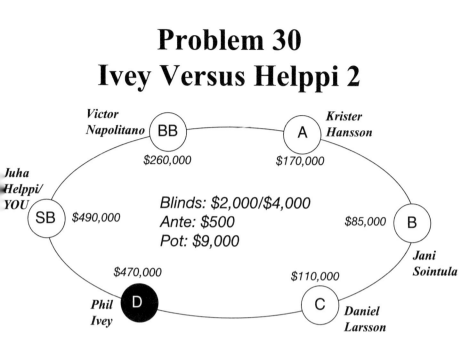

Situation: Later at the same final table of the previous problem. Your playing partner is again Juha Helppi.

Your hand: T♦T♥

Action to you: Hansson, Sointula, and Larsson all fold. Ivey raises to $12,000.

Question 30A: *What do you do?*

A. Call $10,000
B. Reraise to $40,000

Action: You actually call $10,000. Victor Napolitano in the big blind also calls for $8,000. The pot is now $39,000.

Flop: K♦8♠6♦

Question 30B: *What do you do?*

A. *Check*
B. *Bet $20,000*
C. *Bet $40,000*

Action: You actually check. Napolitano checks. Ivey bets $20,000. The pot is now $59,000.

Question 30C: *What do you do?*

A. *Fold*
B. *Call $20,000*
C. *Raise to $60,000*

Action: You actually call $20,000. The pot becomes $79,000. Napolitano folds.

Turn: 9♦

Question 30D: *What do you do?*

A. *Check*
B. *Bet $40,000*

Action: You actually check. Ivey checks behind you. The pot remains $79,000.

River: 6♣

Question 30E: *What do you do?*

A. *Check*
B. *Bet $40,000*

Action: You actually check. Ivey bets $50,000. The pot is now $129,000.

Question 30F: *What do you do?*

A. *Fold*
B. *Call $50,000*
C. *Raise to $150,000*

Action: You actually call. Ivey shows K♣J♥, and takes the pot.

Solution to Problem 30

We've progressed a little farther into the final table, which has now been reduced to six players. Helppi has taken the chip lead by a little bit over Phil Ivey.

Question 30A: Ivey fires at the pot from the button, which was not unexpected. You have the

Obviously you're going to play the hand. But should you call or raise? There are arguments for both plays, so let's review the arguments quickly.

Arguments for calling:

- You're the chip leader, and you're in a pot against the other big stack. You only have a medium pair. You'd like to play the hand small, rather than big.

- You probably have the best hand, so calling is deceptive. Ivey will think your hand is weaker than it really is.

- The big blind has yet to act. If he has a big hand, you'd rather not get caught between him and Ivey.

Arguments for raising:

- You almost certainly have the best hand right now, but it's a hard hand to improve. If overcards come on the flop, you won't know if you have the best hand unless you make a set.

- You're out of position, so you'll be acting before Phil Ivey every round, and if the big blind plays, you'll have to act before him too. If you don't improve your tens, you'll be under constant pressure to make tough decisions later.

- If you call, the pot will be $31,000 and it will cost the big blind $8,000 to call. He'll be getting almost 4-to-1 on his money. So he'll stick around and see the flop with a lot of hands, most of which he would have folded had you raised. By calling, you'll put yourself in a position where your tens have to beat both Ivey and Napolitano.

- A few hands ago, you pushed Ivey out of a big pot with a nice semi-bluff. Ivey will remember that hand, and give you credit for being a tricky player. He won't necessarily believe that your raise means strength. If he has anything at all, he may want to look you up. Once you raise doubts in your opponent's mind, straightforward value bets can be as trappy as any other play.

In my mind, the arguments for raising are much stronger than the arguments for calling. While calling is "trappy" in the sense that it misleads your opponents as to the strength of your hand, you'll have trouble making use of that misdirection when overcards come on the flop and you have to act first. The arguments for raising are more concrete and more compelling. You probably have the best hand now, but it's a hand whose relative strength deteriorates as more cards appear on the board, so make your move now rather than later. If Ivey has an overcard or two, make him pay to see the flop. Eliminating the big blind, who would otherwise represent a second drawing hand, is also important.

Score 4 points for Choice B, reraising to $40,000. No credit for Choice A, calling.

You actually call, and Napolitano in the big blind calls as well. The pot is now $39,000.

The flop comes

You act first.

Question 30B: This would be a pretty good flop against one opponent; in that case you'd be pretty confident you still had the best hand. Against two opponents you're a little more uncomfortable, especially since you act first.

Here, checking makes a lot of sense. You don't need to worry about getting money in the pot, since if both you and the big blind check to Ivey, he'll probably fire away. But if the big blind bets with Ivey yet to act, he probably has something. I like checking, hoping to pick up some information. Score 2 points for Choice A, checking.

One point for Choice C, making the smaller bet of $20,000. A small bet should win if your pair of tens is still best, while it has the added benefit of getting some extra information. If you bet and the big blind calls or raises with Ivey yet to act, you know you're in big trouble.

No credit for the bigger bet of $40,000 (Choice C). It's more than you need to pay for your information.

You actually check, and Napolitano in the big blind checks. Ivey bets $20,000, and the pot becomes $59,000.

Question 30C: You're getting 3-to-1 pot odds from an aggressive player, and you may still have the best hand. Under the circumstances, folding is not an option.

What about raising? If Ivey has nothing, a raise will chase him away. If Ivey has a diamond draw, a raise will stop him from drawing out on you. But if Ivey has a pair of kings, he'll call or reraise, and you'll know you're beaten.

While not a happy choice, just calling is reasonable given the pot odds. Even if Ivey has a king, he'll have to wonder just what you're holding to have called two of his bets, and that might slow him down in the future. Score 3 points for Choice B, calling; no credit for folding or raising.

You call, and the big blind folds. The pot is now $79,000. The turn is the 9♦.

Question 30D: Since you have the T♦, the third diamond on board gives you a diamond flush draw. You can't be sure it's good, since the A♦, Q♦, and J♦ are all out, but it may represent additional outs for your hand. The third diamond should also slow Ivey down, since he'll have to consider that you might have been calling with a diamond draw.

Your hand hasn't gotten stronger, so you can't really bet for value anymore. You don't know where you stand in the hand. If you had just made a diamond flush, you'd probably check, hoping to snap off a bet from Ivey. So check, and see what happens. Score 2 points for Choice A, checking, no credit for Choice B, betting.

You check, and Ivey checks behind you. The pot remains $79,000. The river comes a 6♣.

Question 30E: You didn't make a diamond flush, but on the positive side, the six probably hasn't beaten you, since it paired a card that was already on board. You still have second pair, which may or may not be best. Just check, and see if you can check the hand down. Checking has the additional virtue that it might induce a bluff if Ivey has nothing. Score 4 points for Choice A, checking, 2 points for Choice B, betting $40,000. The bet might save you some money if Ivey stops betting and just calls, since he might have led out with a bigger bet that you would have called.

You check, and Ivey bets $50,000. The pot is now $129,000.

Question 30F: Not a happy choice, but there are three reasons you have to call:

1.   The pot odds of 2.6-to-1 are substantial.

2.   Ivey might be betting with a hand you can beat; he might have a pair of nines or eights, believing it to be the best hand.

3.   You've shown no strength throughout the hand, so Ivey could think you've been on a diamond draw with two high-to-medium cards, including one diamond. In that case, even an ace-high might be best.

You're probably beaten, but the 2.6-to-1 pot odds are good compensation for making sure. Score 3 points for Choice B, calling; no credit for other plays.

Ivey shows his K♣J♥ and wins with a pair of kings.

The Hand From Ivey's Point of View

Now that we know Ivey's actual cards, let's step through the hand from his viewpoint and see what we can learn.

Ivey's pre-flop raise on the button was a perfectly good value bet with K♣J♥. One bonus of an aggressive style is that your value bets are well-concealed and hence more profitable.

Ivey's raise gets two callers, both out of position. What are they calling with? Medium to low pairs, perhaps, or two high cards, or maybe ace-x. Since Ivey is aggressive, he faces more calls than a tight player would.

The flop of K♦8♠6♦ is very good. Ivey has a pair of kings. Both players check to him, and he bets his kings for value. Again, the strength of his hand is concealed by his previous aggressive ways.

He gets a call and a fold. What can the caller have now? Ivey knows Helppi is a strong and dangerous player. Because Ivey could be bluffing, but isn't (this time), Helppi's range of possible hands is very wide. He could have paired the board, or have a pair in the hole, or low trips, or a diamond draw, or maybe two high cards including an ace.

Notice in this last comment the kinds of problems that an aggressive player creates *for himself.* Because his own range of hands is so large, an intelligent opponent will have a similarly wide range of hands. While Ivey is hard to put on a hand, it's more difficult for him to put opponents on hands as well.

The turn comes a 9♦, putting three diamonds on board, and Helppi checks. Ivey has no diamonds, but the nine raises an additional problem. If Helppi did have a king and has been calling with it, there are now few kings that Ivey can beat. He's losing to ace-king and king-queen, tying king-jack, beating king-ten, but losing to king-nine and king-eight (which are now two pair).

Lower kings were unlikely calling cards pre-flop. So Ivey checks as well. (If he is still winning at this point, the slight show of weakness may get him a call on the river.)

The river comes a 6♣, and Helppi checks again. Ivey makes a smallish bet of $50,000. At this point he's probably not certain he's winning, but feels he's a favorite to be winning and should get paid something more if he stands better. In fact Helppi had a lower pair and Ivey collects a nice pot.

If Helppi had check-raised on the end, instead of just calling, would Ivey have called? It's hard to say. From Ivey's viewpoint, he's vulnerable to a lot of hands, including other kings, trips, or a diamond draw, all of which could more or less reasonably account for Helppi's sequence of bets. My guess is that he would probably make the call, but he wouldn't like it.

Problem 31
Ivey Versus Helppi 3

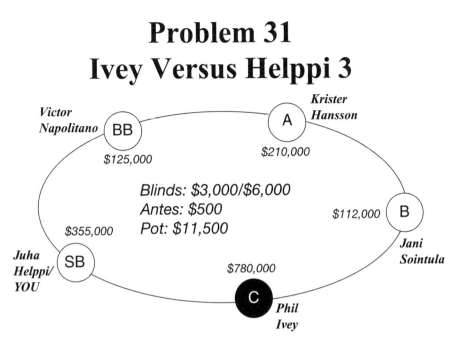

Situation: Later in the same tournament, with the field now reduced to five players. Your playing partner in the small blind is once again Juha Helppi. Ivey's stack is now more than twice that of anyone else at the table.

Your hand: A♠K♦

Action to you: Hanssen and Sointula fold. Ivey raises to $18,000. The pot is now $29,500.

Question 31A: *What do you do?*

A.   Call $15,000
B.   Raise to $60,000

Action: You actually call $15,000. Napolitano in the big blind calls $12,000. The pot is now $56,500.

Flop: A♦A♣7♦

Question 31B: *What do you do?*

A. *Check*
B. *Bet $30,000*
C. *Bet $50,000*

Action: You actually bet $30,000. Napolitano folds. Ivey calls. The pot is now $116,500.

Turn: 5♠

Question 31C: *What do you do?*

A. *Check*
B. *Bet $60,000*
C. *Bet $100,000*

Action: You actually check. Ivey bets $60,000. The pot is now $176,500.

Question 31D: *What do you do?*

A. *Call $60,000*
B. *Raise to $120,000*
C. *Raise all-in ($307,000)*

Action: You actually call. The pot is now $236,500. You have $247,000 left in your stack.

River: 4♠

Question 31E: *What do you do?*

A.   Check
B.   Bet $100,000
C.   Move all-in

Action: You actually bet $100,000. Ivey folds. You take the pot.

Solution to Problem 31

Question 31A: This hand starts in a very similar fashion to the last hand. Two folds, then Ivey raises on the button. And now you look down to see a strong hand — last time a pair of tens, this time the

As with the pair of tens, I think Helppi should reraise before the flop. In this case I would reraise to about $60,000. Helppi has a good hand right now, and being out of position after the flop hurts badly against a strong, aggressive player. Simply winning the hand here isn't a bad result, but if Helppi's bet doesn't win the hand, it will slow Ivey down in the post-flop action.

Against a weak, passive player, calling is a much more reasonable play (although reraising is still good.)

Score 1 point for Choice A, calling, and 4 points for Choice B, reraising.

You actually call $15,000, and the big blind calls for $12,000. The pot is $56,500.

The flop comes

Question 31B: Obviously this is a fantastic flop. You now have trips with top kicker, so your job is to extract the maximum from the other two players. You can start by either checking or betting right now. Let's see how both moves play out.

1. **Bet now, then check on the turn**. Helppi can start with a small bet now, perhaps a little less than half the pot. Ivey can then call or fold. (We'll ignore for now the big blind. If he gets involved, so much the better, but Ivey bet before the flop, and he tends not to go meekly away after he's taken the lead pre-flop.) If Ivey folds, his pre-flop bet was a complete bluff and there wasn't much chance of winning any money this hand. If he calls, then you check on the turn. The combination of the small probe bet on the flop and the check on the turn looks like the action of a player who saw the aces on the flop, said to himself "I can steal this pot if Ivey doesn't have an ace," then backed off when Ivey stuck around. Ivey might go ahead and bet in that situation, putting a second (and larger) bet in the pot.

2. **Check now, then bet on the turn**. If you check first, Ivey will most likely bet. Then you call. On the turn, you bet no matter what comes. Will Ivey call this bet? He might; however, your call on the flop looks a lot stronger than merely betting on the flop. A bet could simply be a steal attempt, but what can a call mean? You've seen Ivey raise before the flop, and now two aces come, and now Ivey bets

again, and now you call. What hand other than a hand with an ace lets you make both the pre-flop call and the post-flop call? Most players in Ivey's position would lose interest in the hand after that sequence.

The first sequence — betting, then checking the turn — gives a better chance of getting two bets in the pot rather than one. Score 3 points for Choice B, betting $30,000. Score 1 point for Choice A, checking, which isn't unreasonable. No credit for the bigger bet. You want to appear to be stealing the pot cheaply, not making a value play.

By the way, if you had recently made this same play at the table, you should vary your play and just check. Remember that your opponents will be trying to remember your preferred bet sequences, so keep moving around whenever both choices are somewhat reasonable.

You bet $30,000. The big blind folds. Ivey calls $30,000. The pot is now $116,500.

The turn comes a 5♠.

Question 31C: That was an excellent sequence. Ivey called your probe bet, and a harmless card came on the turn. Now continue the plan and check, indicating that your bet was a bluff.

Score 2 points for Choice A, checking, no credit for betting.

You check, and Ivey bets $60,000. The pot is now $176,500.

Question 31D: Of course you're going to call. Should you raise? A raise will end the hand if Ivey is bluffing. A raise will also prevent Ivey from drawing to a flush if he has two diamonds or two spades in his hand. Is it worth sacrificing the chance of making more money on the river to eliminate the possible flush draws?

I don't think so. Ivey certainly hasn't played the hand as though he was on a flush draw, and he's unlikely to hit the draw even if he has one. Your main goal here is to double your chips with a big hand. Late in the tournament, you want to make plays that give you the best shot at winning the whole thing, not the plays that let you finish an honorable third. Call, and try to win even more on the river.

Score 3 points for Choice A, calling, no credit for raising.

You actually call. The river comes a 4♠. The pot is now $236,500. You have $247,000 left in your stack, and Ivey has you easily covered.

Question 31E: You must check now, and allow Ivey to bet. To see why this approach is so much better than betting, let's look at the three possible types of hands that Ivey might have right now, and imagine how Ivey would play each hand.

1. **Ivey has a strong hand.** There are a lot of possible hands that Ivey might think are good, including a bunch that *really are* good. (Ivey is beating you with A7, A5, A4, 77, 55, or 44, all hands that fit his bets perfectly well. Since lots of other hands fit his bets well, all of which you beat, you're going all the way with your hand if you can. But it's worth noting that you aren't close to having the nuts here.) Among the hands that Ivey might think are good, but aren't, are hands like AQ, AJ, AT, and possibly KK or QQ.)

2. **Ivey has a medium hand.** Medium hands might be nines, eights, or something like king-seven or queen-seven. The middle pair might be good, but whether Ivey would bet it on the river is questionable.

3. **Ivey has nothing.** Ivey could easily have been bluffing at the pot from the beginning with something like jack-nine.

Let's look at what happens in these three cases, first if we bet, and second if we don't bet:

1. **If Ivey has a strong hand**, it doesn't matter much if we bet or don't bet. If we bet, he will call or raise. If he raises we will move all-in. Alternatively, if we check, he bets, we raise (or call, if he put us all-in). Either way, a lot of money gets in the pot, perhaps our entire stack.

2. **If Ivey has a medium hand**, we may not be able to win money in either case. If we bet, the threat of an ace may make Ivey lay down a medium pair. But if we check, can Ivey bet? That's unlikely, too. Let's see why.

    Before you make a bet on the river, you need to ask yourself a question. "What can my opponent hold that

    a. Explains his bets so far,
    b. Will call my bet, and
    c. I can beat?"

    If there aren't any such hands, then your bet can only lose money (because it will only be called by hands that beat you), and you're better off trying to check the hand down.

    Now if Ivey has been playing with something like king-seven and now has a pair of sevens, what can he beat that will call him? He can only beat a couple of unpaired overcards like king-queen, or a smaller pair. But if you had one of those hands, and were looking at a board of A♦A♣7♦5♠4♠ with king-queen or sixes in the hole, would you call a bet? I wouldn't. By this point in the tournament, Ivey surely assesses Helppi as a strong, tough player, so it's hard to picture him thinking that a bet with a medium pair is a profitable play.

    Conclusion? If Ivey has a medium-strength hand, neither leading nor checking is apt to make any money.

3. **If Ivey has nothing**, he'll fold to a bet. But will he bet if you check? He might, since it's now the only way he can win the

hand! A feeble player might not have the courage to make this bet, but Ivey has plenty of courage. My guess would be that if Ivey felt this was the only way to win the hand, and he wasn't up against a monster, he would bet here between 30 and 50 percent of the time.

Looking at the three cases in sequence, the only case where your play can generate a profit is the third case, where Ivey has nothing. If Ivey has a big hand, you'll either make or lose a lot of money no matter how you play. If he has a medium hand, you probably won't make any money either way. But if he has nothing, you may be able to snap off a bluff.

Score 5 points for Choice A, checking. No credit for either betting play.

You actually bet $100,000, and Ivey folded. (His hand was Q♦8♠, and he had nothing on the end.)

Problem 32
Ivey Versus Helppi 4

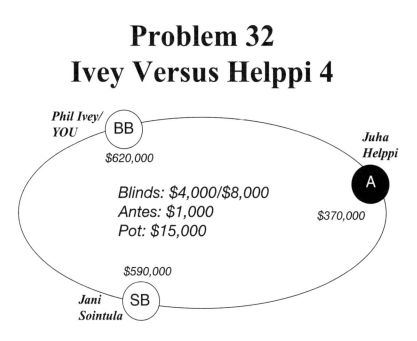

Phil Ivey/ YOU — **BB** — $620,000

Juha Helppi — **A** — $370,000

Jani Sointula — **SB** — $590,000

Blinds: $4,000/$8,000
Antes: $1,000
Pot: $15,000

Situation: Still later in the same tournament. Only three players remain. This time your playing partner is Phil Ivey, still the chip leader, but only by a small amount.

Your hand: T♦9♠

Action to you: Helppi raises to $25,000. Sointula folds. The pot is $40,000.

Question 32A: *What do you do?*

A. *Fold*
B. *Call $17,000*
C. *Raise to $60,000*

Action: You actually call $17,000. The pot is now $57,000.

228 Problem 32

Flop: Q♥8♦4♣

Question 32B: *What do you do?*

A.   *Check*
B.   *Bet $30,000*

Action: You actually check. Helppi bets $50,000. The pot is now $107,000.

Question 32C: *What do you do?*

A.   *Fold*
B.   *Call $50,000*
C.   *Raise to $150,000*

Action: You actually call. The pot is now $157,000.

Turn: A♠

Question 32D: *What do you do?*

A.   *Check*
B.   *Bet $80,000*

Action: You actually check. Helppi bets $75,000. The pot is now $232,000.

Question 32E: *What do you do?*

A.   *Fold*
B.   *Call $75,000*
C.   *Push all-in*

Action: You actually push all-in, and Helppi folds. You take the pot.

Solution to Problem 32

Question 32A: As you move through a tournament, you have to spot your opponent's predilections and betting patterns. Every player has them. A good player, like Helppi, won't be so foolish as to religiously do the same thing every time, but they will have favored ways of handling situations, and over the course of an afternoon, you should be able to spot a few.

If the hands we've seen so far are typical, Ivey has probably noted a couple of Helppi's tendencies:

1. In general, he's fond of playing hands opposite to their true strength. He'll push weaker hands strongly, while checking his very good hands.

2. He likes to bet a good hand on the flop, then check it on the turn, showing weakness. This play sets him up for a profitable move on the river.

He can't do these things all the time of course, or he wouldn't have reached the final three. But he probably does them just often enough so that Ivey has filed them away in his enormous memory bank.

Our first decision, however, doesn't involve any fancy hand reading. Helppi raises on the button at a three-handed table, and the small blind folds. Three-handed, Helppi's bet doesn't necessarily mean much, and Ivey has the

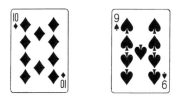

which is good enough to see a flop getting more than 2-to-1 odds, even out of position.

Score 3 points for Choice B, calling, no credit for either folding or raising.

You call. The flop comes

Question 32B: The flop missed you, but gave you an inside straight draw. Right now you know almost nothing about your opponent's hand, and you're out of position, so a check is the prudent play. Let your opponent tell you something, then try to correlate his actions with his previous play. Score 2 points for Choice A, checking, no credit for Choice B, betting.

You check. Helppi bets $50,000. The pot is now $107,000.

Question 32C: You probably have the worst hand right now. But if Helppi doesn't have a queen, you most likely have 10 outs: four jacks, three tens, and three nines. So you're not really in bad shape, and it's always possible that you can take the pot away even if you don't hit your hand. You're getting more than 2-to-1 odds, so just call and see what happens. Score 2 points for Choice B, calling, no credit for anything else.

You call. The pot is $157,000. The turn comes an A♣.

Question 32D: The ace didn't help you, but it does open some interesting possibilities. Just check and see what Helppi does. Score 2 points for Choice A, checking. No credit for anything else.

You check. Helppi bets $75,000. The pot is $232,000.

Question 32E: Now it's time to review the betting and put it together with what you know of your opponent's style:

- Helppi bet before the flop, indicating that he had something.

- Helppi bet after the flop, indicating that the flop helped him, or at least didn't hurt him.

- Now an ace arrives on board, and Helppi bets again, indicating that the ace helped him.

What hand does Helppi have if he had a good hand before and after the flop, and the ace on the turn helped him as well? Trip aces? Ace-eight? Ace-queen? But this is a player who in general has shown he likes to trap a little with his good hands. If you just hit trip aces or top two pair on the turn, even a completely straightforward player would be inclined to give a free card rather than just bet for value and chase his opponent away. Remember, this is not a board loaded with straight or flush possibilities. It's actually a very safe board if Helppi has the hand he's representing.

The more likely explanation is that the ace didn't help Helppi, but he's using its scare value to chase Ivey out of the hand. The proof isn't airtight, but hunches like this combined with some sketchy observations are all you have in poker. Sometimes you have to stake your tournament life on them.

Ivey realizes that his opponent's bets don't quite add up, so he makes the appropriate response — he moves all-in!

Notice that it's not a complete bluff. If Ivey is called, he has at least four outs on the river, and if his suspicions are correct and Helppi is playing with something like a low pair, then he has six more outs, for a total of ten. However, the bluff component of the bet is extremely strong as well. Nothing is more demoralizing than to represent a scare card, only to have your opponent move all-in. Unless Helppi actually has the ace, it's almost impossible for him to call this bet, and Ivey knows that.

Score 5 points for Choice C, moving all-in. It's a world-class play, one that very few players are capable of making. No credit for Choice B, calling. Score 3 points for Choice A, folding, a play for mere mortals.

You actually move all-in, and Helppi folds his 6♠6♣ in the hole.

Why do great players win tournaments? Because they can make plays like this when the opportunity presents itself.

Problem 33
Pot Odds and Calling Ranges

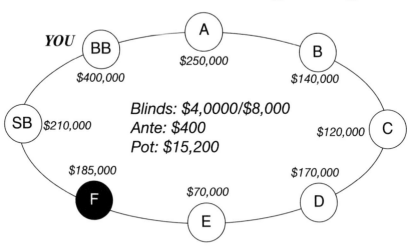

Situation: The final table of a large multi-table online tournament. Player E seems to be a very good player but has recently suffered two big losses that have reduced him to the small stack. This is his third hand since being pummeled. He folded the previous two hands to an early raiser.

Your hand: ??

Action to you: Players A, B, C, and D all fold. Player E moves all-in for $70,000. Player F and the small blind fold.

Question 33: *With which of these hands would you call?*

A. 4♣4♦
B. Q♣J♦
C. A♣6♦
D. 9♣8♣

Solution to Problem 33

Unfortunately for us, we don't have any hard data on how Player E likes to handle a short stack. If we call this hand, both we and the rest of the table will know a lot more. We do know one thing for sure — the pot odds. Since we're in the big blind and we already have $8,000 in the pot, it costs us $62,000 to call. Since the pot contains $85,200, we're getting pot odds of about 1.4-to-1. Put another way, if we call and can win 42 percent of the hands, we'll break even.

Now we need to make an educated guess as to what hands Player E might have. What does he need to push? His M is just under 5. A tight player will have loosened his requirements considerably with an M so low, but he's not necessarily pushing with any two cards yet. (If his M were in the 2-3 range, I might expect him to push with any two cards.)

Lacking any more information, and based on the sort of hands you tend to see when players make a move in this range, I think he might push with any of the following hands:

- Any pair
- Any ace
- KQ, KJ, KT, suited or offsuit
- QJ or QT, suited or offsuit

Some players would push with a lot more hands than this, while others might drop the lowest aces but push with some of the middle connectors like jack-ten or nine-eight, especially suited. But this group, comprising about the top 25 percent of all hands, probably represents a good average of the sort of hands players will push, given a low but not desperate M and three players left in the pot. Most players don't like to push trash hands at the end of a tournament when the money is significant, even though it may be correct to do so. They're much more comfortable pushing hands that at least look like threatening hands.

Against this range, what do you need to call? Assuming you have him comfortably covered (as here), the answer hinges on the pot odds you're being offered. The 1.4-to-1 odds that you're being offered in this problem wasn't selected at random; it's actually a crucial benchmark ratio.

> *When receiving odds of 1.4-to-1, your calling range is almost the same as his pushing range. Once you've estimated his pushing hands, you can call with all but the very worst hands on his list.*

Here, for instance, you should fold hands like ace-deuce offsuit, or king-ten offsuit, or queen-jack offsuit, which are right at the bottom of his list. But you can call with ace-trey suited, or ace-six offsuit, or king-jack suited, all of which are better than the very bottom of his range.

In our problem, score 2 points each if you called with hands A and C, and 2 points each if you folded B and D.

As the pot odds change, so do your calling requirements. As your pot odds rise to 1.5-to-1, you can start to call with hands that are weaker than any in his range. When you reach numbers like 1.8-to-1, you can call with hands that are much weaker than his range. Of course, to get pot odds like that, his stack must be getting smaller and smaller in relation to the blinds, so he's pushing with more and more hands. The effect is that *with high pot odds, he's pushing with most hands, and you're calling legitimately with any two cards!*

The tournament prize structure may require you to make small adjustments to this calling strategy in the following way. The more the prize structure is skewed to first place, the more you want to call with marginal hands, both to knock out players, and to grow your own stack so you can bully the remaining players even more. The flatter the prize structure, the more you want to play a little tighter than the 'correct' strategy, as outlined above. In practice, online tournaments tend to have flatter prize structure (because the organizers want as many players as possible to win significant money and keep playing), while live tournaments often have structures very skewed to first place (because the organizers know that million-dollar prizes build TV ratings). So in general, you should call a little more aggressively in live play than online; oddly enough, this is just the opposite of how most players play.

Problem 34
All-Ins and Pot Odds

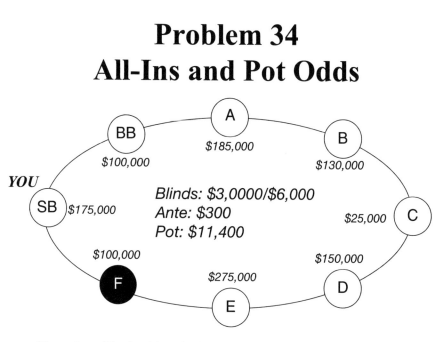

Situation: Final table of a large multi-table online tournament. You're in the small blind. The big blind seems a bit on the tight side, but solid and tenacious.

Your hand: Q♣7♦

Action to you: Players A through F all fold.

Question 34A: *What do you do?*

A. *Fold*
B. *Call $3,000*
C. *Raise to $18,000*
D. *Raise to $25,000*
E. *Push all-in*

Action: You actually raise to $25,000. The big blind calls. The pot is now $52,400.

Flop: A♣7♥2♠

Question 34B: *What do you do?*

A. *Check*
B. *Bet $25,000*
C. *Push all-in*

Action: You actually bet $25,000. The big blind moves all-in for his last $75,000. The pot is now $152,400.

Question 34C: *What do you do?*

A. *Fold*
B. *Call $50,000*

Action: You call and he turns over 9♥7♠. The turn and river come 4♦3♥, and your better kicker wins the pot.

Solution to Problem 34

Question 34A: You're in the small blind, and everyone folds to you. Your hand is a modest

What should you do? Here's how I would rank the five choices:

1. **Choice A, Fold**. No credit. Too tight. Your hand is just slightly above average, but you act first and the big blind may not have anything worth playing. You're entitled to make a try for the pot.

2. **Choice E, All-in**. No credit. Fear of flopping. A normal raise will win the pot if the big blind has nothing. Don't put more than half your chips in jeopardy when you have no idea what you're up against.

3. **Choice B, Call $3,000**. Score 3 points for this conservative choice. True, you're left out of position with a weak hand, and you'll have a hard time after the flop unless you hit a queen or a seven. However, you're taking full advantage of the 3.5-to-1 pot odds you're being offered, which is enormous compensation.

4. **Choice C, Raise to $18,000**. Score 2 points for this more active play. You're giving odds now, but you're making an effort to take the pot.

5. **Choice D, Raise to $25,000**. Score 3 points for the most aggressive play. Raising to four times the big blind, rather than three times, shows that you're serious and gives the big blind weaker pot odds for calling. You not enthused about playing this hand, so make calling a little tougher.

You raise to $25,000, and the big blind calls. The pot is $52,400.

The flop comes

You act first.

Question 34B: An interesting flop. You've hit middle pair, which in heads-up play is a good hand. The ace, however, is a concern. Your opponent didn't reraise before the flop, which is slight, but certainly not conclusive, evidence that he doesn't have an ace. Lots of players would reraise holding an ace, but lots of others would just call and use their position after the flop as a weapon.

I like betting here. I hit part of the flop, and don't know that the ace helped my opponent. Since I raised pre-flop and an ace came, my opponent has to be a little concerned about an ace. There's no reason to refrain from betting. I have a hand, and my opponent has to show me that it's not the best hand. Also, too many overcards to my seven can come on the turn. Score 2 points for Choice B, betting $25,000, and no credit for either checking (too weak) or pushing (too strong).

You bet $25,000. Your opponent pushes all-in for his last $75,000. The pot is $152,400.

Question 34C: You didn't really want to see an all-in, but there it is. No time to panic, however. Let's work our way through the key features of the situation.

The pot has just over $150,000, and you need $50,000 to call. You're getting just over 3-to-1 pot odds to call. Those are huge odds when you have middle pair. To see why, imagine he has the hand you fear. Let's say he called with ace-four offsuit, so now he's made a pair of aces and you're beaten. But you still have outs. The five remaining queens and sevens give you a winning hand, and by the 'rule of four', that gives you close to 20 percent winning chances even if you're losing right now. (The exact number if he holds ace-four is 18.3 percent.) If instead he's holding a pocket pair above your sevens, say a pair of tens, your winning chances are a little better — 20.2 percent in this case.

Those are big numbers. When you're getting 3-to-1 pot odds, you need 25 percent winning chances to call. (Those readers who were backgammon players will be very familiar with this particular ratio.) Even if you were certain you were beaten right now, your out cards are giving you almost all the equity you need to call.

But are you certain you're beaten? After all, suppose he has a seven, just like you. With the short stack, he probably feels this is the perfect time to make a move. Now it's your kicker that's key, and you actually have an excellent kicker with your sevens — a queen. Only one potential kicker beats you, a king. (The ace isn't important because that beats you anyway.) And of course, there's always the chance that he's just semi-bluffing with a couple of high cards, thinking that the flop may have missed you completely. The extra winning chances when he has middle pair or a bluff easily give you the equity to call.

Score 4 points for Choice B, calling, no credit for Choice A, folding.

When I have middle pair in a heads-up confrontation, the determining factor for me is the quality of my kicker. With a good kicker (as here) I'm often willing to go all the way with the hand. With a poor kicker I'm not so happy, because I'm losing to all the top pairs and most of the middle pairs.

Problem 35
Making Moves at the Final Table

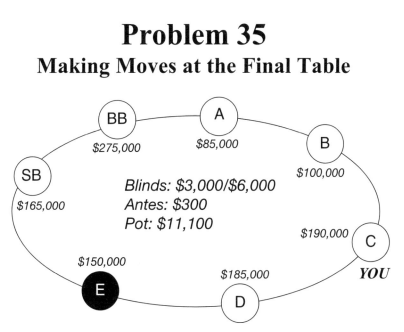

Situation: Final table of a large multi-table online tournament. The table has tightened up since the last small stack was eliminated. In the last two rounds of the table, no hand has gone to the flop.

Your hand: T♠9♠

Action to you: Players A and B fold.

Question 35: *What do you do?*

A.   *Fold*
B.   *Call $6,000*
C.   *Raise to $20,000*

Action: You raise to $20,000. The other players all fold. You take the pot.

Solution to Problem 35

From time to time at a final table, you're going to have to make plays with sub-standard, but not hopeless hands. The blinds are high, and you can hit a streak of very weak hands or poor situations at any time. Without being obvious, you need to steal the occasional pot.

I don't like to move at pots randomly, however. In general, I'm looking for three criteria:

1. **A tight table**. The other players will tell you how eager they are to fight for pots. If all the pots are going to the first player to bet, it may be a sign that, for various reasons, a lot of the players at the table don't really feel like playing right now. Fatigue sets in, players get nervous, people start checking the payout structure, and suddenly you get a lull in the action. This should be a sign to pick up the slack and start moving.

2. **A reasonable hand**. I'm not going to move with a trey-deuce unless everyone else has fallen asleep. But I'm not waiting for ace-queen either. A middle suited connectors is a good, playable hand that's not likely to be dominated if I get called.

3. **Plausible position**. If someone has entered the pot, I can't be bothered. But if it has been folded to me, I'm interested.

Here all the factors are in place, and I'm making a normal raise. If I get called, I'll play the hand as best I can after the flop. But I'm hoping not to get called. If someone reraises, he's probably got a real hand, and I'll fold my suited connectors.

Score 2 points for Choice C, raising. Score 1 point for Choice A, folding, a reasonable play with a weak hand. Also 1 point for Choice B, calling, which is a different, and more difficult approach to making money with the hand. Your aim is to win a bigger pot by astute post-flop play.

Problem 36
Calculating the Right Raise

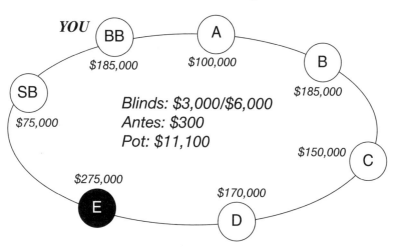

Situation: Final table of a large multi-table online tournament. You're in the big blind with the second-biggest chip stack. The table has in general been playing tight. The big stack is Player E on the button, who has seemed tight and aggressive.

Your hand: 8♦8♠

Action to you: Players A, B, C and D all fold. Player E raises to $22,000. The small blind folds.

Question 36A: *What do you do?*

A. *Fold*
B. *Call $16,000*
C. *Raise to $44,000*
D. *Raise to $56,000*

E.   Raise to $80,000
F.   Push all-in

Action: You actually raise to $56,000. Player E moves all-in. The pot is now $241,000.

Question 36B: *What do you do?*

A.   Fold
B.   Call $129,000

Solution to Problem 36

Question 36A: The

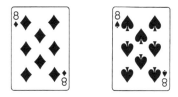

is a good hand in this situation. In addition, you were raised by the button, which might only represent an attempt to steal the pot. The button, however, is also the big stack, and the only player at the table who could knock you out of the tournament; that's a factor you'll need to keep in mind.

You're definitely going to play the hand. You're also definitely going to raise, and try to win before the flop. If you just call, the flop will probably not help your hand, and will likely contain an overcard or two. You'll be out of position and you won't know where you stand — an awkward situation. Better to make a move now.

There's another excellent reason for reraising in this spot. You want to discourage your opponent from raising on the button.

By calling you encourage your opponents to keep attacking your blinds.

No credit for Choice A, folding. Just 1 point for Choice B, calling.

The real question is — how much to raise? Different sized raises have distinct advantages and disadvantages. Let's consider both for a moment.

When you raise a small amount, you give your opponent relatively good pot odds to call. On the other hand, if your opponent reraises you all-in, the pot odds you'll receive will be relatively poor, and you'll have an easier time laying down your hand.

As you raise larger and larger amounts, you give your opponent worse and worse pot odds to call. The upside of these bigger raises is that you've increased the chance that he will lay down his hand if he was stealing or otherwise playing marginal cards. The downside is that if he now turns around and puts you all-in, you will have better pot odds to call (because your remaining stack is smaller relative to the pot), so you will be more locked into the hand.

The situation creates an interesting conundrum: raise too little, and you won't accomplish your goal of chasing away bluffs or marginal hands; raise too much, and you may lock yourself into a hand that you don't really want to play for all your chips.

This problem — deciding exactly how much to raise — doesn't really occur in the early stages of tournaments when your M is high and your stack is deep. If you reraise someone in an early round and he turns around and puts you all-in, his raise will be so large relative to the pot that your exact pot odds won't be a decisive factor. Either you'll have a hand that you want to play for all your chips, or you won't.

But in the late stages of a tournament, where the Ms have begun to dip under 20, calculating the size of your bet or raise may be a very important decision. Let's look at some possible bet sizes in this problem and see what happens.

To start, let's calculate the pot odds for Choice C, where you raise to $44,000. We're actually calculating two different pot odds: the odds your opponent sees when you raise him, and the odds you see if he reraises you all-in.

When he raises to $22,000, the pot becomes $33,100 (it was $11,100 after the blinds and antes). Your stack at this point is $179,000 (you've put in the $6,000 big blind). If you raise to $44,000, you're actually putting $38,000 in the pot; $16,000 to call his raise and $22,000 to raise him. The pot becomes $33,100 plus $38,000, or $71,100. Your stack becomes $179,000 - $38,000, or $141,000. His pot odds to call your bet are $71,100-to-$22,000, or 3.23-to-1.

If at that point he puts you all-in, he puts a total of $163,000 in the pot; $22,000 to call your raise, and $141,000 to raise you the rest of your chips. The pot now becomes $71,100 + $163,000, or $234,100, and it costs you $141,000 to call. Your pot odds are then about 1.7-to-1.

You can crank through the calculations for the other two raise sizes on your own if you want, but all we care about are the relative pot odds being offered. Here's a table of what the odds look like for all three raise sizes:

Your Initial Raise	Opponent's Pot Odds to Call	Your Pot Odds To Call All-in
C to $44,000	3.23-to-1	1.7-to-1
D to $56,000	2.44-to-1	1.9-to-1
E to $80,000	1.84-to-1	2.57-to-1

As you can see, as you increase your initial raise, you reduce his pot odds dramatically, but as a result, you are being offered better and better odds to call his subsequent all-in (if that's what he chooses to do.)

To take the next step, we need to think a little bit about our hand and our opponent. We've observed that he's a tight-aggressive player, and we've already shown some strength by reraising him. What hands can we put him on if, indeed, he reraises all-in? I wouldn't assume that a tight-aggressive player is going to bluff much against the second-biggest stack at the table. On the other hand, Ms are starting to shrink (our M was less than 17 at the start of the hand, his was just under 25) so he can't simply wait for the stone cold nuts to play. I'd guess a player with that profile might push with any of these hands: a pair of eights or better, an ace-jack or better, suited or unsuited. (A looser player might go with a few lower pairs, and maybe an ace-ten or a king-queen, but let's be a little conservative.)

How do our pair of eights match against that range? Better than you might think. We're about 40 percent to win against that particular range of hands, which means we can call his all-in with pot odds better than 1.5-to-1.

That estimate solves our problem neatly. We can call a subsequent all-in no matter which initial bet we pick. Therefore we'll pick the bet that gives him the worst pot odds, and reraise to $80,000. Score 5 points for Choice E, 4 points for Choice D, and 3 points for Choice C.

What about pushing all-in? It's not an unreasonable play. Since we just established that you have to call a subsequent all-in from your opponent. However, a smaller raise serves to disguise your hand. After all, you wouldn't push all-in with a big pair since you would want your opponent to call. But if you push with a medium to small pair, your opponents will quickly figure out what your bets mean. Score 2 points for Choice F, pushing all-in.

Question 36B: In our problem, the player didn't pick the best raise, but our answer was clear in any event. Score 4 points for Choice B, calling, no credit for folding.

Problem 37
Playing on the
Single-Table Bubble — 1

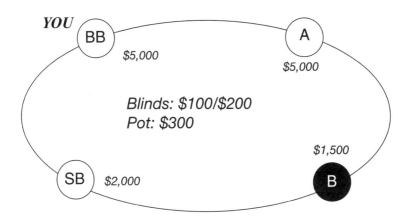

Situation: Online sit-and-go tournament. The tournament pays three players in the standard ratio of 50 percent first, 30 percent second, 20 percent third. Four players remain.

Your hand: ??

Action to you: Player A goes all-in. Player B and the small blind fold. Player A has appeared somewhat loose and doesn't seem to understand the intricacies of bubble play in sit and go tournaments. You believe that he might move all-in with any of the following hands: any pair, any ace, king-jack or better, suited or offsuit, and queen-jack, suited or offsuit.

Question 37: *Which of the following statements is correct?*

A.   *Fold all hands*
B.   *Call with AA only*
C.   *Call with AA and KK only*
D.   *Call with AA, KK, QQ, and AK suited or offsuit*
E.   *Call with AA through TT and AK and AQ, suited or offsuit*
F.   *Call with AA through 88 and AK through AJ, suited or offsuit*

Solution to Problem 37

Playing on the bubble in sit-and-go tournaments is somewhat different from bubble play in larger multi-table tournaments because of the different prize structures. Almost all sit-and-go tournaments have a standard prize structure: 50 percent for first, 30 percent for second, and 20 percent for third. The bubble occurs when just four players remain, and being eliminated on the bubble means the difference between nothing and 20 percent of the prize fund. At the same time, the difference between third prize and first prize is relatively small: third prize is a full 40 percent of first prize.

Contrast these distributions with those of a large multi-table tournament, either live or online. At multi-table tournaments, something like 10 percent of the field will win a prize, but the bubble prize will be tiny, perhaps less that 1 percent of first prize, and you can't win any significant amount of money until you penetrate much deeper into the tournament.

As a result of the difference in prize structures, the optimal bubble strategy in sit-and-gos is very different from the optimal strategy in multi-table events. In multi-table tournaments, the right idea is to play aggressively on the bubble, taking advantage of the many players who just want to cash and get their entry fee back. But in sit-and-gos, simply getting in the money is a significant result, so conservative bubble play is not only reasonable, but optimal.

In Problem 37, you're sitting in the big blind in a bubble situation. Right now you're in good position. The blinds ($100/$200) are relatively low, so your stack of $5,000 represents an M of almost 17. One other player has a stack equal to yours, while the other two players have low Ms and are the prime candidates for elimination.

But suddenly your good position is threatened. The other big stack shoves all-in. You've observed him and he appears to be fairly loose, and to have no real understanding of what's happening. You estimate the range of hands with which he might push is pretty big. What do you need to call?

The answer may surprise many players: You actually need an enormously strong hand to call and risk going out on the bubble! The correct answer is Choice C — "Call with AA and KK only." All other hands should be folded. Score 3 points if you picked that answer. Score 1 point if you picked Choice B or Choice D — your heart was in the right place.

The key factors driving your decision are your large M and the presence of two small stacks. You have enough chips to last awhile, and one of the small stacks should hit a critical situation quickly. You're in such a good position that you need a very, very good hand to risk elimination.

But what about your loose opponent? Can't you take advantage of his looseness in some dramatic way?

Actually, no. If we change his pushing range to something more rational — let's say a pair of eights or better, or ace-ten or better, plus king-queen — then your calling range is just slightly affected. Now you can call with aces, and only aces!

Playing properly on the bubble is a key skill for succeeding in the sit-and-go online tournaments, which are a big part of modern poker. Over the next few problems we'll explore some more aspects of sit-and go bubble play.

Final Note: The theory of playing in single-table tournaments is similar to the theory of playing in satellite tournaments where there are identical prizes for finishing in the last few places. In *Harrington on Hold 'em: Volume II* we showed an example where it was correct to fold aces when on the bubble in a satellite. The situation in sit-and-gos is similar but not quite as extreme because there is now a gradation in the prize structure.

Problem 38
Playing on the
Single-Table Bubble — 2

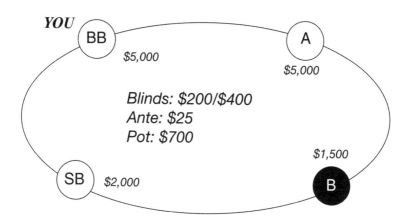

YOU

BB $5,000

A $5,000

Blinds: $200/$400
Ante: $25
Pot: $700

$1,500

SB $2,000

B

Situation: Online sit-and-go tournament. The tournament pays three players in the standard ratio of 50 percent first, 30 percent second, 20 percent third. Four players remain. Compared to the last problem, the blinds and antes have increased.

Your hand: ??

Action to you: As in Problem 37, Player A goes all-in, and Player B and the small blind fold. You think Player A has the same pushing range as before: any pair, any ace, king-jack or better, suited or offsuit, and queen-jack, suited or offsuit.

Question 38: *Which of the following statements is correct?*

A. *Fold all hands*
B. *Call with AA only*
C. *Call with AA and KK only*
D. *Call with AA, KK, QQ, and AK suited or offsuit*
E. *Call with AA through TT and AK and AQ, suited or offsuit*
F. *Call with AA through 88 and AK through AJ, suited or offsuit*

Solution to Problem 38

The situation is the same as the previous problem except that the blinds and antes have increased. Blinds are now $200 and $400, and the antes are $25, so the pot is $700 to start. Your M is now just over 7, while the small stacks have Ms around 2 and 3.

Altering the blinds, as it turns out, has almost no effect on your strategy. Choice C is still the correct answer — call with AA and KK only. Score 3 points for that answer, and 1 point for either Choice B or Choice D. Your situation has deteriorated because your M is smaller, but the situation of the small stacks has deteriorated right along with you. The result is that you are very, very slightly more inclined to play, but not enough to alter your hands against a loose player.

If we make Player A tighten his pushing requirements as in the last problem, so that his pushing range is eights or better, ace-ten or better, and king-queen or better, then you can now call with either kings or aces. The appearance of kings in this case shows that with a lower M, you are just a little more inclined to play, but you still need monster hands.

Problem 39
Playing on the
Single-Table Bubble — 3

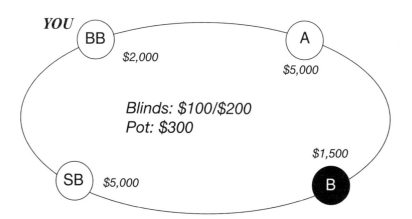

Situation: Online sit-and-go tournament. The tournament pays three players in the standard ratio of 50 percent first, 30 percent second, 20 percent third. Four players remain. You are now one of the smaller stacks, instead of the chip leader.

Your hand: ??

Action to you: As in Problem 37, Player A goes all-in, and Player B and the small blind fold. You think Player A has the same pushing range as before: any pair, any ace, king-jack or better, suited or unsuited, and queen-jack, suited or unsuited.

Question 39: *Which of the following statements is correct?*

A. *Call with AA only*

B. *Call with AA and KK only*

C. *Call with AA, KK, and QQ only*

D. *Call with AA through JJ and AK suited*

E. *Call with AA through TT and AK and AQ, suited or unsuited*

F. *Call with AA through 88 and AK through AJ, suited or unsuited*

G. *Call with AA through 44, AK through A9, suited or unsuited, and KQ*

Solution to Problem 39

We've returned to the $100 and $200 blind structure of Problem 37, but now we've altered the stack sizes. This time you have one of the smaller stacks, at $2,000, and are being put all-in by one of the players with $5,000. As before, you estimate that he has a relatively loose pushing requirement. What do you need to call?

You might think that with the second-smallest stack and an M of less than 7, your calling requirements might be pretty loose. Many players might pick Choice G, which indeed would leave them a favorite in the majority of situations.

But the best answer is Choice D: "Call with AA through JJ and AK suited!" While your requirements aren't as tight as when you had the big stack, they're still extremely tight. You're only calling with the top 2 percent of your hands. In third place, you can't take the chance of being knocked out on the bubble with anything but a monster hand, even if you know your opponent is willing to push with a lot of mediocre hands. Score 3 points for picking Choice D, and 1 point for either Choice C or Choice E.

As a side note, if Player A had the tighter pushing range of the last two problems (eights or better plus ace-ten or better plus king-queen, suited or unsuited) your calling requirements would rise still further, to a pair of queens or better, a little looser than in the last two problems, but still very, very tight.

Conclusion: An M of 7, while low, still gives you time to wait for a better hand to commit all your chips.

While our arguments for playing tight on the bubble may seem generally reasonable, especially when you have a big stack (as in the previous two examples), this example probably bothers some readers. After all, here you are in third place, with a relatively small stack, yet we're advocating being extremely tight nonetheless. To illustrate what's really going on more clearly, we're going to take you through a close examination of what really happens to your equity in the tournament when you call in these situations.

Caution: The rest of this problem involves more mathematical calculations that some readers may find uncomfortable. If so, just skip the rest of this problem and go on to Problem 40. But if you're really curious and want to see what's actually happening, read on.

We're going to start by calculating each player's cash equity at various stages of the hand, and then look at the changes in equity for each possible result. For analysis purposes, we'll assume that the players are playing for a $1,000 prize fund, with prizes of $500 first, $300 second, and $200 for third. Fourth place, of course, gets nothing.

Calculating the equity isn't easy, but it can be done with a systematic approach. We'll start by calculating the equity of the four players before the hand actually starts. We'll designate the four players as Players A through D, with the following chip stacks:

- Player A: $5,000
- Player B: $5,000

- Player C: $2,000
- Player D: $1,500

Since the player's equity depends on the exact chances that each player has of finishing first, second, third, and fourth, we have to calculate those probabilities first. That requires building the following table of probabilities:

Table I: Probabilities of finishing first through fourth before the hand.

Player	Stack	First	Second	Third	Fourth
A	$5,000	0.370	0.329	0.244	0.057
B	$5,000	0.370	0.329	0.244	0.057
C	$2,000	0.148	0.193	0.279	0.380
D	$1,500	0.111	0.150	0.232	0.507

Each entry in the appropriate cells of this table shows the probability of a given player finishing in a given spot. Player A, for example, is one of the co-leaders with a $5,000 stack. He has a 37 percent chance of finishing first, a 32.9 percent chance of finishing second, a 24.4 percent chance of finishing third, and only a 5.7 percent chance of finishing dead last. (We're assuming, of course, that all the players are equally skilled.)

Before we explain how these numbers are calculated, notice that the matrix obeys all the common-sense conditions one might expect. Players A and B, with equal stacks, have identical probabilities of finishing in all four positions. Players A and B, with the biggest stacks, have a larger probability of finishing first than any other position. Player D, with the smallest stack, has the smallest chance of finishing first and the largest chance of finishing fourth. The sum of each column equals 1.0 (someone has to finish in each position) and the sum of each row equals 1.0 (each player must finish somewhere).

So where do the probabilities come from? Let's start with the column that contains the probabilities of a first-place finish for each player, since it's the easiest to calculate. Each player's chance of finishing first is simply the ratio of his chips to the total number of chips in play. Player A, for example, is 37 percent.

$$0.37 = \frac{\$5,000}{\$13,500}$$

For Player D, it's 11.1 percent.

$$.111 = \frac{\$1,500}{\$13,500}$$

Calculating the second-place probabilities gets a little trickier. To calculate the chance that Player A finishes second, for instance, you have to perform three separate calculations:

1. First, assume that Player B finishes first. (We know from the first-place column that this event has a probability of 37.0 percent.) Player A's chance of finishing second is the ratio of his chips ($5,000) to the total number of chips for the three remaining players, A, C, and D. This total is $8,500. So A's chance of finishing second, *given that B finished first*, is 58.8 percent.

$$.588 = \frac{\$5,000}{\$8,500}$$

The chance of the two events occurring together (B finishing first, then A finishing second) is 0.370 times 0.588, or 0.218.

2. Second, perform the same calculation for the case where C finishes first. If C finishes first (14.8 percent of the time),

there are $11,500 in chips left for the other three players, so A's chance of finishing second now is 43.5 percent.

$$.435 = \frac{\$5,000}{\$11,500}$$

The chance of these two events occurring together (C first, A second) is 0.148 times 0.435, or 0.064.

3. Finally, calculate the chance of D finishing first and A finishing second. The answer is 0.046.

The total chance that A finishes second is the sum of these three probabilities or 0.329.

$$0.329 = 0.218 + 0.064 + 0.046$$

Using spreadsheets to do the calculations simplifies the process considerably, as you might imagine.

Calculating the third-place probabilities uses the same idea, but requires more bookkeeping. There are 12 possibilities for the first- and second-place finishers (A first, B second, then A first, C second, all the way to D first and C second.) For each of those 12 situations, two players remain in contention for third, and each has a chance proportional to his chips divided by the total number of chips held by the two remaining players. Each of the 12 cases contributes a probability of finishing third for the two remaining players. Total all the contributions over the 12 cases, and you have the third-place probabilities.

The fourth-place probabilities don't need to be calculated directly, since all the probabilities for a given player need to add to 1.000.

Once the probabilities for a given situation are complete, you can use them to calculate the information that's of real interest, namely the equity for each player as of that point. Those equities are as follows:

**Table II:Equity for each player
before the hand is played, given a prize
distribution of $500 first, $300 second, and $200 third.**

Player A	$332.63
Player B	$332.63
Player C	$187.71
Player D	$147.02

Calculation of these numbers is pretty simple. Just multiply the probability of a given player finishing in a given position by the prize for that position, and add the amounts for each player. For Player A, the computation looks like this:

$$\$332.63 = (0.370)(\$500) + (0.329)(\$300) + (0.244)(\$200)$$

Some players try to approximate these equities by multiplying the total prize fund by a given player's share of the chips at that moment. For Player A, that approximation would yield $370, not far from the actual figure. However, using that method produces equities that are too high for the chip leaders and too low for the trailers.

Using this method, we can calculate equities for each possible result of a given hand and compare them. Let's go ahead and do that for the three possible outcomes in Problem 39:

1. Player A pushes and Player C folds
2. Player A pushes; Player C calls and wins
3. Player A pushes; Player C calls and loses

Without boring you with the details of the calculations, here's what the three sets of equities look like:

Table III: Equity for each player
after the three possible results of Problem 39.

Player	Column 1: A Pushes, C Folds	Column 2: A Pushes, C Calls and C Wins	Column 3: A Pushes, C Calls and C Loses
A	$343.97	$242.41	$394.32
B	$330.75	$324.56	$353.69
C	$175.35	$293.97	$0.00
D	$149.93	$139.06	$251.99

So far so good. To start, take a look at the first column, where Player C folds to Player A's all-in move. If Player C folds, he loses a little equity compared to his situation before the hand, while A gains some equity. However, the equity changes are not restricted to A and C, although they were the only players directly involved in the hand. Player B loses a little bit, since A has now taken the lead, while Player D gains some equity, since he has moved closer to Player C.

The really interesting columns, however, are the second and third, which summarize what happens when Player C calls and puts his tournament on the line. To see more clearly what's going on, let's create a new table, which shows only the changes in equity when C calls.

Table IV: Equity changes for
each player when Player C calls.

Player	Column 2 - Column 1 Gains/losses when C calls and wins	Column 3 - Column 1 Gains/losses when C calls and losses
A	-$101.56	+50.35
B	-$6.19	+22.94
C	+$118.62	-$175.35
D	-$10.87	+102.06

Let's look at the last column first. When C calls and loses, he loses his whole equity of $175.35, the equity he would have had by folding. (Notice where this equity goes, by the way. Relatively little of it goes to Player A. Most goes to Player D, who is now assured of the $200 third prize.)

So by calling, Player C risks a total of $175.35. But what does he expect to gain from this risk? Look at the first column. If he wins, his gain in equity is a mere $118.62! And that's the crux of C's problem — despite his precarious position in the tournament, he still has a lot more to lose than to gain from an all-in confrontation.

In fact, the ratio of his potential loss to his potential gain is

$$\frac{\$175.35}{\$118.62}$$

a whopping 1.48-to-1, or almost exactly 3-to-2. By calling, he's actually laying odds, not getting odds, and to be in a profitable situation, he needs to be, on average, about a 60-to-40 *favorite* in the hand when he calls! What kinds of hands make him a 60-to-40 favorite against Player A's pushing range? Only a mix of the very highest pairs and ace-king suited will do. Hence his extreme tightness when calling.

Let's make one last observation before we let this problem go. Take a look at the risk-reward ratio for Player A, the big stack. When Player C calls and wins, Player A is the big loser, with an equity loss of $101.56. But when C calls and A wins, most of C's equity loss goes elsewhere! Player B collects $22.94, and lowly Player D collects a whopping $102.06. Player A's gain is a measly $50.35. Player A's loss-to-gain ratio is almost exactly 2-to-1, meaning Player A needs a very strong hand as well to justify an all-in move.

Because of the unusual distribution of equity gains and losses, bubble play requires generally very conservative play from everyone in the hand, as long as the Ms are reasonably high. In this example the blinds totaled $300, so the Ms ranged from Player D at 5, to Player C at a little over 7, to Players A and B who are around 17. Those Ms are high enough so that caution must predominate.

Problem 40
Playing on the
Single-Table Bubble — 4

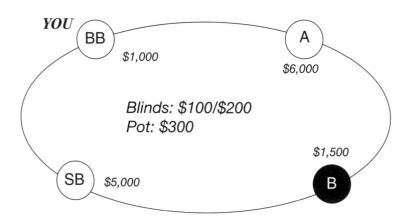

Situation: Online sit-and-go tournament. The tournament pays three players in the standard ratio of 50 percent first, 30 percent second, 20 percent third. Four players remain. Now your stack is very small, with an M of a little over 3.

Your hand: ??

Action to you: As in Problem 37, Player A goes all-in, and Player B and the small blind fold. You think Player A has the same pushing range as before: any pair, any ace, king-jack or better, suited or unsuited, and queen-jack, suited or unsuited.

Question 40: *Which of the following statements is correct?*

A. *Call with AA through JJ and AK suited*
B. *Call with AA through TT and AK and AQ, suited or unsuited*
C. *Call with AA through 77, AK through AJ unsuited, AK through AT suited*
D. *Call with AA through 44, AK through A9, suited or unsuited, and KQ suited*
E. *Call with any pair, any ace, and any two cards ten or higher*

Solution to Problem 40

We've kept the $100 and $200 blind structure, but now we've shrunk your stack to just $1,000. Your opponent remains the same wild man as before. We saw last hand that reducing your stack from $5,000 to $2,000 only created a couple of extra calling hands. Surely reducing you to the smallest stack at the table, with an M of just over 3, must have a dramatic effect, or does it?

Well, it has an effect, but the effect is not as dramatic as you might think. The correct answer is now Choice C, "Call with AA through 77, AK through AJ unsuited, AK through AT suited." Score 3 points for that choice, and 1 point for Choice B or Choice D. With an M of just 3 and a somewhat loose opponent, you can open your calling requirements a bit, but you still have to exercise caution and play with reasonable hands if you're going to venture a call that can eliminate you.

What if we had the tight opponent of the last few hands, instead of the loose opponent? In that case your calling requirements once again rise drastically, to a pair of jacks or better and ace-king, suited or offsuit. In the real world, however, I wouldn't make the assumption that I was facing such a tight opponent. Most players play pretty loose on the bubble, much looser than they theoretically should, and even if I saw an opponent sitting out a few hands, it's more likely that he just hit a run of low cards than that he turned into a locksmith at this stage.

This hand, I think, most clearly illustrates the huge difference between sit-and-go bubble play and real tournament bubble play. In a large tournament, when you have a short stack and you're nearing the bubble, it's routine to call with hands like those in Choice E above: the pairs, the aces, and the paint cards. But we're making those plays in big tournaments because the low-level prizes are insignificant compared to the really big prizes at the final table. (Insignificant is a relative term, of course. To all the online qualifiers who won their way into the 2005 World Series of Poker in online satellites, the $15,000 prize for getting into the money might have looked very significant indeed. But compared to the million-dollar prizes waiting for those who made the final table, it really wasn't.)

But in a sit-and-go tournament, when you're on the bubble, you're already on the verge of significant money. Consider this: when you move from fourth to third, you make 20 percent of the prize fund. When you move from third to second, you only gain another 10 percent of the prize fund. And the final move from second to first only gets you an additional 20 percent. Viewed this way, the transition from bubble status to in-the-money status is as big or bigger than any other transition in the tournament.

Problem 41
Playing on the
Single-Table Bubble — 5

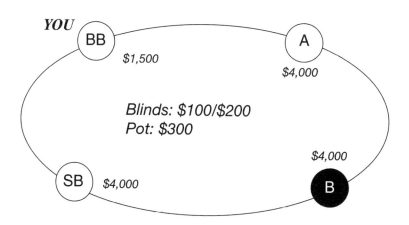

Situation: Online sit-and-go tournament. The tournament pays three players in the standard ratio of 50 percent first, 30 percent second, 20 percent third. Four players remain. Unlike the previous problem, you are now the only low stack in the tournament.

Your hand: ??

Action to you: As before, Player A goes all-in, and Player B and the small blind fold. You think Player A has the same pushing range as before: any pair, any ace, king-jack or better, suited or offsuit, and queen-jack, suited or offsuit.

Question 41: *Which of the following statements is correct?*

A.   *Call with AA through 99, and AK and AQ, suited or offsuit*
B.   *Call with AA through 66, AK through AT suited, and AK through AJ offsuit*
C.   *Call with any pair, AK through A8, suited or offsuit, and KQ, KJ, QJ suited or offsuit*
D.   *Call with any pair, any ace, and any two cards ten or higher*

Solution to Problem 41

Now we've changed the stack sizes so you are the only small stack with an M of 5, while the other three players all have big stacks with Ms a little over 13. Not only are you in danger, but there are no other short stacks. How much does this affect your calling requirements?

Once again, your weakening position allows you to loosen your requirements, but only by a little bit. The correct answer here is Choice B. "Call with AA through 66, AK through AT suited, and AK through AJ offsuit." Score 3 points for Choice B and 1 point each for Choice A and Choice C.

If you believed that Player A had tight pushing requirements (eights or better, ace-ten or better, king-queen), then your calling requirements again get very strict. You can only call with jacks or better plus ace-king suited or offsuit. Life isn't easy on the bubble!

Problem 42
Playing on the
Single-Table Bubble — 6

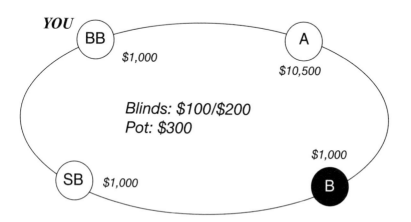

Situation: Online sit-and-go tournament. The tournament pays three players in the standard ratio of 50 percent first, 30 percent second, 20 percent third. Four players remain. In our last example, you have one of three equal (but tiny) stacks, battling a big bully stack.

Your hand: ??

Action to you: One huge stack and three small stacks at the table. Player A has been brutalizing the table for some time with raises when first to act. You now believe that he will, in fact, go all-in with any two cards when first to act. Once again he goes all-in, and both the button and the small blind fold.

Question 42: *Which of the following statements is correct?*

A. *Call with AA through 88, and AK suited*
B. *Call with AA through 66, and AK through AJ, suited or offsuit*
C. *Call with any pair, AK through A8, suited or offsuit, and KQ, KJ, QJ suited or offsuit*
D. *Call with any pair, any ace, and any two cards ten or higher*

Solution to Problem 42

Another variation on a now-familiar theme. Player A has most of the chips at the table and is simply pushing all-in when he's first to act. Your two colleagues have already folded. (Cowards!) What do you need to stand up to this bully?

Quite a bit, actually. You may have a small stack, but you're firmly in contention for a money prize, and that's hugely important. Either of the other small stacks could go out at any time. Your correct answer is Choice A: "Call with AA through 88, and AK suited." Score 3 points for that choice. The big stack doesn't matter much any more; you're playing against the two smaller stacks, and you need a big hand to risk going out on the bubble. Score 1 point for Choice B, and no credit for the other loose calls.

If we change Player A to the 'tight' player of the last few examples (pushing with eights or better, ace-ten or better, and king-queen), then his tightness plus the other two tiny stacks makes you super-tight once more: you can only call with aces or kings.

If Player A is the 'loose' player of the previous examples (pushing with any pair, any ace, and queen-jack or better), you can only add queens to your list of calling hands. Notice this key fact: changing Player A from 'loose' to 'pushing with any hand' only enabled you to add five hands to your calling list: JJ, TT, 99, 88, and AK suited. It's your chip situation versus the other players, and not Player A's pushing requirements, that's the main driver of your strategy.

All of these exceptionally high calling requirements are driven by the fact that you will be knocked out on the bubble if you call and lose. If you are the big stack and are being put all-in by one of the smaller stacks, you're in no danger of being eliminated, so your calling requirements are much more normal: any pair or any two reasonably high cards will suffice.

Problem 43
Hansen Versus Deeb
— Putting the Story Together

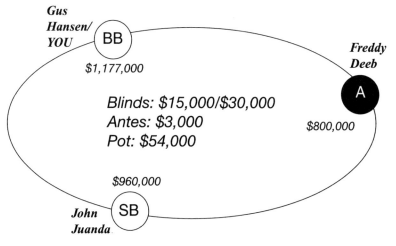

Situation: Final table of the 2002 Bellagio Five-Diamond Classic. Your playing partner in the big blind is Gus Hansen, in the process of winning his first major WPT event.

Your hand: Q♥5♥

Action to you: Freddy Deeb, on the button, raises to $80,000. John Juanda folds. The pot is now $134,000.

Question 43A: *What do you do?*

A. *Fold.*
B. *Call $50,000*
C. *Raise to $200,000*

Action: You actually call $50,000. The pot is now $184,000.

Flop: K♦4♣2♥

Question 43B: *What do you do?*

A. *Check*
B. *Bet $80,000*
C. *Bet $150,000*

Action: You actually bet $80,000. Freddy Deeb calls. The pot is now $344,000.

Turn: 7♥

Question 43C: *What do you do?*

A. *Check*
B. *Bet $80,000*
C. *Bet $200,000*

Action: You actually check. Freddy Deeb checks. The pot remains at $344,000.

River: Q♦

Question 43D: *What do you do?*

A. *Check*
B. *Bet $80,000*
C. *Bet $200,000*
D. *Push all-in*

Action: You actually bet $80,000. Freddy Deeb raises to $250,000. The pot is now $674,000, and it costs you another $170,000 to call.

Question 43E: *What do you do?*

A. *Fold*
B. *Call $170,000*
C. *Raise all-in*

Action: You actually call. Deeb turns over 6♥3♥, and you win the pot with your pair of queens.

Solution to Problem 43

Question 43A: Even in three-player poker,

doesn't constitute a particularly strong hand. Gus doesn't mind calling with these sorts of hands, even out of position, to see what the flop brings. Here he's getting pot odds of 2.6-to-1, and Deeb is a trappy player who could be fooling around. It's a marginal play. I would be inclined to fold, but I'd probably call once in a while with a hand of this strength. Gus is more likely to play.

Score 2 points for Choice A, folding and 2 points for Choice B, calling. No credit for raising.

Gus calls $50,000, bringing the pot to $184,000. The flop comes

Question 43B: Gus has no information about Deeb's hand beyond the fact that Deeb raised from the button pre-flop. In three-handed poker, a pre-flop raise from the first player to act doesn't necessarily mean much. Although the flop has missed Gus, it contains only one card above a four, so it likely missed his opponent as well.

Checking may just induce a bet from the pre-flop raiser, a bet that you can't call. Betting is better since this flop will have missed most hands, many of which will fold.

Score 4 points for Choice B, betting $80,000. Score 2 points for Choice A, checking. Also no credit for Choice C, betting $150,000, too much if Deeb really has a hand.

Gus bets $80,000, and Deeb calls. The pot is $344,000. The turn comes the 7♥.

Question 43C: The 7♥ is a helpful card for Gus, giving him a flush draw. But what about Deeb? What hands can he have that justify the pre-flop bet and the post-flop call? Let's run through some possibilities.

- **The big hands.** The big hands here are the three sets of trips and perhaps ace-king and king-queen. All these hands would have bet pre-flop, and all are strong enough to just check after the flop, hoping to set a trap.

- **The other kings.** This group includes everything from king-jack down to about king-seven. (The weaker kings probably don't raise pre-flop.) Many players, however, would raise with these hands after Gus bet on the flop.

- **Lower pairs.** The pairs from jacks through sixes would certainly justify a raise pre-flop. (Queens and fives are less likely since Gus has one of each card.) With the king showing, they might only call after Gus's bet. A pair of sevens just became trips. If he bet before the flop with low cards, he might have a pair of fours or deuces now.

- **An ace.** If Deeb holds an ace and a medium or low card, he would have bet before the flop and probably just called after Gus's bet, whether or not he paired the low card.

- **Straight and flush draws.** If Deeb bet before the flop with low cards, he might have a straight draw, and the arrival of the 7♥ makes flush draws possible. If he has hands of this type, he's looking for a free card on the turn.

That's a big list, and Gus is losing to most of the hands on it, except the draws. Betting now doesn't make much sense. Checking, however, should draw some useful information. Why? Let's turn the problem around and see things from Deeb's point of view. If Deeb has trips, or a king, or a medium-to-high pair, does he want to bet on the turn or wait until the river? Clearly betting on the turn would be right. If Gus has nothing but is on some sort of draw, he may call a bet on the turn, but he'll fold on the river with nothing. If Gus has a little something, like a pair of sevens or fours, he might call on the turn for value, but he'll probably fold on the river if another scary high card comes. So Deeb has plenty of reason to bet his value hands right now, before it's too late.

Gus checks. Score 5 points for that play (Choice A). Don't put any more money in the pot if your analysis indicates you're beaten and your opponent has shown he's playing. No credit for the betting plays.

Deeb now checks. The pot remains at $344,000. The river comes a Q♦.

Question 43D: A new card, and a new piece of information. Deeb didn't bet on the turn after all. Was he slow-playing a big hand?

And the arrival of the queen now gives Gus a hand. It's only second pair, but if Deeb has a king, did he expect to make money checking the turn and betting the river?

Deeb's check on the turn means that the pair of queens are probably the best hand right now. Score 4 points for Choice B, betting $80,000, which might get some more money in the pot if Deeb had a lower pair. No credit for Choice A, checking, which probably won't make any money, and no credit for Choice D, pushing all-in. Also no credit for Choice C, making a big bet. If Deeb has a pair lower than your queens, this is probably more money than he wants to call with a king and queen on board.

Gus bets $80,000. Deeb raises to $250,000. The pot is now $674,000. It costs you $170,000 to call.

Question 43E: Is this a bluff, or has Deeb been trapping all along? The pot odds, at 4-to-1, are pretty good, so you should be inclined to call unless you're sure you're beaten.

Let's assume Deeb had a big hand after the turn — kings with a good kicker, or trip sevens or fours or deuces. What would he do?

He would have to assume that Gus had one of four hands: nothing, a draw, a lower pair, or a real good hand.

● **If Gus had nothing,** the slightly better play is to check and hope that either Gus catches a card on the river that's good enough to let him call a bet or decides to bluff. I say "slightly better" because, although checking is clearly correct, Gus won't have many apparent outs and this play won't make money very often.

- **If Gus has a draw,** then betting on the turn is correct by a lot. If you put your opponent on a draw, you want to bet because it's a profitable bet (you'll win most of the time) and because he won't call after he misses his draw.

- **If Gus has a lower pair,** you also want to bet on the turn, not so much to make him pay for his outs (since he doesn't have many) but because a scare card could easily land on the river that would make him fold.

- **If Gus has a real good hand** as well, then it doesn't matter much which street you bet. One of you will lose a lot of money on the hand, and if the money doesn't go in on the turn, it will go in on the river.

So if Deeb had a big hand on the turn, it's pretty clear he was supposed to bet then. But he didn't. That doesn't prove he didn't have a big hand; it only demonstrates that he *may not* have had a big hand. But when you're getting 4-to-1 pot odds, you don't need proof beyond a reasonable doubt. Just the reasonable doubt is enough to justify your call.

Score 5 points for Choice B, calling. No credit for Choice A, folding. Also no credit for Choice C, going all-in. Remember, you only have second pair. Just because you believe that you may be even money or a slight favorite to win the hand doesn't imply that you want to get most of your stack invested.

Gus actually calls, and Deeb was on a bluff with the 6♥3♥. Gus wins the pot.

When you're bluffing, you want to imagine that you have the hand you're representing, and play accordingly. *This isn't easy.* You should give your imaginary hand just as much thought, and reason the hand out just as carefully, as if you held the real article.

That way your moves will tell a consistent story, one your opponent can believe.

Problem 44
Corkins Versus Hellmuth
— Playing a Middling Hand

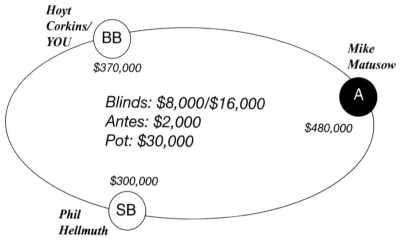

Hoyt Corkins/ YOU — BB — $370,000

Mike Matusow — A — $480,000

Phil Hellmuth — SB — $300,000

Blinds: $8,000/$16,000
Antes: $2,000
Pot: $30,000

Situation: Final table of the ESPN 2005 Poker Superstars II tournament. Three players remain. Your playing partner is Hoyt Corkins in the big blind.

Your hand: 8♥4♦

Action to you: Mike Matusow folds and Phil Hellmuth calls for $8,000. The pot is now $38,000.

Question 44A: *What do you do?*

A.   Check
B.   Raise $30,000

Action: You actually check.

285

Flop: Q♣8♦3♥

Action: Hellmuth checks. The pot remains $38,000.

Question 44B: *What do you do?*

A.   *Check*
B.   *Bet $20,000*

Action: You actually check.

Turn: 5♣

Action: Hellmuth checks.

Question 44C: *What do you do?*

A.   *Check*
B.   *Bet $20,000*

Action: You actually bet $20,000. Hellmuth raises to $70,000.

Question 44D: *What do you do?*

A.   *Fold*
B.   *Call $50,000*
C.   *Raise all-in*

Action: You actually call for $50,000. The pot is now $178,000.

River: 7♣

Action: Hellmuth bets $65,000. The pot is $243,000.

Question 44E: *What do you do?*

A. *Fold*
B. *Call $65,000*
C. *Raise all-in*

Action: You actually call $65,000. Hellmuth shows J♦2♣, and you collect the pot.

Solution to Problem 44

Hellmuth picks up the J♦2♣ and elects to call from the small blind. He's just fooling around with a weak hand, looking to see what develops and relying on his ability to outplay opponents after the flop.

Question 44A: Score 2 points for Choice A, checking with the

Hellmuth called instead of raising, which might show some weakness, but your hand *really is* weak, so stay out of trouble and just check. No credit for raising.

The flop comes

Hellmuth checks again. He's missed the flop, but that doesn't mean he can't win the hand, even out of position. He checks to see if Corkins will tell him anything, while keeping his investment low.

Question 44B: Corkins elects to check, which I think is a mistake. Right now he has middle pair, which in two-player poker is a pretty good hand, especially in position. Hellmuth's call pre-flop and check post-flop have not yet indicated any real strength, so it's reasonable for Corkins to think he has the best hand. Moreover, his situation is much more likely to get worse instead of better. If an eight lands on the board, he'll have a lock hand, but probably won't get any action. Only the arrival of one of the last three fours will give him a strong hand that might win a big pot. However, he has to be scared that any card higher than an eight coming on the turn could beat him. That's a lot of bad cards (aces, kings, jacks, tens, and nines) and just five really good cards, so time is not on his side.

Score 4 points for Choice B, betting $20,000. Score 2 points for Choice A, just checking.

Having voted for betting, I should mention that many good players would play the hand the same way Corkins played it: checking, looking to play small-ball, but also looking to perhaps get Hellmuth involved in a hand where he doesn't have anything. When you go in that direction, you're more likely to have to make some tough calls in situations where the board is threatening and you still don't have much. Of course, a similar scenario might develop after betting. However, once you bet, you do know that any moves your opponent makes are made in the knowledge that you have shown strength.

I'm actually more likely to check with top pair in similar situations. Fewer cards can appear that are frightening, and I'm strong enough to get involved in a bigger pot.

Corkins, however, does check and the turn comes the 5♣.

The five is not a threatening card, so Hellmuth now checks, planning to check-raise. He has nothing, but Corkins hasn't shown anything either, despite being given two chances to bet. So Hellmuth reasonably believes the hand is winnable. He elects the check-raise in preference to a simple bet because it represents more strength, and with a jack-deuce, Hellmuth would like to squelch resistance and take the pot down right now. (The check-raise also wins more money when it works.)

Question 44C: The five didn't hurt and probably didn't affect Hellmuth one way or another. You've now seen a pre-flop call and two checks from Hellmuth. Your pair of eights looks very good right now, and there's no reason not to bet. A half-pot bet should be plenty under the circumstances to take down the pot. Score 3 points for Choice B, betting $20,000, and no credit for Choice A, checking.

You bet $20,000, and Hellmuth check-raises to $70,000. The pot is now $128,000.

Question 44D: Hellmuth is representing a queen. He may have it, he may not. Hellmuth is certainly capable of check-raising you without a hand, and you're well aware of this.

In reality, you have second pair, which is a pretty good hand heads-up, and the pot is offering you 2.5-to-1 odds. Those are excellent odds for second pair, and even better odds against an aggressive player known for skillful post-flop play. Remember that you've indicated no strength until your bet on the turn, so Hellmuth simply can't credit you with a good hand yet.

Score 4 points for Choice B, calling. No credit for Choice A, folding.

What about raising? It's very aggressive, but are there any hands you can beat that will call your raise? Raising here announces that you aren't afraid of top pair, but in fact you're very much afraid of top pair. If Hellmuth has nothing, a raise will make him go away, but you'll beat him in a showdown anyway, so that's not a huge achievement. Skip the raise, and let your position and pot odds do the work. No credit for Choice A, raising.

You actually call $50,000, and the pot becomes $178,000. The river card is a 7♣.

Hellmuth now has to decide what to do. Corkins called (but didn't reraise) a check-raise with a board of Q♣8♦3♥5♣ (with two clubs). The obvious holding that accounts for the call is either a queen with a low kicker or an eight. The only open-ended straight draw that could have just connected is a holding of precisely six-four. (A nine-six holding just connected as well, but that represented an inside straight draw.) Would he have called with just a five or a trey in his hand, for a low pair? It's a dangerous play. Perhaps he had two clubs plus a low pair, say the 9♣3♣. His additional outs would have made the last call pretty easy.

By delaying his first raise until the turn, Hellmuth hasn't actually learned very much. All he knows for sure is:

- Corkins didn't have enough to bet either pre-flop or post-flop, and

- Corkins had enough to call a check-raise, but not enough to reraise.

Unless he missed his straight draw, whatever Corkins had is enough to win, since Hellmuth has exactly nothing.

Now Hellmuth has to ask the big question: *Can Corkins be bluffed out on the river, and if so, how big a bet will it take?*

So far both sides have invested about $90,000 in the hand. Hellmuth has about $210,000 left, while Corkins has him covered with about $280,000. What hands might Corkins have? From our previous analysis, they break into three main groups:

1. **The big hands:** a flush, a straight (both unlikely) or top pair, weak kicker.

2. **The medium hands:** second pair.

3. **The weak hands:** one of the bottom pairs, or perhaps a busted straight draw.

The big hands aren't likely, which is good since Hellmuth can't chase Corkins off any of those hands anyway. If Corkins holds a weak hand, Hellmuth may be able to get rid of him with a sufficiently big bet. However, what if Corkins holds one of the medium hands? Here Hellmuth would have to rely on whatever observations he'd been able to make while playing with Corkins. Having seen Corkins on quite a few final tables in the last couple of years, he seems to be a real bulldog with his medium-strength hands. While he may not bet them aggressively, he's doesn't like to lay them down, especially with reasonable pot odds.

Putting the whole picture together, I think Hellmuth either has to check and concede the hand, cutting his losses, or make a substantial bet, more than $100,000, which will chase Corkins off the weak hands and might make him lay down second pair rather than risk his whole tournament.

Hellmuth actually bet $65,000, which raises the pot to $243,000 and gives Corkins 4-to-1 odds to call.

Question 44E: Corkins has second pair and 4-to-1 odds against an aggressive and trappy opponent. He correctly realizes he can't lay the hand down for that price, and calls. Score 4 points for Choice B, calling, no credit for folding or raising.

On the end, Hellmuth needed to make a bigger bet to give himself a chance to win the pot. I think $110,000 to $120,000 is the right amount, but I wouldn't squawk if he had moved all-in. A six-figure bet seems much more threatening than a five-figure bet, even if the absolute dollar amounts are close, and is more likely to get the opponent to go away.

Problem 45
Negreanu Versus Arieh
— Handling an Aggressive Opponent

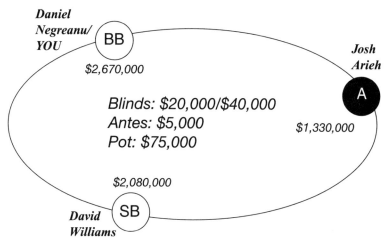

Daniel Negreanu/YOU — BB — $2,670,000

Josh Arieh — A — $1,330,000

Blinds: $20,000/$40,000
Antes: $5,000
Pot: $75,000

David Williams — SB — $2,080,000

Situation: Final table of the Borgata tournament of 2004, part of the World Poker Tour. Only three players remain. Josh Arieh and David Williams have been extremely aggressive throughout the final table. Daniel Negreanu started out by playing his standard small-ball game, but has loosened a bit under the onslaught of Williams and Arieh. Your playing partner in the hand is Daniel Negreanu in the big blind with a small chip lead over David Williams.

Your hand: 9♣6♣

Action to you: Josh Arieh limps for $40,000. David Williams, in the small blind, folds.

294 Problem 45

Question 45A: *What do you do?*

A. *Check*
B. *Raise $60,000*
C. *Raise $100,000*

Action: You actually check. The pot is now $115,000.

Flop: T♣5♣3♦

Question 45B: *What do you do?*

A. *Check*
B. *Bet $40,000*
C. *Bet $65,000*
D. *Bet $100,000*

Action: You actually bet $40,000. Josh Arieh calls. The pot is now $195,000.

Turn: 7♦

Question 45C: *What do you do?*

A. *Check*
B. *Bet $60,000*
C. *Bet $100,000*
D. *Bet $200,000*

Action: You actually check. Josh Arieh bets $225,000. The pot is now $420,000.

Question 45D: *What do you do?*

A. *Fold*
B. *Call $225,000*
C. *Raise to $650,000*

Action: You actually call $225,000. The pot is now $645,000. You have about $2.3 million left, Josh has just over a million.

River: 4♥

Question 45E: *What do you do?*

A. *Check*
B. *Bet $250,000*
C. *Bet $550,000*
D. *Push all-in*

Action: You actually bet $550,000. Josh Arieh moves all-in for his last $1,020,000, raising you $470,000.

Question 45F: *What do you do?*

A. *Fold*
B. *Call $470,000*

Action: You actually call, and Arieh shows J♣9♦ for a jack-high hand. Your 7-high straight wins the pot and knocks Arieh out.

Solution to Problem 45

Arieh is first to act and limps for $40,000 with the J♣9♦. It's a reasonable play. The cards are close together and he'll have position throughout the hand. The limp is also a little unusual for him since he's been playing very fast at this final table. This slightly out of character move may induce some extra caution from his opponents.

Williams folds the T♥3♠ in the small blind. I agree. It's too weak to play even getting 5-to-1 pot odds.

Question 45A: Negreanu checks the

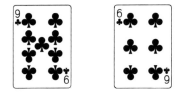

a completely sensible play for a weak hand that will be out of position. Score 2 points for Choice A, checking, no credit for raising.

The pot is now $115,000. The flop comes

Question 45B: You didn't hit the nine or the six, but it's still a reasonably good flop. No high cards that might have hit Arieh's hand, a flush draw (for you), and some chances of a runner-runner straight (for you).

Against a tight player, Negreanu might elect to check this flop and try to get a free card. Against Arieh, who's been playing fast all day, that approach isn't likely to work. A check will probably result in a big bet from Arieh, which Negreanu will have to call, since the bet may well represent a complete bluff.

Negreanu elects instead to make a probe-sized bet of $40,000. It's not a value bet (since he doesn't have anything yet), and it's not an attempt to win the pot right away (since Arieh will have such good pot odds that he could reasonably call with almost anything.) Rather, it's a defensive bet, designed to hold off a bet from Arieh while retaining the initiative in the hand.

Against a tight player, I think a check would be the most reasonable play. Against Arieh, I like betting, but I think Daniel's amount is too small. The trouble with a probe bet against a super-aggressive player is that he'll call with a lot of hands, and you won't have learned much from your bet. I would have bet something closer to half the pot, about $65,000. That forces Arieh to pay a price to stick around.

The $40,000 probe bet is very much in keeping with Daniel's style. He likes these little bets, and at a table with a mix of strong and weak players in the early and middle parts of a tournament, they tend to be very successful. A lot of players think to themselves "I've got a marginal hand, I could play it or not. Hey, this guy might be one of the two or three best players in the world, I don't need the aggravation, I'll find a better spot to put my money in," and give up the hand, and Daniel pulls down another pot with a minimal investment of chips. But Arieh's not going to think that way, so a bigger bet is required.

Score 4 points for Choice C, betting $65,000. Score 2 points for Choice A, checking, and Choice B, betting $40,000. Checking allows Arieh to take the initiative, while betting less just encourages an aggressive player like Arieh to stick around with almost anything. No credit for Choice D, betting $100,000, too big a bet for such a weak hand.

Negreanu actually bets $40,000, making the pot $155,000.

Arieh now calls. With his J♣9♦, it's not a call made for value. As yet Arieh has nothing, just an overcard to the board and some vague chances for a straight. But Arieh believes he can win this hand down the road, based on a combination of factors:

- **He may have as many as six outs**. If Negreanu doesn't have a ten in his hand, then hitting either his jack or his nine may give him a winning hand. Some of the outs may not be live, or might help Negreanu's hand in some way. But it's reasonable to suppose that he has on average between four and five outs legitimately. He might also get a back-door flush or straight, which adds a little to his count of outs.

- **He's getting more than 4-to-1 odds on this call**. Those are big odds, and good players are predisposed to play when they see those kind of odds in a murky situation. If Negreanu doesn't bet on the turn, then Arieh's call here will let him see two cards, so his four or five outs turn into eight or ten outs, and he's getting almost the right price for eight or ten outs.

- **Negreanu hasn't shown any real strength yet**. He checked in the big blind (when he could have raised) and made a small probe bet on the flop, which could mean almost anything. It's reasonable for Arieh to think that he might be able to take the hand away somewhere down the road, even if he doesn't make any legitimate hand.

Would I make this call? Probably not. By nature I play a tighter game than Arieh, and this call is certainly out on the edge of permissible plays. So far at this final table, Negreanu has played reasonably tight. He doesn't normally like to lead out at pots, but here he's leading, saying in effect "I like this pot a little bit." With no hand yet, I'd be inclined to let it go and stay out of trouble. But Arieh's had great success with a very fast and aggressive style, and this call is perfectly consistent with his general approach to the game.

Arieh calls. The pot is now $195,000. The turn card is the 7♦.

Question 45C: The seven gives Negreanu some new outs. He now has fours and eights to make a straight, in addition to the clubs which make a flush. That's a total of 15 outs on the river. (The eights aren't actually outs since they give Arieh a higher straight, but Negreanu can't know that.)

It's hard to be sure what Negreanu's proper play should be. Both checking (hoping for a free card) and betting about half the pot (possibly winning the pot while discouraging a bet from Arieh) look completely reasonable. I've made both moves in this sort of situation from time to time. Score 3 points for both Choice A, checking, and Choice C, betting $100,000. Just 1 point for Choice B, betting just $60,000. Another probe-sized bet just signals weakness. No credit for Choice D, betting $200,000, which is too big a bet for the situation.

Negreanu checks.

Arieh now overbets the pot, putting in $225,000. He's decided the pot is winnable, since Negreanu has made three modest moves in a row:

1.   He just checked before the flop, instead of raising.

2.   He made a small probe bet after the flop, instead of a larger bet.

3.   He checked on the turn, instead of betting.

Why the big bet instead of a smaller bet of perhaps two-thirds of the pot? Negreanu must have some outs at this point, and the more Arieh bets, the worse are Negreanu's calling odds. But the simplest explanation is that he has nothing, and he'd really like Negreanu to go away. The bigger the bet, the more likely your opponent will fold a marginal hand.

The pot is now $420,000.

Question 45D: Negreanu now has to put in $225,000 to call a pot of $420,000. He's getting more than 1.8-to-1 on his money. Deciding whether to call or not is now partially an exercise in mathematics and partially a matter of reading the situation at the table.

- **The math**: Negreanu may have as many as 15 outs. (It's possible some of the outs are nullified, but there's no way to know. In fact, the three eights that are not clubs are not outs.) If he truly has 15 outs, then of the 46 cards he hasn't seen, he has 31 losers and 15 winners, so he's slightly more than a 2-to-1 underdog. The pot is getting large, and Arieh is showing some interest, so there's a reasonable chance of substantial implied odds. In fact, Arieh's whole stack could be at risk if Negreanu hits, particularly if it's one of the straights. On the math alone, calling looks like at most only a small error.

- **The situation**: Arieh has been pushing aggressively throughout the entire final table, so his bet may just be a bluff. This is particularly possible since Negreanu's own bets have not shown any real strength. Knowing this doesn't help, however, since Negreanu's own hand is so weak (nine-high) that any card above a nine can beat it. So the math will have to be the deciding factor.

So the situation doesn't really help, but on the math alone Negreanu can squeeze out a call. He's getting close to the right price just on his draw, and the implied odds, while hard to quantify, must be there. As a bonus, there's a chance that if he hits his hand, he may be able to knock out a dangerous opponent. At a tough final table, that's a good tie-breaking consideration. Score 4 points for Choice B, calling. No credit for raising or folding.

Negreanu actually calls. The pot is now $645,000. The river card is a 4♥, giving Negreanu a 7-high straight.

Question 45E: The 7-high straight doesn't lock up the hand. An eight-six is the nuts, giving a ten-high straight. In addition, any six will split. But Daniel's hand is good enough that he wants to get as much money as possible in the pot and see what happens. How to do this depends on what he thinks Arieh might have:

- If Arieh has nothing, he won't call a big bet. He might, however, try to run a bluff if he thought that was his only play to win. In that case, the right play is to check, hoping to induce a bluff.

- If Arieh has a straight, it doesn't matter whether Negreanu bets or not; all the money will get to the center of the table.

- If Arieh has one or two pair, we get the most interesting cases. Arieh might have started with a ten in his hand and had top pair all along, or started with seven-five, hit the 5♣ on the flop (accounting for his call) and the 7♦ on the turn (accounting for his big bet). With these hands, Arieh might check if Negreanu checks, but will almost certainly call a bet if Negreanu bets. Here it's right for Negreanu to make a solid bet. The exact size is the issue.

No credit for Choice D, pushing all-in. That's too likely to scare away the hands with one pair, and might even make Arieh reluctant to call if he has two low pair.

No credit also for Choice A, checking. Even for an aggressive player, Arieh's play so far indicates that he has something, and Negreanu's call on the turn indicates that he has something as well. Checking is too likely to result in no money going in the pot.

The decision between Choices B and C, betting $250,000 and $550,000, is a tough one. The $250,000 will get called by any hand that isn't a complete bluff, even though it smells strongly like a suck bet. $550,000 is about three-quarters of the pot, and it's also a little more than half of Arieh's remaining chips. But at this stage of the tournament, Arieh will have trouble laying down a real hand. I think, given the betting Negreanu has seen, that $550,000 has a reasonable chance of being called. Score 2 points for Choice B, betting $250,000, and 4 points for Choice C, $550,000.

Negreanu bets $550,000; the pot is now almost $1.2 million.

Arieh now pushes all-in, attempting to steal the pot with nothing. It's a serious blunder, for two reasons.

1. **The pot odds**. Arieh's all-in puts a total of $2.2 million in the pot, but only represents a raise of $470,000. Negreanu is getting pot odds of 4.7-to-1 to call on the end. Any hand that could make a legitimate bet can call those odds. The idea of a big bluff on the river is to put money pressure on your opponent or threaten him with the loss of his whole stack. That can't happen here, because Arieh doesn't have enough money left to exert any pressure. He can only win the pot if Negreanu is on a bluff.

2. **Negreanu's style**. Making a random bluff on the river after missing a draw is a beginner's play. It's not Negreanu's style at all. He'll bluff on the river, but only after setting the situation through earlier play that implies a strong hand. (Take a look at his hand against Freddie Deeb, at the end of *Harrington on Hold 'em: Volume II.*) Negreanu's sudden big bet on the end after tentative play through indicates just what in fact happened — he hit a real hand at the end.

Of course, it's easy to criticize from the sidelines, and in fact Arieh's aggressive play was what had brought him to the final table in the first place. Always remember that the kind of cool, reasoned analysis we're making here is much easier to do in the quiet of the study than in the chaos of the spotlight.

Question 45F: With a straight and huge pot odds to boot, Daniel calls. Score 4 points for Choice B, calling, no credit for folding. He probably thought he was calling for a split, since any six in Arieh's hand would have split the pot.

Problem 46
Heads-up: Calling
an All-in When Trailing

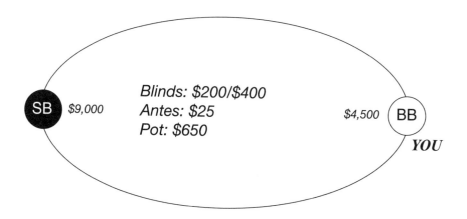

SB $9,000

Blinds: $200/$400
Antes: $25
Pot: $650

$4,500 BB

YOU

Situation: Heads-up in an online sit-and-go tournament. Your opponent has played a solid and perceptive game throughout the tournament. You've been playing heads-up for about 20 hands. So far the pots have been small.

Your Hand: ??

Action to you: The small blind pushes all-in.

Question 46: *With which of the following hands would you call?*

A. QQ
B. AK offsuit
C. 99
D. AT suited

303

Solution to Problem 46

When an opponent who's been playing conservatively suddenly pushes all-in, it raises some questions. Does he have a huge hand? If he has a huge hand, why didn't he play more slowly, trying to squeeze me for a bigger profit? Is he trying to bluff me with a medium-strength hand? Is he just trying to steal the pot, figuring I can't call?

In practice, players usually have reasonable hands when they push all-in, even with a sizeable chip lead. It's very rare to see someone jeopardize their whole tournament with a bluff, even though such a bluff is very likely to work. It's better to assume that you're up against a pretty strong hand and play accordingly.

Fortunately, your calling requirements are fairly insensitive to exactly what range of hands your opponent is using for pushing. Take a look at your calling requirements in these two cases:

1. **Your opponent is very tight, and will only push with a premium hand:** pairs from AA down to TT, and AK or AQ. In this case you can profitably call only with AA, KK, QQ, or AK, suited or unsuited.

2. **Your opponent is moderately tight, and will push with both premium hands and some not-so-premium hands:** pairs from AA down to 77, plus AK, AQ, AJ, AT, and KQ, suited or unsuited. In this case your profitable calling range is AA, KK, QQ, JJ, TT, AK and AQ, suited or unsuited.

Notice in comparing these two lists you're calling with AA, KK, QQ, and AK in either case, and you're throwing away pairs under tens and anything weaker than ace-jack. The only difference is that against the looser player you're calling with jacks, tens, and ace-queen, while throwing them away against the tight player.

Score 2 points each for calling with Choices A and B, plus 2 more points each for folding Choices C and D.

Problem 47
Heads-up: Calling
an All-in When Leading

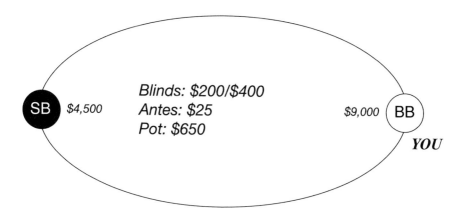

Blinds: $200/$400
Antes: $25
Pot: $650

SB $4,500

$9,000 BB

YOU

Situation: Heads-up in an online sit-and-go tournament. The same players as before. Your solid, strong opponent has been playing small-ball. This time you are the chip leader.

Your hand: ??

Action to you: The small blind pushes all-in.

Question 47: *With which of the following hands would you call?*

A. QQ
B. AK offsuit
C. 99
D. AT suited

Solution to Problem 47

While many players realize that they need to be cautious when calling a bet that could eliminate them, they aren't so cautious when holding a lead. In that case, they tend to call with a wider range of hands in the hope of ending the contest right away.

In fact, if Ms are reasonably high — here they are 15 and 30, and your estimate of the opponent's pushing range is the same, then your calling ranges are identical whether you're leading or trailing at the time. If we make the same estimate about our opponent as we did in the last problem, then our calling hands are exactly the same:

1. If he has a very tight pushing range (AA through TT, plus AK and AQ), then call only with AA, KK, QQ, or AK, suited or unsuited.

2. If he has a looser pushing range (AA through 77, plus AK through AT and KQ, suited or unsuited), then add jacks, tens, and ace-queen to your calling range.

Score 2 points each for again calling with Choices A and B, and another 2 points each for folding Choices C and D.

As your lead becomes larger, can you loosen your range? *Yes, but only if you believe that he has loosened his pushing requirement.* If you think he will still only push with strong hands, then you will hardly change your calling requirements at all.

Problem 48
Negreanu Versus
Williams — Sending a Message

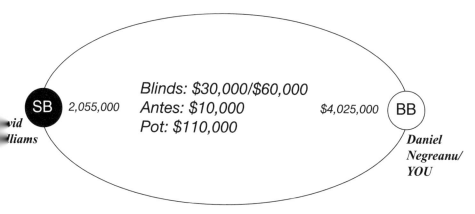

Blinds: $30,000/$60,000
Antes: $10,000
Pot: $110,000

SB 2,055,000

$4,025,000 BB

*vid
liams*

*Daniel
Negreanu/
YOU*

Situation: Early in the heads-up session at the 2004 Borgata Open between Daniel Negreanu and David Williams. Your playing partner is Daniel Negreanu. Negreanu has been playing his characteristic small-ball throughout the final table. David Williams has for the most part been hyper-aggressive. However, he tends to slow down with his bigger hands.

Your hand: A♦4♣

Action to you: David Williams calls for $30,000. The pot is now $140,000.

Question 48A: *What do you do?*

A.   *Check*
B.   *Raise to $70,000*
C.   *Raise to $200,000*

Action: You actually check. The pot remains $140,000.

Flop: Q♥J♦3♦

Question 48B: *What do you do?*

A.   *Check*
B.   *Bet $70,000*
C.   *Bet $140,000*

Action: You actually check. Williams bets $60,000. The pot is now $200,000.

Question 48C: *What do you do?*

A.   *Fold*
B.   *Call*
C.   *Raise to $120,000*

Action: You actually call. The pot is now $260,000.

Turn: 6♦

Question 48D: *What do you do?*

A.   *Check*
B.   *Bet $70,000*
C.   *Bet $140,000*

Action: You actually check. Williams checks behind you. The pot remains $260,000.

River: J♣

Question 48E: *What do you do?*

A. *Check*
B. *Bet $70,000*
C. *Bet $140,000*

Action: You actually check. Williams bets $100,000.

Question 48F: *What do you do?*

A. *Fold*
B. *Call*
C. *Raise $300,000*

Solution to Problem 48

Williams limps with J♥9♠, a perfectly good play. We know from *Harrington on Hold 'em: Volume II,* because of the pot odds and position, you're entitled to limp with any two cards before the flop. What you do then depends on how your opponent responds.

Question 48A: Negreanu has an ace, which is a very strong card heads-up. But

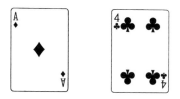

isn't a strong ace, and he'll be out of position for the rest of the hand. Out of position, I like to have stronger hands for my raises. In addition, Williams, who has been playing very aggressively for most of the final table, has now elected to limp rather than raise. That's a little scary; I'd actually feel more comfortable if my aggressive opponent were raising. Negreanu probably feels the same way too. Since Negreanu's natural style is small-ball, he elects to check. I like that play.

Score 2 points for Choice A, checking. No credit for Choice B, a small raise. You will get called, because of the pot odds, and you've just managed to get more money in the pot to no good end. Two points for Choice C, raising $200,000, a bit more than the pot. It's a good play to end the hand right now, when you don't have position. If your opponent comes over the top, you can still get away from the hand.

Negreanu actually checks. The flop comes

The pot is $140,000.

Question 48B: There are two diamonds on board, and Negreanu has the ace of diamonds, which is a little something. But basically the flop has missed him, and the queen and the jack are two scary cards which may have hit his opponent. Score 2 points for Choice A, checking. No credit for any bet.

Negreanu actually checks.

Williams now bets $60,000. He's hit middle pair, which is very big at heads-up. He wants to get more money in the pot, and Negreanu shouldn't have any trouble calling this bet. The pot is now $200,000.

Question 48C: The pot odds here are very good. It costs Negreanu $60,000 to see a pot of $200,000, which is 3.3-to-1. Those are big odds. In addition, Negreanu has an overcard to the board. In heads-up play, there's rarely a pair in your opponent's hand, and most flops miss, so an overcard is a much bigger deal than at a full table. Negreanu's ace gives him a reasonable chance of having the best hand right now. So he calls.

Score 3 points for Choice B, calling. No credit for Choice A, folding, which ignores the big pot odds, or for Choice C, raising, which overestimates the strength of your hand.

Negreanu actually calls, and the pot is now $260,000. The turn comes a 6♦.

Question 48D: The diamond on the turn gives Negreanu a diamond draw, and the three remaining aces are probably outs as well. Negreanu would like a free card here, and it's possible Williams won't be so interested in betting into what might be a made flush. Negreanu therefore checks. Score 3 points for Choice D, checking, no credit for betting any amount.

Williams now has a tough problem. He bet on the flop and got a call. Presumably the call meant something, but what? To Williams, the possibilities look about as follows:

- **A queen**. If Negreanu had a queen and made top pair, a raise was the likely response to Williams' bet. But he only called. He might be slow-playing, but that's a slightly unusual play, so this is a less likely holding.

- **A jack**. Now both players would have a pair of jacks, and Williams' nine kicker might or might not be best. But two jacks are already accounted for, so this holding is less likely as well.

- **A trey**. Even bottom pair is a good holding heads-up. This would account for the call on the flop and the check on the turn. Negreanu would have just five outs on the river.

- **An overcard**. Negreanu could have an ace or a king, and figure his overcard might be good. A possible holding. Negreanu would have three outs on the river.

- **A flush**. Two diamonds would account for his call, in which case he just hit a monster.

- **A flush draw**. One diamond might also account for his call, in which case he has nine outs.

- **A straight draw**. Ace-king would have raised before the flop, but king-ten and ten-nine might have called.

Some of the holdings have Williams beaten already, while others are unlikely to draw out on the river. If he were sure that Negreanu was still on a flush or a straight draw, he'd want to bet now. But other possibilities abound, so Williams elects to keep the pot small.

Williams checks. The river comes a J♣.

Question 48E: The jack didn't help Negreanu's hand. It also didn't hurt it, since he was beaten by a pair of jacks anyway. It's still possible Negreanu's hand can win a showdown, but there's no reason to put more money in the pot. Score 2 points for Choice A, checking. No credit for any bet. Negreanu actually checks.

Williams now has trip jacks. It's almost certainly the best hand, unless Negreanu was slow-playing a flush or a pair of queens in the hole, both of which look very unlikely given the lack of betting. How much can Williams bet that will be paid off? He elects to bet $100,000, about 40 percent of the current pot. Negreanu will get 3.5-to-1 odds to call, which should be enough to tempt him if he has a pair or even an overcard. If he doesn't have as much as an overcard, he won't call any bet. Williams bets $100,000. The pot is now $360,000.

Question 48F: Negreanu elects to call the final bet with just an ace in his hand. At this point, he undoubtedly thinks he's beaten, so why call? The 3.5-to-1 odds are part of the answer, but there are two other good reasons:

1. **Curiosity**. Negreanu wants to know what Williams has. It's not just some whim or an idle curiosity. Negreanu at this point remembers all the cards that have come and the bets that have been made. (All top players remember this stuff.) Now he wants a hand to associate with all the bets and checks. The more hands he can see, the better picture he can draw of his opponent and how he plays. Given the pot odds he's getting, $100,000 is a relatively cheap price to pay for some solid information. (If you're finding it hard to put "$100,000" and "cheap" in the same sentence, remember that there's over $6,000,000 in chips on the table, so this bet represents less than one-sixtieth of the chips in play.)

2. **Sending a message**. Aggressive players will push you off the table if you let them. In a heads-up session, you won't have time to wait for the big hands that will let you call or reraise with confidence. You have to make stands with hands of lesser quality. By calling with an ace-high, Negreanu is sending a message: "I don't need a big pair to call you, pal." In the future, Williams will know that trying to steal a pot with nothing just might cost him all his chips. Like a chess master sacrificing a pawn for attacking chances, Negreanu is sacrificing part of a bet to slow his opponent down.

Score 3 points for Choice B, calling. No credit for Choice C, raising. One point for Choice A, folding, which is probably the correct play in a vacuum.

Problem 49
Negreanu Versus
Williams — Big Pot, Big Hand

Blinds: $30,000/$60,000
Antes: $10,000
Pot: $110,000

SB $3,480,000

BB $2,600,000

Daniel Negreanu/ YOU

David Williams

Situation: A few hands further in the heads-up session at the 2004 Borgata Open. Your playing partner is again Daniel Negreanu.

Your hand: K♠2♦

Action to you: You are first to act.

Question 49A: *What do you do?*

A.   *Fold*
B.   *Call $30,000*
C.   *Raise $140,000*

Action: You actually call $30,000. Williams checks. The pot is $140,000.

315

316 Problem 49

Flop: 6♣6♠3♠

Action: Williams checks.

Question 49B: *What do you do?*

A. *Check*
B. *Bet $60,000*
C. *Bet $120,000*

Action: You actually check.

Turn: 9♠

Action: Williams checks.

Question 49C: *What do you do?*

A. *Check*
B. *Bet $60,000*
C. *Bet $120,000*

Action: You actually bet $60,000. Williams raises to $200,000. The pot is now $400,000.

Question 49D: *What do you do?*

A. *Fold*
B. *Call $140,000*
C. *Reraise to $500,000*

Action: You actually call $140,000. The pot is now $540,000.

River: 6♦

Action: Williams bet $500,000. The pot is now $1,040,000.

Question 49E: *What do you do?*

A. *Fold*
B. *Call $500,000*
C. *Raise all-in*

Action: You actually call $500,000. Williams shows the 9♥9♣, for nines full of sixes, which beat your trip sixes.

Solution to Problem 49

Question 49A: A king in heads-up is worth a call all by itself, and here Negreanu will have position to go along with his

Score 2 points for Choice B, calling. No credit for folding, which is much too conservative, or raising, which is overly optimistic.

Williams has a pair of nines, and elects to check them rather than raise. It's a move consistent with how he's played the heads-up session — trapping with his big hands and aggressively attacking with his weaker hands. Here, however, he's overdoing things. When a high card comes and he gets action, he'll have to spend the whole hand wondering if he's beaten. If two high cards come and he gets action, he'll want to throw the hand away. To make matters worse, he's out of position in the hand. To make matters still worse, Negreanu only limped, so there may not be big action on the hand unless Negreanu hits something, which could be very bad news.

Right now, the blinds and antes are big enough so that just taking down the pot is an accomplishment. I'd stick in a decent-sized raise here, perhaps another $100,000 or so. A pair of nines is potentially just too dangerous a hand to slow-play.

Williams actually checks, and the pot remains at $140,000. The flop comes

Williams checks again. This check I like. The flop is innocuous and Williams' overpair is very likely to be good. The only danger is that Negreanu may not take the bait.

Question 49B: Negreanu still has nothing, just an overcard to the board. In addition, Williams' refusal to bet should be a little disquieting. When aggressive players refuse to bet, you should be suspicious. Score 3 points for Choice A, checking, no credit for betting.

Negreanu actually checks, and the pot remains at $140,000. The turn comes a 9♠, putting three spades on board.

Williams has made a full house, nines full of sixes. There's a potential flush or flush draw on board, and Williams is hoping that Negreanu has a spade in his hand or, ideally, has already made his flush. But he can't do anything to discourage Negreanu, so he checks.

Question 49C: Williams has passed on three chances to bet, so it's entirely possible he has nothing. In addition, Negreanu has a flush draw as a fallback position. It's time to just take the pot down if that's possible, or at least try to build the pot in case the flush draw hits. If Williams has a spade, and the flush hits, Negreanu's king of spades could let him win a monster pot.

Score 3 points for Choice B, the direct play, betting $60,000. Around half the pot should be the right amount to bet here. This bet will win the pot if it's immediately winnable.

One point for Choice A, checking, which is another way to play the hand, although I don't like it quite as much. The idea is twofold: your king-high hand might be enough to win a showdown, and since you have a draw, you're happy to see another card for free.

No credit for Choice C, the big bet of $120,000, which is too much money given that your hand is only king-high.

Negreanu actually bets $60,000.

Williams can now spring his trap. He doesn't want to overbet, because he wants Negreanu sticking around if he has a flush draw. But he needs to get some more money in the pot right now, to set up an even bigger profit on the river.

He actually raises to $200,000, which is a very nice-sized raise. It makes the pot $400,000, so Negreanu will be getting almost 3-to-1 to stick around. If Negreanu has a flush draw plus an overcard, he'll think he has 12 outs, and he'll be getting the right price even without any implied odds. If he has only a flush draw, he'll need implied odds to make the call work, but this bet will indicate that the implied odds are there. Nice play.

Question 49D: Negreanu has now learned that Williams has something. His best guess is probably that Williams has a nine in his hand, perhaps jack-nine or ten-nine, and has just made top pair. If so, Negreanu has 12 outs — all nine spades and the three kings. Even if Williams has been slow-playing a bigger hand, like three sixes, most flush cards should win for him. He's close to getting the odds he thinks he needs, and there's no way he can read Williams for a made full house, so a call is correct and pretty automatic. Score 3 points for Choice B, calling, and no credit for folding or raising.

Negreanu actually calls $140,000. The pot is now $540,000. The river card is a 6♦, putting three sixes on board.

Williams now makes an excellent play, betting $500,000. If you've played with Negreanu for any length of time, you know that he tends to regard big bets on the river as bluffs, attempts to salvage a hand that didn't connect. It's a reasonable assumption against weak players, a dangerous assumption against experienced and observant players. The conservative play would be for Williams to bet something like $250,000, an amount that Negreanu (or anybody else) would call with any kind of hand because of the pot odds. Williams presses, betting a number that suggests he might be trying to buy the pot, and puts his curious and suspicious opponent to the test.

Question 49E: Negreanu now has a real problem. He's missed his hand, but he still has trip sixes with a king kicker. Williams might have the same sort of hand he has — just a flush draw that missed, but with a weaker kicker. He's being offered a little more than 2-to-1 by the pot, but it's a big pot now, and if he's wrong, the lead will change hands.

I can understand Negreanu's suspicion of the betting he's seen so far. Williams' check-raise on the turn seems to say that he hit a nine. But most of his nines — A9, K9, Q9, J9 — would probably have bet on the flop. The board was weak. Daniel hadn't shown any strength. The overcards might be good. So put in a bet and find out. The check on the flop followed by the check-raise following a nine doesn't quite add up. This opponent had mostly been playing his strong hands weakly and his weak hands strongly. So maybe he's doing it again. You're getting 2-to-1 odds to find out, so...

But two other key ideas are in operation here, and they argue strongly against the call:

1. **You need a big hand to play a big pot.** Now, we're playing heads-up, so "big hand" is a relative concept. But calling half a million with just a king-high — I can't do it.

2. **The play of the last hand.** Negreanu has just demonstrated that he's capable of calling on the end with just a high card, thereby sending a message to Williams. However, if you send a message to a smart, alert opponent, *you have to assume that the message was received.* Williams now knows that Negreanu can call with just a high card. *Therefore Williams is betting a hand that can beat a high card.* Therefore you fold.

Score 3 points for Choice A, folding, and no credit for Choice B, calling.

Negreanu actually calls and loses to Williams' full house.

Problem 50
Negreanu Versus Williams
— Pushing With a Monster?

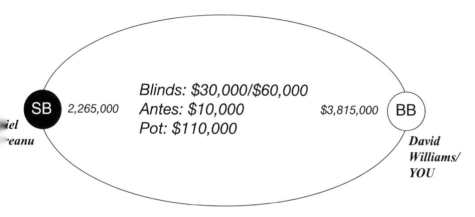

Blinds: $30,000/$60,000
Antes: $10,000
Pot: $110,000

SB 2,265,000

$3,815,000 BB

iel
eanu

David
Williams/
YOU

Situation: A few hands further in the heads-up session at the 2004 Borgata Open. Your playing partner is now David Williams in the big blind. You have recently taken the lead in the match and now have over 60 percent of the chips. Negreanu has been playing small-ball. You have been very aggressive.

Your hand: K♠4♥

Action to you: Negreanu limps for $30,000.

Question 50A: *What do you do?*

A.   *Check*
B.   *Raise $100,000*

Action: You actually check. The pot is now $140,000.

Flop: A♥Q♣T♥

Question 50B: *What do you do?*

A. *Check*
B. *Bet $60,000*
C. *Bet $100,000*

Action: You actually check. Negreanu bets $60,000. The pot is now $200,000.

Question 50C: *What do you do?*

A. *Fold*
B. *Call*
C. *Raise to $120,000*

Action: You actually call. The pot is now $260,000.

Turn: J♠

Question 50D: *What do you do?*

A. *Check*
B. *Bet $100,000*
C. *Bet $200,000*

Action: You actually check. Negreanu checks behind you. The pot remains $260,000.

River: 6♠

Question 50E: What do you do?

A. Check
B. Bet $100,000
C. Bet $200,000
D. Push all-in

Action: You actually bet $200,000. Negreanu calls and shows A♣6♥. Your straight beats his two pair.

Solution to Problem 50

Negreanu is first to act before the flop and picks up A♣6♥. It's a good hand heads-up, and since he'll be in position for the rest of the hand, it's a hand that's strong enough for raising. It's not so strong, however, that you're unhappy if you take the hand down right here. I'd raise with the hand, probably $100,000 or $120,000. Negreanu, however, likes to play these sorts of hands slow and small, so he just limps. It's a play consistent with his approach to this match.

Question 50A: The king is a nice card, but the four kicker is pretty weak, and you'll be out of position for the rest of the hand. So a raise here with the

is on the loose side. I like just checking. Score 3 points for Choice A, checking, and no credit for raising.

Williams actually checks, and the pot is $140,000. The flop comes

Question 50B: It's a dangerous-looking flop, but your king gives you an inside straight draw, and if Negreanu limped with a couple of low cards, you might have the best hand right now. But it's much too dangerous to lead out with a bet. Score 3 points for Choice A, checking; no credit for either of the two betting plays.

Williams actually checks.

Negreanu, with his pair of aces, bets $60,000. Since he only limped before the flop, the ace in his hand is somewhat concealed. If Williams has either a queen or a ten, he may get action this hand.

The pot is now $200,000.

Question 50C: Negreanu has made a small bet, but it's put you in a difficult position. You're getting better than 3-to-1 odds to call. Those are tempting odds, but you must analyze carefully where you stand here. Right now your hand falls into one of three categories:

1. **You have the best hand right now.** Negreanu limped with two low cards, and is now making a probe bet to steal the pot. The best situation.

2. **You don't have the best hand now, but hitting your king or making your straight will give you the best hand.** Negreanu has a pair lower than your king, either because he started with a low pair or he had a queen or a ten and just hit

his hand. You're about a 3.5-to-1 underdog to hit your king or make your straight with two cards to come, and there's no guarantee you'll get to see the second of those two cards.

3. **You don't have the best hand now, and you need to hit a jack to win.** Negreanu has paired an ace, or hit two pair. You're almost 11-to-1 to hit your jack on the turn, and again no guarantee that you'll still be around when the river card is dealt.

Now you have to ask yourself, "How has my opponent been playing?" Negreanu has been playing tight, keeping the pots small, but pressing his good hands when he has them. Since he could have checked but bet instead, it's reasonable (but not certain) to assume he has some piece of the flop. If so, the first possibility goes away, and you need to hit either a king or a jack to win the hand.

Hitting the king, however, is a very double-edged result. You'll then be out of position, second-best to an ace, and way behind if Negreanu holds a jack. You'll never know where you stand in what might become a big pot. That's very dangerous in no-limit hold 'em.

Hitting the jack is a great result. You'll have the best hand and you'll know it. But you're bucking 11-to-1 odds on the next card, with no reason to believe that your implied odds, if you hit the straight, will be big enough. Remember that if the jack actually comes, the board will be A-Q-J-T. Your possible straight will be very obvious, and you may not be able to get any action on your hand.

All in all, you've got a collection of possibilities, none of which look quite good enough to keep on playing. Just let the hand go. Score 3 points for Choice A, folding. One point for Choice B, calling. No credit for the berserko play of raising (Choice C).

You actually call. The pot is now $260,000. The turn comes a J♠.

Question 50D: You've filled your straight, and now the problem is extracting the maximum from the hand. Since Negreanu has been showing strength so far, find out if he will continue to bet the hand. If so, he'll do your work for you. If not, you'll have to make some money on the river. Score 3 points for Choice A, checking. One point only for Choice B, betting $100,000, which might tell Negreanu he has to let it go. No credit for Choice C, betting $200,000, after which you might not get paid at all.

For Negreanu, this looks like a very dangerous card, giving Williams a straight if he holds a king. Negreanu still only holds top pair, and that looks a little less impressive now. So he prudently checks.

The pot remains $260,000. The river is a 6♠.

Question 50E: No time left to fool around. You're first to act, so you have to bet your straight or risk making no more money on the hand. Negreanu checked on the turn, so you can't assume he'll bet on the river. No credit for Choice A, checking.

Choice B, betting $100,000, is too cautious. It will certainly get called, since Negreanu will be getting 3.6-to-1 pot odds and he probably has something at this point. But it won't make you very much money. Remember, part of your call on the flop was predicated on the idea of making money *after hitting your straight*. You were almost an 11-to-1 underdog to get the straight, and you invested $60,000 in the call. That means you need to make some pretty big money when you do hit the straight, to make up for all the times you throw away your hand on the turn or river and abandon the $60,000. If you're only going to bet $100,000 on the river, you couldn't (reasonably) make the call on the flop. No credit for betting $100,000.

Choice C, betting $200,000, is better. The bet is very likely to be called, especially by Negreanu, who has shown that he likes to look up these river bets. By getting more money in the pot, you're getting closer to the payoff you need to justify your earlier call, so your play is more consistent. It's a prudent play, one that will very likely put another $200,000 in your stack. Score 2 points for Choice B.

However, Choice D, pushing all-in, is best! Score 5 points for that play. The reason is that while you will mostly win an extra $200,000 with Choice C, betting $200,000, and you'll mostly get nothing when you push all-in, the extra money when you do get called is so huge that you have to push if there's almost any chance that you'll be called.

Consider the respective payoffs. Negreanu started the hand with $2,265,000 in chips, and so far you've each put $130,000 in the pot, so he has $2,135,000 left. Compare $2.1 million to $200,000 — it's 10.5 times bigger! That means that if there's as much as a 9 percent chance that he'll call the all-in move, you'll make more money (on average) by pushing. In addition, of course, you'll end the tournament, which is a little extra bonus.

While there's no way to precisely evaluate the chance that he'll call the all-in move, it's reasonable to assume that it's always bigger than 10 percent. He might have trips or two pair, or even a lower straight. He might decide your bet is so big it "must" be a bluff. After all, you've been aggressive throughout the final table, making big bets and bigger raises. They haven't all been backed up by big hands, and Negreanu knows this. Negreanu has shown that he can make great folds, but he can also make tough calls. This might be such a time. The payoff is so huge that you must give him a chance to call when you have a monster hand.

You actually bet $200,000.

The six on the river gives Negreanu two pair, aces and sixes. He's getting 2.3-to-1 on the call, so he properly calls. He could easily be facing a lower two pair than his own. Your straight beats his two pair.

Scoring the Problems

Use this section as a scoresheet for recording your answers and their associated point value. The maximum number of points available is shown for each part of each problem.

Problem 1: (3)_____

Problem 2: (4)_____

Problem 3
    3A: (3)_____
    3B: (3)_____
    3C: (3)_____
    3D: (3)_____

Problem 4
    4A: (3)_____
    4B: (3)_____
    4C: (4)_____
    4D: (3)_____
    4E: (4)_____
    4F: (4)_____
    4G: (5)_____

Problem 5
    5A: (3)_____
    5B: (2)_____
    5C: (4)_____
    5D: (2)_____

Problem 6
    6A: (5)_____
    6B: (4)_____
    6C: (4)_____
    6D: (4)_____
    6E: (4)_____
    6F: (4)_____

Problem 7
    7A: (2)_____
    7B: (3)_____
    7C: (3)_____
    7D: (3)_____
    7E: (2)_____
    7F: (2)_____

Problem 8
    8A: (3)_____
    8B: (2)_____
    8C: (2)_____
    8D: (3)_____
    8E: (2)_____
    8F: (2)_____

332 Scoring the Problems

Problem 9
  9A: (3)_____
  9B: (3)_____
  9C: (3)_____
  9D: (5)_____
  9E: (3)_____
  9F: (3)_____

Problem 10
  10A: (3)_____
  10B: (4)_____
  10C: (4)_____

Problem 11
  11A: (2)_____
  11B: (4)_____
  11C: (4)_____
  11D: (4)_____
  11E: (3)_____
  11F: (3)_____

Problem 12
  12A: (3)_____
  12B: (3)_____
  12C: (3)_____
  12D: (4)_____

Problem 13
  13A: (4)_____
  13B: (3)_____
  13C: (3)_____
  13D: (3)_____

Problem 14
  14A: (4)_____
  14B: (3)_____
  14C: (3)_____
  14D: (3)_____

Problem 15
  15A: (3)_____
  15B: (4)_____
  15C: (3)_____
  15D: (2)_____
  15E: (3)_____

Problem 16
  16A: (3)_____
  16B: (4)_____
  16C: (3)_____
  16D: (3)_____
  16E: (4)_____
  16F: (5)_____

Problem 17
  17A: (4)_____
  17B: (4)_____
  17C: (5)_____

Problem 18: (5)_____

Problem 19
  19A: (3)_____
  19B: (4)_____
  19C: (3)_____

Problem 20
    20A: (3)_____
    20B: (5)_____

Problem 21: (5)_____

Problem 22
    22A: (2)_____
    22B: (3)_____
    22C: (3)_____
    22D: (3)_____
    22E: (4)_____

Problem 23
    23A: (2)_____
    23B: (3)_____

Problem 24
    24A: (5)_____
    24B: (3)_____
    24C: (3)_____

Problem 25
    25A: (3)_____
    25B: (3)_____
    25C: (2)_____
    25D: (3)_____
    25E: (3)_____
    25F: (3)_____

Problem 26
    26A: (2)_____
    26B: (4)_____
    26C: (4)_____
    26D: (3)_____

Problem 27
    27A: (2)_____
    27B: (3)_____
    27C: (3)_____
    27D: (4)_____
    27E: (4)_____

Problem 28
    28A: (2)_____
    28B: (2)_____
    28C: (3)_____
    28D: (4)_____

Problem 29
    29A: (3)_____
    29B: (3)_____
    29C: (4)_____

Problem 30
    30A: (4)_____
    30B: (2)_____
    30C: (3)_____
    30D: (2)_____
    30E: (4)_____
    30F: (3)_____

Problem 31
    31A: (4)_____
    31B: (3)_____
    31C: (2)_____
    31D: (3)_____
    31E: (5)_____

Problem 32
    32A: (3)_____
    32B: (2)_____
    32C: (2)_____
    32D: (2)_____
    32E: (5)_____

Problem 33
    (a): (2)_____
    (b): (2)_____
    (c): (2)_____
    (d): (2)_____

Problem 34
    34A: (3)_____
    34B: (2)_____
    34C: (4)_____

Problem 35: (2)_____

Problem 36
    36A: (5)_____
    36B: (4)_____

Problem 37: (3)_____

Problem 38: (3)_____

Problem 39: (3)_____

Problem 40: (3)_____

Problem 41: (3)_____

Problem 42: (3)_____

Problem 43
    43A: (2)_____
    43B: (4)_____
    43C: (5)_____
    43D: (4)_____
    43E: (5)_____

Problem 44
    44A: (2)_____
    44B: (4)_____
    44C: (3)_____
    44D: (4)_____
    44E: (4)_____

Problem 45
    45A: (2)_____
    45B: (4)_____
    45C: (3)_____
    45D: (4)_____
    45E: (4)_____
    45F: (4)_____

Problem 46
    (a): (2)_____
    (b): (2)_____
    (c): (2)_____
    (d): (2)_____

Problem 47
    (a): (2)_____
    (b): (2)_____
    (c): (2)_____
    (d): (2)_____

Problem 48
    48A: (2)_____
    48B: (2)_____
    48C: (3)_____
    48D: (3)_____
    48E: (2)_____
    48F: (3)_____

Problem 49
    49A: (2)_____
    49B: (3)_____
    49C: (3)_____
    49D: (3)_____
    49E: (3)_____

Problem 50
    50A: (3)_____
    50B: (3)_____
    50C: (3)_____
    50D: (3)_____
    50E: (5)_____

The maximum number of points, if you answered all the problems correctly, is *591*. Use the following guidelines to get an idea of where you stand:

- **500 or more:** World-class. Probably already making a fine living from the game.

- **400 or more:** A very good player who should show a solid profit in big tournaments.

- **300 or more:** A player with a solid base of skills to build upon.

- **200 or more:** A player whose game needs work in many key areas.

- **Under 200:** An intermediate or beginner-level player.

Categorizing Your Errors

Do your errors fall into systematic groups? This chart may help you find out. For each play where you didn't earn the maximum number of points, find the play you actually made in this listing of choices and circle it. When you're done with the book, check and see if any particular category has an unusually high number of errors. That's an area where you may need improvement.

Pre-Flop Errors

Over-reliance on "reads:" 1b

Over-betting pots: Betting too much with a good hand, thereby reducing the chance of making money. 1c

Loose play. Betting or raising without a good combination of hand and position: 1d, 1e, 4Bc, 7Ac, 7Bc, 8Ab, 8Ac, 9Ac, 9Bc, 10Ab, 10Ac, 11Ac, 12Ab, 12Ac, 13Ac, 19Ac, 19Ad, 20Ac, 22Ac, 23Ac, 27Ac, 28Ac, 29Ac, 32Ac, 43Ac, 44Ab, 45Ab, 45Ac, 48Ab, 49Ac, 50Ab

Loose play. Setting up a potentially big pot without a premium hand: 2, 5Ac, 5Ad

Loose play. Moving all-in unnecessarily: 34Ae, 36Af

Passive/aggressive play. Calling with a weak hand out of position: 4Ab, 7Bb, 27Ab

Properly sizing your initial bet. Getting enough money in the pot but allowing some weak hands to stick around: 6Ab, 6Ad, 14Ab, 36Ac, 36Ad

Under-betting. Giving weaker hands the correct odds to hang around: 3Ac, 17Ab, 17Ac, 34Ac

Tight play. Folding when your hand is playable: 3Aa, 5Aa, 9Aa, 9Ba, 19Aa, 19Ba, 20Aa, 20Ba, 22Aa, 23Aa, 26Aa, 29Aa, 32Aa, 34Aa, 35Aa, 36Aa

Tight/passive play. Calling when you need to raise: 3Ab, 17Aa, 19Bb, 20Bb, 24Ac, 25Ab, 30Aa, 31Aa, 35b, 36Ab

Passive play. Betting too little when you need to put your opponent to a decision for all his chips: 24Ac

Passive play. Folding when you need to push all-in: 21

Correctly calling or folding all-in bets: 33, 36Ba

Technically incorrect calls in short-table situations: 46a-46d, 47a-47d

Technically incorrect sit-n-go bubble plays: 37, 38, 39, 40, 41, 42

Post-Flop Errors

Proper sizing later bets. Balancing the need to get money in the pot with a good hand with the need to prevent drawing hands from getting the right odds to continue: 5Bc, 5Bd, 6Bb, 6Bd, 6Db, 6Dd, 6De, 6Ea, 6Fa, 15Bc, 15Cc, 17Bb, 17Cb

Slow-playing hands. Improperly slow-playing a hand when the goal should be to chase away draws and isolate on a single opponent: 6Aa

Fear of playing the hand. Making huge bets or all-in bets in an attempt to end a hand rather than play a hand: 4Dc, 4Ec, 6Ae, 6Be, 7Cd, 7Dc, 11Cc, 15Cd, 16Ac, 16Bb, 16Bc, 17Bd, 20Bd, 22Bc, 22Bd, 34Bc

Excessively tight play. Checking when you need to bet, either to clarify the hand, to try to win the pot, to get more money in the pot, to restrain an aggressive player, or to bluff an opponent: 3Ba, 3Ca, 4Ea, 5Ba, 6Ba, 9Da, 10Ba, 10Ca, 11Ea, 15Ba, 16Aa, 17Ba, 17Ca, 25Ba, 27Ba, 27Ca, 28Ca, 31Ba, 34Ba, 43Ba, 44Ba, 44Ca, 45Ba, 49Ca

Excessively tight play. Folding when a call or raise is reasonable: 11Da, 12Ad, 12Da, 13Aa, 13Ba, 13Ca, 14Aa, 15Aa, 16Ca, 23Ba, 24Aa, 25Ca, 29Ba, 29Ca, 32Ca, 44Da

Betting too little against a known aggressive opponent: 24Cb, 24Cc, 45Bb, 45Cb

Betting out of position when checking is better: 8Bb, 8Bc, 8Cb, 8Eb, 28Bb, 30Bb, 30Bc

Betting too much for the weakness of your hand: 3Bc, 3Cc, 4Fb, 4Fc, 5Bb, 5Bc, 9Dc, 9Dd, 16Cc, 16Cd, 25Bc, 25Cc, 27Bc, 27Cc, 28Bc, 43Bc, 43Dc, 43Dd, 43Ec, 44Dc, 44Ec, 45Bd, 45Cd, 49Cc

Betting when you need a free card: 48Db, 48Dc

Folding hands good enough to call: 6Ca, 8Da, 11Aa, 11Ba, 11Fa, 22Ca, 22Da, 24Ca, 26Ca, 30Ca, 43Ea, 44Ea, 48Ca, 49Aa

Walking into traps. Betting or raising when you're not likely to be a favorite: 3Dc, 3Dd, 3De, 6Cc, 6Cd, 8Dc, 8Fc, 9Cb, 9Cc, 9Eb, 9Ec, 9Fc, 12Bb, 12Bc, 12Cb, 12Cc, 12Dc, 12Dd, 13Bc, 13Cc, 13Dc, 13Dd, 14Bb, 14Bc, 14Cb, 14Cc, 14Db, 14Dc, 15Db, 15Dc, 15Dd, 15Ec, 15Ed, 19Cb, 19Cc, 25Db, 25Dc, 25Eb, 25Fc, 26Bb, 26Cc, 26Db, 26Dc, 27Db, 27Dc, 27Ec, 29Bc, 30Cc, 30Db, 30Eb, 30Fc, 32Bb, 32Cc, 43Cb, 43Cc, 48Bb, 48Bc, 48Cc, 48Eb, 48Ec, 48Fc, 49Bb, 49Bc, 49Dc, 50Bb, 50Bc

Ignoring pot odds when deciding to fold or call: 3Da, 8Fa, 13Da, 15Ea, 18, 30Fa, 34Ca, 48Fa, 49Da

Calling or raising big bets with weak hands: 9Fb, 49Eb, 49Ec, 50Cb, 50Cc

Calling instead of raising. Getting too little money in the pot: 7Da, 22Ba

Missing a chance to steal a pot or make a semi-bluff: 23Bb, 39Cb, 39Cc

Betting too much with a strong hand. Chasing your opponent away: 6De, 6Ec, 7Eb, 7Ec, 7Fc, 11Dc, 11Dd, 11Ec, 16Dc, 16Dd, 22Cc, 22Cd, 22Dc, 31Bc, 31Cb, 31Cc, 31Db, 31Dc, 50Db, 50Dc

Betting too little when bluffing: 10Bb, 10Cb

Failure to trap. Betting a hand that should be checked: 4Cb, 4Cc, 4Cd, 4Db, 7Cb, 7Cc, 24Bb, 24Bc

River Errors

Betting when you should check to induce a bluff: 31Eb, 31Ec, 32Db

Betting when only better hands can call: 5Db, 5Dc

Betting too little with a monster. Not maximizing your big hands: 50Eb, 50Ec

Checking a hand that must be bet: 7Fa, 11Ca, 16Da, 22Ea, 28Da, 43Da, 50Ea

Calling on the river when probably beaten: 4Ga, 25Fb, 27Eb

Failing to move all-in when situation dictates: 16Ea, 16Fa, 16Fb, 22Ec, 32Ea, 32Eb

Index